Personal Relationships. 1:
Studying Personal Relationships

Personal Relationships. 1:

Studying Personal Relationships

Editors
STEVE DUCK and
ROBIN GILMOUR

Department of Psychology
University of Lancaster, England

1981

ACADEMIC PRESS
A subsidiary of Harcourt Brace Jovanovich, Publishers
London New York Toronto Sydney San Francisco

ACADEMIC PRESS INC. (LONDON) LTD.
24/28 Oval Road,
London NW1

United States Edition published by
ACADEMIC PRESS INC.
111 Fifth Avenue
New York, New York 10003

British Library Cataloguing in Publication Data

Personal relationships.

   Vol. 1
   1. Interpersonal relationships
   I. Duck, Steven W.
   II. Gilmour, Robin
   301.11   HM132   80-41360

   ISBN 0-12-222801-4

Filmset by Colset Private Ltd, Singapore

Printed in Great Britain by
Whitstable Litho Ltd, Whitstable, Kent

Contributors

G. M. ANDREYEVA, Sub-department of Social Psychology, Department of Psychology, Moscow State University, Moscow, USSR.

ROBERT L. BURGESS, Division of Individual and Family Studies, Henderson Human Development Building, Penn State University, University Park, PA 16802, USA.

DONN BYRNE, Department of Psychology, State University of New York at Albany, 1400 Washington Avenue, Albany, New York 12222, USA.

HUBERT FEGER, Lehrstuhl Psychologie II am Institüt fuer Psychologie der Rhein. Westf. Techn. Hochschule, Templergraben 55, 5100 Aachen, West Germany.

LEONID J. GOZMAN, Sub-department of Social Psychology, Department of Psychology, Moscow State University, Moscow, USSR.

ELAINE HATFIELD, Department of Sociology, University of Wisconsin-Madison, Madison, Wisconsin 53706, USA.

ROBERT A. HINDE, MRC Unit on the Development and Integration of Behaviour, University Sub-department of Animal Behaviour, Madingley, Cambridge CB3 8AA, UK.

JOHN J. LaGAIPA, Department of Psychology, University of Windsor, Windsor, Ontario, Canada N9B 3P4.

BARRY McCARTHY, School of Psychology, H Block, School of Social Studies, Preston Polytechnic, Livesey House, Corporation Street, Preston PR1 2TQ, UK.

I. L. MANGHAM, Centre for the Study of Organizational Change and Development, University of Bath, Claverton Down, Bath BA2 7AY, UK.

MICHAEL D. NEWCOMB, Department of Psychology, University of California at Los Angeles, Los Angeles, California 90024, USA.

DAVID PRZYBYLA, Department of Psychology, State University of New York at Albany, 1400 Washington Avenue, Albany, New York 12222, USA.

JANE TRAUPMANN, Center for Research on Women, Wellesley College, 828 Washington Street, Wellesley, Massachusetts 02181, USA.

Preface

It is perhaps natural — or, at least, understandable — that the very earliest attempts to explain personal relationships should be characterized by untested personal intuitions, lack of systematic attack on the issues, and an experimental approach that focused on manageable but minute details of very localized or limited parts of the putative general process. This was undoubtedly the case in the relevant research that was available until about the mid-1970s. Recently, however, researchers in a variety of research disciplines seem to have detected that improvements in (unrelated) research techniques and general theoretical advances have moved us to the point where the topic of personal relationships can become a feasible one for more useful research. Indeed, it promises to be a new area of research in its own right, and one that will be characterized at once by systematic records of real-life relationships and by more soundly and generally based conceptual statements. All of us recognize in our daily experience many varieties of personal relationship, each — or so it seems — with different features and facets, different histories and different significance to us. Yet researchers in individual disciplines have only recently begun to improve on the existing poor grasp of the processes or concepts involved. At the same time, it is a welcome thing that, because of general shifts of social attitudes, personal relationships are being accepted as an area suitable for — and even in urgent need of — social scientific study.

The study of personal relationships is thus clearly destined to establish itself firmly as an important new area that transcends, though it draws from, a number of existing lines of work. Interestingly, it is one that has many distinct strands to its history and no clear descent from the traditions of any given academic discipline. On the one hand it has a large inheritance from the social-psychological research on interpersonal attraction (IPA), but on the other hand it emerges also from ethology, sociology, and social anthropology with a considerable legacy from the helping professions, clinical psychology and guidance counselling. The unique value of this exciting new area is its synthesis of the specific recent advances in each of these component approaches, but at the same time, their fusion in turn improves the individual constituents by broadening and deepening their singular contributions.

Indeed, as social psychologists we are concerned that this is specifically true in the

vii

case of the contribution made by our own discipline. For, although IPA (Interpersonal Attraction) research on its own has been one of the fastest-growing research areas in social psychology since 1960, researchers have so far very little grounds for complacency about the value of their research taken by itself. It has often been criticised (both rightly and wrongly) for such things as triviality, artificiality, lack of generalizability, mistaking the purpose of its work, and failing to contribute anything practical to the store of knowledge drawn on by those who guide, advise about or untangle the relationships of real people. Now, however, it is likely that the disappointment that many people rightly felt about IPA research will soon be replaced with optimism as the work transfuses itself into the study of personal relationships which promises to offer truer insights into the dynamics of real-life relationships. Research has now developed beyond the specifics of initial attraction, beyond laboratory study of acquainting, and beyond the conceptual inadequacies of attending merely to the stimulus properties of both partners (or, worse, of only one partner) in an encounter. In the last decade, interest has grown vigorously in the development of relationships, in the real-world meanings and events of relationships, and in the sociocognitive processes that occur once two people start interacting as acquaintances. Theoretical representations of "relationship development" have been improved, and methodological advances have followed this burgeoning of interest and potential, such that the possible contribution of social psychology to the new field of personal relationships is assuming at once a centrality and an excitement. For example, whilst "social psychiatrists" have always been interested in failures of relationship, social psychologists have also recently begun to focus on the retrospective explanation, and on the dynamics, of general relationship breakdown. Whilst social anthropologists and sociologists have had a steady interest in description and comparison of relationships, a clearer understanding of the meaning of such things has grown along with the development of new methods involving social psychological analysis of longitudinal development of naturalistic relationships.

It is clear that, at least in part, this growing-up of IPA research has been impelled by the changing emphases in social psychology generally. As a reflection of this, the imbalance of emphasis that developed in social-psychological work on interpersonal attraction — and against which there has been such a justifiable and productive reaction — was the tendency to overemphasize attitudinal and intrapsychic phenomena and to act as if the evaluative responses studied by most experimental social psychologists were all that there was to personal relating. This appearance was misleading not only as a representation of personal relationships but also as an indication of the true position of many of the experimental workers themselves since many wrote as if they recognized the narrowness of their approach, whilst acting otherwise. Of course, such work has clarified important parts of the relevant processes, but has also illustrated that exclusive attention to such things is ultimately narrow, impedimental and misleading. We welcome the fact that future developments contributed by social psychologists are also likely to reflect the broader general developments taking place in the social-psychological enterprise as a whole (Duck, 1980a, b), which in this context will take the form of an increasingly complex methodology that is capable of assessing, measuring and studying relationship dynamics as they occur and unfold in natural settings (Wiggins, 1979).

As social psychologists we dwell on this particular thread of the descent of the new area of personal relationships research not because it is the most important but because it is the most familiar to us, and because it simultaneously demonstrates the limitations of unidisplinary approaches to personal relationships. For instance, critical and basic taxonomic work, without which the field could not coalesce, was first done by Hinde (1979), an ethologist, and it is surely no coincidence that one constituent discipline (social psychology) had overlooked (and, incidentally, on its own lacks the necessary skills to employ usefully) those ideas and approaches which an expert from another academic subculture soon demonstrated as essential vehicles of progress. Clearly, the birth of a truly collaborative science of relationships across many disciplines would be a welcome means of combining the valuable compon_... of each constituent into a forceful assault on the general problems.

What lends the general argument more force is precisely that other workers, starting from these different theoretical cultures, have ended up making similar points. Thus Hinde (1979) has argued that many disciplines can contribute expertise to the understanding of human relationships and he goes on to assert that research on personal relationships is the basis of a science that will unite the work, interests and conceptual bases of a variety of previously independent academic subdisciplines. It is true that many sorts of theorists and researchers have the topic of "personal relationships" within their research areas: as noted above, the ethologist, social anthropologist and sociologist have clear and important overlap, through this topic, with the work of experimental social psychologists, clinical psychologists, family relations psychologists, developmental psychologists, students of adolescence and many workers in social psychiatry. Each of these groups has, over the years, ploughed an independent furrow in the same field, but the convergence of interests, of methodologies and of solutions to research problems has steadily become inevitable.

Apart from bringing in perspectives from their original disciplines, workers in the new area of personal relationships are now likely to be able to create a concerted theoretical assault on key problems. For instance, the study of the natural development and classification of relationships is urgently needed as a springboard to the solution of a variety of problems. We do not know enough about the development of children's relationships — although much research effort has been expended on mother–infant relationships, often with wild claims about the influence of such relationships upon the future adult relationships of the child. Until we know more clearly the nature of relationships and their changes through adolescence, such research cannot be properly placed or understood. Likewise we know next to nothing about the role of personal relationships in prevention of disease or mitigation of the effects of old age, although some work suggests that failures of relationships can actually lead to physical deterioration. Indeed, as a general point, the time is ripe for us to work towards an understanding of decay and dissolution of relationships of all kinds (rather than simply of marriage). Furthermore, there is a need for a greater emphasis on the clinical application of work in this field, starting with an understanding of the "pathologies" of relationships, leading on to improvements in the treatment of clinical populations, and then extending through the whole area of "social handicap" or deficit (which includes most people at some time or another). The next few years will see the solution to at least some such problems and we are confident that, in ten years' time, the enormous practical benefits of study in this area will also be ripe for gathering.

As research has slowly evolved to the point where such claims are more credible, there have been a number of texts that have helped by laying out or illustrating the wide range of work in interpersonal attraction (Huston, 1974; Duck, 1977c; Mikula and Stroebe, 1977; Berscheid and Walster, 1978); some texts which have attempted to shift the theoretical emphasis towards a better understanding of the dynamics of relationships (Duck, 1977b; Burgess and Huston, 1979; Kelley, 1979); and some texts which have focused on specific questions or local areas within the general research field of interpersonal attraction (Byrne, 1971; Duck, 1973; Clore, 1975; Foot *et al.*, 1980). No text has yet attempted all three. Indeed, the breadth of the topic makes the task an unlikely or impossible one for any single text, notwithstanding the importance of the area and its interest both to a wide range of researchers and to workers in the helping professions.

When we first began to plan texts, however, we originally envisaged ones that would be generally focused on the important research into disturbances in relationships — but as we elaborated our original conception we began to see the necessity to cover a range of conceptual issues first, and also then to map out what was known about the development of relationships before the reader was pointed towards disturbances in them and their dissolution. Accordingly, we proceeded to prepare lists of topics for four separate but cognate volumes, each dealing with its own particular set of related issues but yet having a clear place in relation to the other volumes of the set. Each was intended to stand on its own but to gain strength from its association with the others; thus there is a family relationship among the volumes — separate but complementary. Each one covers a wide range of work into personal relationships by writers with a variety of academic backgrounds and so reflects the variety of perspectives that exists in the area. The four volumes in the set are: the present volume, "Personal Relationships. 1: Studying Personal Relationships", which deals with conceptual, methodological and topographical issues in the study of relationships (see below); "Personal Relationships. 2: Developing Personal Relationships", which deals with issues in the explanation of development of intimacy in relationships as well as with relationships developmentally through the life-span; "Personal Relationships. 3: Personal Relationships in Disorder", which deals with breakdown of relationships, disorders of certain types of relationships, and the relationships of disordered people, and "Personal Relationships. 4: Dissolving Personal Relationships" which deals with the ending of relationships.

Despite the advantages of such a set, the four volumes are not claimed to offer an exhaustive coverage of the field of personal relationship research. What we hope to do through this quartet is to accelerate the emergence of personal relationships as an interdisciplinary research perspective; to show its coherence as a body of knowledge; to map out the range and kind of terrain that the subject holds; and to encourage the fullest possible exploration and creative practical development of that territory. These are large, but, we believe, important objectives; and the extent to which they are successfully achieved in the developing stages of the field will eventually help to determine the extent to which ensuing research will ultimately produce practical benefits in the field of human relationships.

The present volume, "Personal Relationships. 1: Studying Personal Relationships", is our first step towards the above goals. Specifically, our aims in constructing this volume were to cover conceptual, methodological, and topographical issues in the study of personal relationships in such a way that the variety in such work was well represented. For reasons given above, we did not seek to cover exhaustively the whole set of questions that a reader might expect to find in a volume with this title. Rather our main concern was to address central issues and present a representative array of approaches. We chose, then, to focus on two sorts of problem area: first, the general problems that face a researcher in this field; secondly, some specific questions that arise in the conceptualization and study of particular sorts of relationships. This bipartition of the subject matter of the volume yielded the two Sections that the book now contains.

Section One, The Nature and Study of Personal Relationships, opens with a chapter by Hinde, the distinguished ethologist, who outlines the requirements of a science of personal relationships and makes some extremely valuable seminal suggestions for our achievement of that goal. McCarthy, a social psychologist, then considers the methodological and conceptual issues that face a person wishing to do constructive research in the area, and the clarity of his writing helps to elucidate both unexplored dilemmas which have to be faced and the problems which research still needs to address. A significant and instructive chapter by two Soviet social psychologists, Andreyeva and Gozman, next explores the explicit and implicit influences of social context on personal relationships both in their conceptualization by researchers and in their conduct by individuals in society. La Gaipa, an American social psychologist in the sociological tradition, considers the specific influences on the social systems in which relationships are conducted and points out the important (but inadequately explored) consequences of individuals' *other* relationships on any particular relationship that is chosen for study. The final chapter by Feger, a prominent member of a European team of network analysts, presents a number of ways in which the structural, interactional and diagnostic properties of relationships may be formally represented.

Section Two, Some Aspects and Examples of Personal Relationships, contains the thinking of a variety of workers whose interests centre on different sorts of, or contexts for, the study of personal relationships. To an extent, the selection and ordering of a given list is bound to be arbitrary and arguable, but we believe that we have selected here a collection of illustrative chapters which depict the kinds of different problems in the study of different relationships. The chapters show a variety of both methodological styles and theoretical approaches as well as indicating the enormous range of topics that merit investigation. Chapters cover sexual relationships (Przybyla and Byrne), cohabitation (Newcomb), intimacy (Hatfield and Traupmann), marital and family relations (Burgess), and relationships at work (Mangham). There is no coverage here of children's relationships, adolescent relationships, or courtship growth, since these are among the topics reserved for the companion volume "Personal Relationships.2: Developing Personal Relationships"; while clinical considerations are to be found in the third volume, "Personal Relationships. 3: Personal Relationships in Disorder", nonetheless, the chapters in the present volume fulfil their part in the set by providing instructive and varied insights into research on personal relationships by serving as an introduction both to the area of personal relationships as a whole and to the other volumes in the quartet in particular. The range of conceptual issues covered here itself indicates the magnitude of the task of understanding personal relationships whilst the chapters in Section Two particularly and in the other volumes indicate the values of such understanding, not only as an academic advance but also as a practical step forward.

In constructing this volume we tried hard to retain and realize our original conception of the book when the detailed editorial work began. In this we were given noble assistance by the contributors and we readily acknowledge that debt. Contributors were very efficient in producing drafts and responding to editorial promptings and suggestions. Indeed, the fact that the manuscript was submitted on time (a very rare event in publishers' experience) testifies to the collaborative efficiency of the whole enterprise. We wish also to express our thanks to Phil Levy for his advice and guidance in the various areas where his expertise far exceeds our; and to our colleagues Ceri Roderick and Charles Antaki for their helpful comments, their general support and their encouragement. Furthermore, we wish to acknowledge

publicly our heartfelt appreciation of willing, skillful and extensive secretarial assistance given by Jane Dickinson, Ann Parker, Hazel Satterthwaite and Sylvia Sumner,
who typed, retyped, re-retyped and helped uncomplainingly with our increasingly
unreasonable demands.

Having thus implied strenuously that all responsibility for remaining errors is
diffused, editors customarily at this point go on to deny the implication and take the
blame themselves. This we do gladly : we just hope that there aren't too many of
them.

University of Lancaster   Steve Duck
May, 1980   Robin Gilmour

Contents

CHAPTER 5

Analysis of Social Networks   91
HUBERT FEGER

Section II

Some Aspects and Examples of Personal Relationships

CHAPTER 6

Sexual Relationships   109
D. P. J. PRZYBYLA and DONN BYRNE

CHAPTER 7

Heterosexual Cohabitation Relationships   131
MICHAEL D. NEWCOMB

CHAPTER 8

Intimate Relationships: 165
A Perspective from Equity Theory
ELAINE HATFIELD and JANE TRAUPMANN

For Christina

Für Elise

Section I
The Nature and Study of Personal Relationships

CHAPTER 1

The Bases of a Science of Interpersonal Relationships

Robert A. Hinde

The study of interpersonal relationships forms the meeting point of a number of different scientific disciplines, but the central focus of none. Psychiatry, although crucially concerned with how an individual is affected by his relationships with others, usually sees those relationships from the perspective of one participant, rather than as entities in their own right. Developmental psychology is in a similar position: whilst the child's relationships with others are important determinants of its development, the primary concern is with the child as an individual. Personality theory focuses on differences between individuals, but focuses very little on the differences between, or on the effects of, the relationships they form. Amongst social psychologists, most of whom are primarily interested in the social behaviour of individuals, alone or in groups, there has been an increasing interest in relationships; but the power of experimental methods has biased research towards short-term interactions and away from more enduring relationships. Other social sciences, such as sociology and anthropology, also have an interest in, but not an over-riding concern with, interpersonal relationships.

Of course there have been representatives of many of these disciplines who have made interpersonal relationships their prime concern — family therapists, exchange theorists, and others. But there is as yet no integrated body of knowledge, encompassing all relevant disciplines, and focusing on inter-personal relationships. This chapter is based on the view that to concentrate on the research and conceptual problems posed by dyadic relationships would not only be timely, and if successful might bring inestimable practical gains, but could also be a powerful force for cohesion among diverse branches of social science.

Some support for this view is presented in the next Section, in the course of a discussion of the nature of interpersonal relationships. The rest of the chapter is concerned with two matters deemed crucial for building a science of interpersonal relationships: the provision of an adequate descriptive base; and the integration of some of the diverse theoretical approaches already in the field. These issues have already been discussed in more detail elsewhere (Hinde, 1979); here limitations of space permit me only to summarize some of the main points.

The Nature of Interpersonal Relationships

General observations

The behavioural and affective/cognitive aspects of interpersonal relation-ships are almost inextricably intertwined. Considering first the former, in colloquial usage the term "relationship" implies a series of interactions between two individuals known to each other. By an interaction I mean one or more interchanges of the type: A does X to B and B does Y back again, for as long as they do not undergo a marked change in content. How long an interaction must continue, or how many interactions must occur, before two individuals can be said to have a relationship is an arbitrary matter which it is hardly profitable to pursue. But we do not speak of two strangers who meet in the street as immediately having a relationship, reserving the term for cases where the interaction is affected by past interactions or is likely to influence future ones. Of course two individuals can be said still to have a relationship even if they do not meet for a long period: in such a case "relationship" refers not to an actual sequence of interactions, but to a potential for patterns of interactions which are likely to be of certain general types, though their precise form will be determined by future events.

To describe the behavioural aspects of an *interaction*, it is necessary to specify first what the participants are doing together — whether they are talking, fighting, kissing, or what. Often, however, what they are doing is less important than its quality — are they kissing dutifully, passionately or politely. The use of the term "quality" here carries no implications that such properties cannot be treated quantitatively.

The qualities of an interaction may also include reference to the relation between the behaviour of the two participants — are they behaving synchronously or in conjunction with each other, and to what extent can their behaviour be seen as directed towards, or achieving, a common goal? We may note here that such issues concern properties of the way in which individuals *interact*, and are not relevant to the behaviour of individuals in isolation.

To describe the behavioural aspects of a *relationship*, it is necessary to specify not only the content and quality of the component interactions, but also their frequencies or relative frequencies, and how they are patterned in time. For example the nature of a mother–child relationship varies not only with how often the mother cuddles the child, but also with how often she does so *relative to* the frequency with which the child seeks to be cuddled.

Thus, just as interactions involve emergent properties not relevant to the behaviour of individuals in isolation, so also do relationships involve properties not relevant to their component interactions. It is indeed essential to remember that we must come to terms with phenomena at several different levels of complexity — individual behaviour, interaction, dyadic relationship, and beyond that, social structure: each level involves properties not relevant to the previous one (Hinde, 1976). Partly for that reason, the social behaviour that an individual shows may provide little guide to the extent to which he has formed, or has the capacity to form, social relationships. People may be sociable and yet direct their social behaviours promiscuously, or reticent yet devoted — see data in Hinde (1978b). Thus studies of social behaviour provide no substitute for studies of social relationships.

The discussion so far has concerned only the behavioural aspects of relationships. The behaviour of the participants often provides the primary source of data to an outsider, and some would argue that it is the behaviour of the participants each to the other that is ultimately important. But we have already mentioned that a relationship may continue over periods in which the participants do not meet or communicate with each other. It is also the case that what actually happened in an interaction may be less important than what the participants thought happened, or how they thought they felt (e.g. Valins, 1966), and what the partner is like may be no more important than what he is perceived to be like (e.g. Levinger and Breedlove, 1966; Murstein, 1971). Furthermore individuals evaluate both the component interactions and the relationships in which they participate. They may also be concerned about the view they believe their partner holds of them; about the extent to which they have the opportunity to behave, and have actually behaved, in ways they would like to behave; and about the extent to which their partner feels satisfaction in the relationship. Such evaluations influence the future course of the relationship. It is thus necessary for studies of interpersonal relationships to be concerned not only with their behavioural but also with their affective/cognitive aspects. Whilst relationships involve a series of interactions in time, that is certainly not all there is to it. We shall return to this issue shortly.

The position of studies of relationships within psychology

Studies of interpersonal relationships must come to terms not only with phenomena at a number of levels of analysis — social behaviour, social inter-actions and social relationships — each with both behavioural and affec-tive/cognitive aspects, but also with dialectics of at least two types. On the one hand lies a dialectic between social relationships and the personalities of participating individuals, and on the other that between relationships and the various social influences that determine their nature. This requires a digression.

Psychologists with diverse theoretical viewpoints have long held that the child's developing personality is markedly influenced by his relationships with others, and especially by his relationships with the members of his nuclear family (e.g. Freud, 1938; Sullivan, 1953; Mead, 1934; Cooley, 1956; Bowlby, 1969; Laing, 1962). Of course this does not mean that those relation-ships are the sole determinants of personality; newborns already have their own special characteristics, differing from each other in reflex and behav-ioural characteristics, in the stimuli they present, in their activity, and in their responsiveness to care-givers (e.g. Bell, 1974). These differences may be perceived by adults as involving differences in cuddliness, manageability, or other dimensions that affect the ongoing relationship. But within limits set by congenital characteristics or potentialities, the relationships in which the developing child is involved influence its developing personality.

Early relationships are of special importance primarily because the range of possible courses that development could take is then widest: subsequent relationships can act only within the potentialities left by earlier influences. Thus personality characteristics with considerable persistence may be laid down: although the consistency of the personality attributes usually mea-sured by psychologists has on the whole been rather low (Mischel, 1968; 1973), this must be regarded as a reflection of the techniques used rather than an indication that all individual characteristics are impermanent. We are all conscious of constant threads running through our lives, and sensitive testing can reveal them (e.g. Block, 1977). Nevertheless it is a reasonable assumption that any close personal relationship leaves its mark: there is a real sense in which we are those we have loved — or hated.

But whilst individual personality is influenced by relationships experi-enced, the nature of the individual reciprocally affects the relationships that he enters, and how he behaves within them. Since each relationship involves two individuals, its nature must be in some measure determined by both of them. For practical reasons, this does not necessarily mean that the course of every relationship is absolutely predictable from the known characteristics of the participants. Whether our data come from personal acquaintance, from observation, or from tests, we can never be certain that we have all the information necessary to predict the properties of a relationship with a particular (also incompletely known) other person.

The psychologist must thus come to terms with a dialectic: relationships influence the nature of individuals, and individuals influence the relationships they enter. Recognition of this dialectic highlights an imbalance in psychology: whilst much energy has been devoted to studying the characteristics and behaviour of individuals, relationships have been studied primarily from the viewpoint of one or other participant, and not in their own right. For this reason alone there is a need for a science, or subscience, of interpersonal relationships.

The second type of dialectic arises from the fact that every relationship exists in a social setting. There are two issues here. First, both participants in a relationship have relationships also with other individuals, and these other relationships may both influence and be influenced by their relationship with each other. Secondly, their relationship will be affected by norms of the culture in which they live — they may strive to build a good marriage, to exploit their employees, to help or hinder each other according to standards accepted in the societies in which they have lived. But at the same time such norms are developed, transmitted and refurbished through the agency of the dyadic (and higher-order) relationships that constitute the society. It is thus necessary to come to terms not only with the dialectics between personality and relationship, but also with those between relationships and society.

These obligations, however, also indicate the potential importance of studies of interpersonal relationships within the social sciences. A science or subscience of interpersonal relationships could help to bridge the gap between the study of personality and social psychology on the one hand, and between social psychology and sociology on the other. In such a task developmental psychology, concerned with the differences between and effects of early relationships, would also play a crucial role.

The present status and requirements of a subscience of interpersonal relationships

Whilst the study of interpersonal relationships has considerable potential for integrating subdisciplines within psychology, that is of trivial importance in comparison with its potential relevance for everyday life. It would be unnecessary and trite to emphasize the importance of personal relationships

to each one of us, but it is pertinent to ask why, then, a science of interpersonal relationships does not exist already. By asking such a question, I
have no intention of belittling the extensive knowledge already accumulated
by clinicians, social psychologists, anthropologists and other scientists, not
to mention the work of novelists and biographers. But a "science" implies an
integrated body of knowledge, and even those who focus on interpersonal
relationships must admit that their study as yet lacks integration.

Some responsibility for this could be ascribed to prejudices from outside
science, or to the inherent complexity of the subject matter. For present purposes, however, we may concentrate on two issues.

One concerns the need for an adequate descriptive base. Only when we
have more means for ordering the phenomena to be explained can the generality of descriptive generalizations or explanatory hypotheses be assessed.
The diversity of the phenomena makes the provision of an adequate descriptive base of crucial importance.

The second issue arises from the fact that many students of interpersonal
relationships, starting from a particular theoretical position, have attempted
only to establish the effectiveness of their own approach. This has involved
either attempts to establish the range of applicability of one paradigm (e.g.
Byrne, 1971), or to pit one theory or paradigm against its rivals (e.g. Ajzen,
1977). Largely (though not by any means completely) lacking have been
attempts to integrate them. Yet in the study of interpersonal relationships the
need for integration is of special importance. Relationships have both behavioural and affective/cognitive aspects; they depend on interactions yet
involve more than interactions; their parts must be studied but so must the
whole; they must be related to the personalities of the participants and to the
social context in which they exist. Thus understanding of their dynamics
requires diverse concepts, and an integrated subscience of relationships
demands that the relationships between those concepts be established. This is
a task on which only limited progress is at present possible, but recognition of
its urgency may facilitate further advance.

In the next two sections these issues will be considered in turn.

The Description of Interpersonal Relationships

The aim of description is to be selective, not comprehensive. Selection must
be guided both by the problems to be solved, and by the theories thought
likely to be useful in solving them. In selecting it is difficult to avoid being
influenced by our pet theories, and we can certainly never divest ourselves
entirely of the cultural spectacles we inevitably use in perceiving social

phenomena. But whilst selective description can never be entirely objective, the possibility of bias can be minimized through awareness of the dangers.

An adequate science of interpersonal relationships must be concerned both with close "personal" relationships and with formal or "role" relationships. A descriptive system must thus embrace dimensions relevant to a wide range of relationships. It must also discriminate both between gross categories of relationships — between teacher–pupil, mother–child and husband –wife relationships, for example — and also between relationships within those broad categories — how this husband–wife relationship differs from that.

It is possible to study a wide range of relationships, measure many of their characteristics and then reduce the data by factor analysis or some comparable technique to a limited number of dimensions. Such an approach has been used with considerable success in some contexts (e.g. Lorr and McNair, 1963; Becker, 1964; Maxwell and Hage, 1969; Wish *et al.*, 1976). The last authors, for instance, derived by multidimensional scaling techniques four dimensions: (i) cooperative/friendly vs competitive/hostile; (ii) equal vs unequal; (iii) intense vs superficial; and (iv) socio-emotional/informal vs task-orientated/formal. The use of such dimensions provides a powerful means of data reduction, and an escape from the morass of detail into which studies of interpersonal relationships could easily sink.

But there are problems. If objective measures of behaviour are used, or if specific questions are asked, selection in the data collected is inevitable, and the dimensions abstracted from the analyses are inevitably influenced by that selection. And if subjects are asked to describe their relationships, it is impossible to assess how far their descriptions are affected by implicit theories as to what relationships should be like ("We are married so we must understand each other" — cf. Bruner and Tagiuri, 1954) or distorted to achieve consistency between beliefs ("I must love him if I have looked after him all these years"). The dimensions abstracted may thus imply that aspects of the relationship are inter-related when such is not in fact the case — an issue likely to be important for understanding its detailed nature.

This is not to deny that the ways in which the participants perceive a relationship have a crucial influence on its course. A relationship is, as we have seen, likely to be affected both by what actually happens and by what the participants perceive to happen, the latter including the comparisons they make with what they believe should happen. And what they perceive to happen will be at least affected by what actually happens. It thus seems that description must embrace both what actually happens and what is perceived to happen, and that three or four dimensions are likely to be inadequate for at least some purposes.

However, at present it seems wise to acknowledge that we do not yet know *precisely* what to describe and measure, so that it is prudent to attempt to specify merely what *sorts of issues* are likely to be helpful. In trying to specify these categories of dimensions selection with its inherent dangers is still inevitable, but it is sensible not to discard as preliminary guidelines the qualities we use in everyday life — we may well have been shaped to be aware of those characteristics of relationships that are important to us (Humphrey, 1976). However, for the reasons given above, a rather finer level of analysis than colloquial labels such as "loving", "competitive", and so on must be attempted.

In the following pages, eight categories of criteria that seem valuable for describing relationships will be mentioned. They concern the properties of the relationship itself, and not the demographic or personality characteristics of the participants. Each category may later be refined into one or a number of dimensions, with each dimension assessable in terms of one or a number of intercorrelated measures. The list moves from behavioural measures more useful in differentiating gross types of relationships to those concerned more with thoughts and feelings.

Content of interactions

The initial categorization of relationships that we make usually refers primarily to what the participants do together. "Mother–child" or "doctor –patient" relationship refers to the activities of the individuals concerned. Although "mother–child" might seem to refer to biological characteristics, we do not regard an adopted child as having a "mother–child" relationship with his natural mother.

Such labels are possible only because, within any one culture, there are regularities in the ways in which interactions are grouped within relationships. These regularities are in part biological: the properties of any relationship involving a child are in part a consequence of its immaturity. But utilitarian and conventional issues are also important. Thus the interactions now expected in father–child relationships differ considerably from those usually found a few decades ago.

Just because such societal norms are so important in determining what goes on within relationships of particular types, labels such as "parent-child" or "husband–wife" relationships are often used to refer not to what the participants in such a relationship actually do, but what they are expected to do in the society in question — to their rights and duties. Parents may strive to create a good parent–child relationship, and the implications of the label serve as a determinant of their behaviour.

The contents of the interactions within relationships may be used to differentiate not only major classes of relationships, but also to distinguish between relationships within those classes. For example, Collins *et al.* (1971) compared 60 marriages in which the husband was a neurotic outpatient with 60 control marriages: the husband's contribution to household duties and child care was smaller in the former group.

Diversity of interactions

Some relationships involve many types of interaction (multiplex). Others, such as those between drinking companions or business colleagues, may involve only one (uniplex) or a few. The distinction depends in part on the level of analysis: a mother-infant relationship could be called uniplex (involving only maternal–filial responses) or multiplex (involving playing, nursing, protecting and so on). Yet the dimension is an important one, for the greater the variety of interactions, the richer may be the effects of interactions on interactions. Furthermore, the more things two individuals do together, the more aspects of their personalities are likely to be revealed to each other, and the more experiences they share.

Qualities of interactions

As we have seen, what two individuals do together may be less important than how they do it. However, just how many qualities of interactions should be recognized is unknown; perhaps repertory grid techniques could provide an answer. Whilst the difficulties of measurement are considerable, a few inter-related categories of characters have proved useful.

(a) Intensity — do the participants whisper, talk or shout; do they follow or chase each other? Interpretation of intensity may depend on the context — whispering may indicate either affection or collusion.

(b) Content and presentation of verbal material. In interpreting verbal material, a distinction must be made between "locutionary meaning" and its "illocutionary" or "perlocutionary force" as assessed from its intended or actual effects (Austin, 1962). For example "May I have the salt?" is not a question but a request, and "It's a nice day" may have little to do with the weather but have a marked effect on the relationship. The meaning may also be affected by prosodic (e.g. intonation, stress) and paralinguistic (e.g. supporting gestures) features associated with the verbal utterance (e.g. Rutter and Brown, 1966).

(c) Non-vocal communication. This may be a powerful indicator of the quality of an interaction, even in the absence of verbal communication (e.g. Ekman and Friesen, 1969, 1975; Argyle, 1975). Whilst the signals that have been most studied hitherto are the stereotyped and culturally accepted ones, the importance in close personal relationships of idiosyncratic signals must not be forgotten.

(d) Measures of relations between the behaviour of the two participants. Included here would be measures of the sensitivity of one partner to the other's signals (e.g. Sander, 1977), and of the extent to which the behaviour of each meshes with that of the other (e.g. Hinde and White, 1974; Hinde and Simpson, 1975; Stern, 1977).

It will be apparent that a given quality may apply to some or to all the interactions in a relationship, and to the behaviour of one or both partners. However, where a label appears to apply to only one partner, we must remember that it was elicited by the other, and is thus to some extent a property of both.

Finally, the content of an individual's behaviour, or of an interaction, may be dissociated from the quality or style with which it is expressed. The issue has been made with force by Goffman's (1959) distinction between the expressions an individual *gives* and those he *gives off*. A similar distinction, between the *explicit* content of a message and its *command* or *metacommunicational* aspect, was made by Bateson *et al.* (1956; see also Watzlawick *et al.*, 1967).

Relative frequency and patterning of interactions

Here we are concerned with several different issues.

(a) Clusters of co-varying properties. Many judgements about relationships depend on multiple criteria, and we may be more willing to apply a given label, when more criteria are met. For example, in studies of rhesus monkeys the frequency with which mothers approached their infants, the frequency with which they initiated close contact, and the frequency with which they restrained their infants, were intercorrelated and provided a dimension that could be called "maternal protectiveness" (Simpson and Howe, in press). (It is important to remember also that types of behaviour indicative of the same quality may be alternatives to each other, and might then be negatively correlated.)

(b) Ratio and derived measures. For some purposes relative frequencies may be more revealing than, or may relate to different properties from, absolute measures (Hinde and Herrmann, 1977). Thus a measure of how often a couple made love relative to the frequency with which one or other partner desired it would tell one more about sexual satisfaction than would the absolute frequency of making love.

(c) Relations between heterologous interactions. Some properties of relationships can be regarded as emergent from the relative frequencies of interactions of different sorts. Thus a monkey mother who often rejected her infant's attempts to gain contact might be labelled as "rejecting" (in the context of that relationship), and one who frequently picked the infant up as "possessive". But if she frequently did both, or seldom did either, she might be labelled as "controlling" or "permissive". The labels depend on the relative frequencies of interactions of different sorts, not on any one particular type.

(d) Patterning of interactions. Differences in the patterning of interactions between two relationships may be of great significance, even though the frequencies are similar. A mother–child relationship will differ according to whether the mother picks up the baby only when it is crying or only when it is not crying, even though the frequency of picking up and crying are the same in both cases. Furthermore, the sequencing of positive and negative outcomes provided by one partner for the other may affect the future course of the relationship (e.g. Gergen, 1969; Sigall and Aronson, 1967).

Reciprocity vs complementarity

Relationships differ in the extent to which the various interactions are reciprocal or complementary. A reciprocal interaction is one in which the participants show similar behaviour, either simultaneously or alternately, as when in play one child chases another and then the roles are reversed. A complementary interaction is one in which the behaviour of each participant differs from, but complements, that of the other.

Relationships in which all interactions are reciprocal are probably rare, but those between peers, colleagues or drinking companions may approach this condition. By contrast relationships in which all interactions are complementary are common: most relationships in hierarchical organizations such as businesses and armies are of this type. However, in close personal relationships there need be no congruence in the degree or direction of complementarity in different aspects of the relationship: the interactions may show complex patterns of imbalance. Furthermore, the complementarity may involve many different properties — dominance/subordination, maleness/femaleness, achievement/vicariousness, nurturance/succorance, etc.

Similarity or complementarity in behaviour, or in needs, is likely to be related to similarities or differences in personal characteristics. Dimensions of reciprocity and complementarity may thus be related to the considerable volume of work on the importance of similarities and differences between the participants in a relationship. On the one hand there is considerable evidence that spouses and friends are likely to resemble each other in a variety of sociological and psychological characteristics. Furthermore, attitude similarity, and to a lesser degree similarity in personality, can be conducive to interpersonal attraction. Amongst the suggestions that have been made as to why perceived similarity should be attractive, those likely to have the widest validity are that perceived similarity is associated with consensual validation, that it facilitates communication, and that it leads to positive beliefs (see, for examples, Byrne, 1971; Clore and Byrne, 1974; Ajzen, 1977; Duck, 1976–1977b). On the other hand, there is also evidence that differences can contribute to the building of interpersonal relationships, especially if they involve complementary needs and thereby allow the partners to satisfy each other (e.g. Winch, 1958).

Unfortunately much of the earlier literature involved a supposition that either overall similarity or overall difference, assessed along one or more dimensions in tests outside the relationship, is of primary importance for friendship choice or for the building of a personal relationship. There are several reasons why this is an oversimplification. For one thing, some types of interaction require similarity in behavioural propensities, whilst others require difference of a complementary sort: incompatibility may rest on lack of opportunity either to do things together as equals, or to behave in a nurturant, submissive or some other complementary fashion. A second issue is that personality characteristics assessed in non-interactive tests do not always have a high relevance to real-life situations. And related to this, in real-life relationships there are considerable opportunities for the partners to accommodate to each other's needs, or to satisfy some of their needs outside the relationship.

However, recent work has been designed with more awareness of these problems, and it has been recognized that reciprocity and complementarity may each be important to different extents in different contexts and in different aspects of any one relationship (e.g. Schutz, 1960; Hendrick and Brown, 1971; Seyfried, 1977). Furthermore, what is important may change with the stage of the relationship — whilst attitude similarity may be important early on, personality compatibility may be more important when the relationship has developed, and similarity in the ways in which the participants see the world at a still later stage (e.g. Duck, 1973, 1977a,b; Duck and Craig, 1978). And with regard to the satisfaction of needs outside the relationship, some more clinically orientated workers are now focusing on the extent to which individuals' needs are met in the whole constellation of their relationships (Weiss, 1974).

Intimacy

The extent to which the participants reveal all aspects of themselves to each other is a crucial dimension of many relationships. A number of techniques to assess the degree of self-revelation between two individuals have been devised. Jourard (e.g. 1971) has devised a Self-disclosure questionnaire which characterizes individuals along a scale from "disclosers" to "non-disclosers". Altman and Taylor (1973) have used an instrument which assesses self-disclosure in specific situations or relationships. This involved 671 items relevant to self-disclosure which were classed by one group of judges into *a priori* topical categories (e.g. marriage, family, etc.) and rated for intimacy by another group. It is thus possible to assess degree of intimacy in various aspects of personal experience. Whilst such an instrument may be closely culture-bound, it represents a promising start.

Interpersonal perception

We are concerned here with the relations between the views held by the participants in a relationship about themselves, about each other, and about objects and people outside their relationship. Several different issues are involved. At the lowest level, behavioural meshing would not be possible unless each partner's view of the other were reasonably close to reality. Secondly, their feelings about each other may affect, and be affected by, the extent to which each perceives the other to agree about the rest of the world (e.g. Newcomb, 1956, 1961): a wife's feelings about her husband may be influenced by her perception of the extent to which he loves the baby that she loves. Thirdly, the course of a relationship may be affected by the extent to which each participant understands the other and feels him or herself to be understood — that is, by the extent to which his view of himself coincides with his view of his partner's view of him. And beyond these, each partner may evaluate his perception of his own behaviour, his partner's behaviour, and the relationship, in ways that will affect its future course.

Such issues can be investigated by asking the participants in a relationship to fill in an attitude or personality questionnaire from a number of viewpoints. For instance, Drewery and Rae (1969) requested husbands and wives to fill in the Edwards Personal Preferences Schedule from three points of view — "Myself as I am" (1), "My spouse as I see him/her" (2) and "Myself as I think my spouse sees me" (3). A variety of comparisons were then possible. Thus Husband's (1) vs Wife's (1) assesses similarity and difference between their views of themselves; Husband's (2) vs Wife's (1) compares whether the husband's view of his wife corresponds to her view of herself; Husband's (3) vs Wife's (2) concerns the extent to which the wife perceives the husband as he believes her to perceive him; and each partner's (1) vs (3) concerns the extent to which he or she feels understood. A related approach has been carried even further by R.D. Laing (e.g. 1969).

Another approach which must be mentioned here concerns the use of Personal Construct Analysis (e.g. Kelly, 1955, 1970; Fransella and Bannister,

1977) to assess similarities in the manner in which individuals construe the world. As indicated above, such similarity may be an important correlate, and perhaps a prerequisite, for friendship (Duck, 1973).

Commitment

One of the most important aspects of some close personal relationships, but one that has been little studied, concerns the extent to which the partners are committed to it. Commitment is used here in a general sense to refer to the extent to which the partners in a relationship either accept their relationship as continuing indefinitely or direct their behaviour towards ensuring its continuance or optimizing its properties.

Commitment arises naturally from the processes inherent in the formation of a relationship, though it may also become overtly recognized by the participants in a private pledge, or recognized more widely in a public one. It is useful to distinguish between commitment for continuity (i.e. for continuation of the relationship) and commitment concerning consistency in or nature of content. A parent of a teenage daughter may be happy to maintain continuity irrespective of consistency; a lover may continue to be committed to continuity only if the content of the relationship changes; and a householder may be committed to consistency in his relationship with his neighbour but mind not at all if the neighbour moves away. It is also useful to distinguish between commitment imposed from outside (exogenous commitment), as in arranged marriages or kin relationships, and endogenous commitment which arises within the dyad. These may have very different consequences.

The course of a relationship may be affected not only by the degree of commitment of the two partners, but by the extent to which each believes in the other's commitment. The increased vulnerability which arises with intimacy is tolerable only if accompanied by a belief that the partner will not exploit it, and absence of faith in the other's commitment to continuity in spite of limited change could inhibit personal growth.

So far there seem to have been few attempts to assess commitment (but see Peplau *et al.*, 1978), though it seems a not impossible task.

Summary

These eight features are not to be considered in any sense absolute. They are listed as providing a convenient way to pigeon-hole data: the precise characteristics that will prove useful, and the precise ways in which those characteristics are to be measured, remain to be worked out. Nor is it suggested that this is the only way in which aspects of interpersonal relationships could be classified. Assessments of more global properties, such as the extent to which a relationship was caring, affectionate or competitive, might each draw on aspects relevant to several of these features; it would, however, be an open issue how far the different sorts of data would be correlated. For further details and for discussion as to the extent to which the level of analysis is appropriate, the extent to which the features are sufficiently inclusive, and the extent of their overlap, the reader is referred elsewhere (Hinde, 1979).

Principles of Dynamics

Description is, of course, not an end in itself, but a means towards understanding how interpersonal relationships work, towards comprehending their dynamics. Several sources of generalizations, principles or theories that seem likely to contribute to this end are available. These derive from a vast amount of research, observational and experimental, and it would not be feasible to review them here. Rather the aim of this section is to illustrate how, if they are to be useful, they must be linked to an adequate system for describing relationships. These sources can be considered under four headings.

Social issues

Every relationship is set in a nexus of other relationships, and may be influenced by the relationships that each participant has with other individuals. Furthermore, the nature of every relationship is influenced by the norms current in the society — husband and wife compare their relationship with marriage as idealized in their society, and parents strive to build "good" parent-child relationships.

These norms lie along a continuum from those that are obligatory to those that are merely expected. Marriages must be consummated, but tenderness between husband and wife is merely expected to a degree which varies amongst subcultures even within our own society; and parents are required to show a certain minimum level of child care, but may or may not teach their children how to play football. Norms also lie along a continuum from those that are general throughout the whole society to those that are limited to a subculture or group within the society. Indeed insofar as norms may be acquired during earlier life from significant others, they may be almost idiosyncratic (e.g. Toman, 1971: Teevan, 1972). Whilst reference to idiosyncratic norms could be regarded as a contradiction in terms, this postulation of a continuum between such issues and society-wide norms is intended to emphasize possible similarities in mode of action even though mode of acquisition, sanctions and consequences may differ.

Such cultural norms may have a profound effect on the ways in which individuals behave within relationships. For example, 30 years ago Komarovsky (1946) documented the ways in which girl students, interacting with men, attempted to play down their academic qualities in an effort to present a persona which they believed to be attractive, and Peplau (1976) has shown that "traditional" vs "modern" sex role attitudes affect the behaviour of women interacting with their boyfriends even in an artificial test situation.

Now the courses of interindividual relationships, whether of a close personal or more formal and public kind, depend on evaluations of the relationship by the participants. These are relative to the standards they have brought to the relationship by virtue of their past experience. Thus understanding of the dynamics of interpersonal relationships must depend on adequate descriptions both of how each participant perceives the relationship, and of how he would like it to be (e.g. Tharp, 1963; Murstein, 1972; Quick and Jacob, 1973; Kelley and Thibaut, 1978; Kelley, 1979). However even this may not be sufficient, for how people perceive their relationship and how they would like it to be may not be reflected in their behaviour. Data on what they actually do are therefore also essential.

Interpersonal perception

Each participant in a relationship assesses his own behaviour, his partner's behaviour, and the relationship. In doing so, he attributes enduring dispositions to his partner, and on the basis of these predicts possible future courses for the relationship. Theories concerned with how partners perceive and assess each other are therefore crucial for understanding the dynamics of relationships. To emphasize the importance of linking such theories to a descriptive base, one example will suffice. Individuals form positive and negative attitudes towards objects (physical and social) in the world. If two individuals like each other and perceive each other to have similar attitudes towards an object or person, a state of balance will exist. However, if they like each other but see each other as having dissimilar attitudes, imbalance will be present. A, who likes fishing, is more likely to like B if he perceives B likes fishing. If he likes B but perceives that B does not like fishing, imbalance will occur. If A expects the relationship to be a continuing one, and considers the fishing issue to be important to it, he may attempt to restore "balance". For instance he may decide that he does not care all that much about fishing anyway, or he may convince himself that B does like fishing, really (Heider, 1958; Newcomb, 1961; Kelley, 1971).

Now on this paradigm it could be expected that, if John likes Jill and Jack likes Jill, John would like Jack. In practice this is by no means necessarily the case. Newcomb (1971) points out that attraction is not unitary, and will vary with how the participants see the nature of the relationships in which they are involved: John may see Jack as a male friend in some contexts and as a rival in others. In other words, the application of balance theories to real-life situations may be crucially related to the nature of the relationships involved. A descriptive base is essential.

Exchange and interdependence theories

We are concerned here with theories that share the assumption that social behaviour is in large measure determined by the rewards and costs, or expectations of rewards and costs, consequent upon it (e.g. Homans, 1961; Thibaut and Kelley, 1959; Kelley and Thibaut, 1978; Kelley, 1979; Blau, 1964; Walster *et al.*, 1978). Whilst some emphasize the rewards and costs arising from particular interactions, others (e.g. Kelley and Thibaut, 1978; Kelley, 1979) stress the interdependency inherent in any relationship: successful interaction involves the continuity of the relationship, and thus the satisfaction of both participants. They stress also that in addition to obtaining direct outcomes (rewards and costs) in specific interactions a participant in a relationship may obtain (and affect his partner's ability to obtain) symbolic, abstract outcomes from displaying dispositions (for instance, to be cooperative, dominant, altruistic) that he likes to see himself as having.

For a number of reasons, it appears that the utility of such theories must be linked to an adequate means for describing relationships.

(a) The problem of measurement   The problem of measuring the rewards exchanged and costs incurred in real-life situations must ultimately be crucial to the exchange theorist. Considerable progress has in fact been made, in part because it is possible simply to ask people about their relative values (e.g. Walster *et al.*, 1978), but one point must be borne in mind. The value of many of the resources exchanged in interpersonal interaction, such as social approval or gestures of affection and love, vary with the context. Profits and costs must be assessed in relation to their meanings to the individual concerned. The words "I love you" mean something different in husband–wife, girl–boy and girl–teacher relationships. Furthermore the same words will change in value with the stage in the relationship. Thus generalizations about value must be related to an adequate description of the relational context in which the interaction takes place.

(b) The problem of what is fair   In different relationships, and even within one relationship, the participants may have different views about what is fair. One may consider that each should obtain equal outcomes, another that outcomes should be related to costs incurred, and yet another that they

should be related to needs. Lerner (1974) has pointed out that the rules of justice that prevail may depend on the nature of the relationship. Equality seems to be important amongst younger children, equity (each person's outcomes related to his contributions) becoming more important with age. In general, equality or the relating of outcomes to needs (so-called "Marxist justice") tends to characterize personal relationships, and equity is more usual in formal or role relationships. Thus what is considered to be fair varies with the nature of the relationship (Lerner *et al.*, 1976). Of course this does not imply that the participants in a relationship will necessarily agree on the means of assessing what is fair: parents may allocate resources amongst the children according to need, while the children seek equality in their outcomes.

(c) Categorization of resources   Most exchange theories have been based on principles of learning derived from studies of animals working for food rewards. However the properties of the resources used in interpersonal exchange may differ markedly from those of food (Blau, 1964). Foa and Foa (1974) have suggested that the resources used in interpersonal exchange can be categorized into six classes — money, goods, services, love, status and information. The labels refer primarily to categories of meaning assigned to actions. They suggest that these overlapping categories can be arranged in a circular order (as indicated, with information adjacent to money): instances are more similar, the nearer the categories in this circular arrangement. Amongst the dimensions they discuss are concreteness, with status and information rating least and goods and services rating highest on this dimension; and particularism, referring to how much it matters from whom the resource is received. Money is low on this dimension because the value of money is not usually affected by whom it comes from, whilst love is high because it matters very much who it is who says "I love you". The Foas also suggest that whilst giving money depletes the donor's own resources by the amount given, giving love augments them. Whilst the Foa's scheme can be criticized on a number of grounds, there is also much that makes intuitive sense (Hinde, 1979). That resources differ in their properties is an issue that can no longer be neglected. Furthermore, as we have seen, the meanings assigned to actions (e.g. saying "I love you") vary with the context of the relationship. A categorization of resources must thus be married to a categorization of relationships.

Description in terms of positive and negative feedback

Same aspects of the development of interpersonal relationships can be described as involving positive or negative feedback. There is for instance a considerable literature on the manner in which loving promotes loving, competitiveness promotes competitiveness, giving promotes giving, intimacy promotes intimacy, and so on (e.g. Bateson, 1958; Newcomb, 1961; Backman and Secord, 1959; Rubin, 1975; Stroebe, 1977). However, loving does not always promote loving: it sometimes leads to rejection by the other partner. Similarly, giving can lead merely to selfish acceptance. Important problems are therefore posed — in what circumstances does loving lead to loving, or giving to giving? Such questions demand an adequate description of the relationships in question, perhaps coupled with an understanding of the dialectic with personality.

Similarly some relationships have homeostatic or self-stabilizing properties. Mother–infant relationships, though disturbed in the short-term by a period of separation, often regain their original course in the medium term (Hinde and McGinnis, 1977). However some relationships, such as parent-child or teacher–pupil relationships, carry the seeds of their own destruction or transmutation in the long run: some unhappiness could perhaps be saved if this were recognized in advance. The teasing aspect of such issues demands an adequate descriptive base.

These examples perhaps suffice to illustrate the ways in which an adequate descriptive base both is a prerequisite for, and can facilitate the development of, theories concerned with the dynamics of interpersonal relationships. In addition to principles concerned with dynamics, in the long run we shall also need theories concerned with the effects of personality on relationships and relationships on personality. Here the way ahead is much less clear, but attachment theory, as discussed by Bowlby (1969, 1973, 1980), offers a promising start by focusing on the nature and consequences of the mother–child relationship.

Integration of Concepts

The literature on interpersonal relationships is scattered amongst many different disciplines. And within each discipline, it would seem that each group of investigators has been more disposed to try to tackle the complexities of interindividual relationships with their own conceptual tools than to try to specify the relations between their endeavours and those of others. This is not to say that such attempts have been lacking (e.g. Curry and Emerson, 1970; Chadwick-Jones, 1976; Duck, 1977b; Walster *et al.*, 1978; Kelley, 1979), but it is still the case that the various paradigms and theories in the field have little coherence.

One route towards integration would be to relate the various descriptive and explanatory concepts used in the different approaches. Such a task would be one of considerable complexity, and I could not essay it here. Rather, in keeping with the tone of the rest of this chapter, I shall try to indicate the sort of route that, it seems to me, must be taken. The concepts at present used in the study of interpersonal relationships fall into three major categories, as follows.

1. Descriptive terms. These can be further subdivided into:

(a) those that refer to items of behaviour or action, whether they be discrete actions (e.g. frown) or to categories of action defined with reference to a common causal basis or a common goal (e.g. signal, aggressive behaviour), or to sequences of actions extended over time (e.g. interaction, episode);

(b) descriptions of the properties of interactions, such as terms referring to the qualities of the actions of one or both participants (e.g. solicitude) or to the relations between their actions (e.g. meshing, disconfirmation);

(c) descriptions of the properties of relationships, based on multiple interactions (e.g. competitive).

2. Intervening variables or hypothetical constructs used in explanations of the properties of relationships These include concepts used in the analysis of individual behaviour, and commonly found in S-R theories — for instance, motivation, learning, and reward or reinforcement. Such terms are susceptible to operational definition; at any rate, for use within restricted theoretical systems, though they may also have implications about process (e.g. Kling and Riggs, 1971). However, such terms are likely to prove either unnecessarily cumbersome, or inadequate, for studies of interpersonal relationships. A more cognitive approach is essential — as is apparent from the manner in which exchange theories, though starting from S-R concepts, have been forced almost immediately to bolster them up with cognitive ones. Interpersonal relationships can be discussed only against a background of the assumption that individuals, though often buffeted by physical, psychological or social forces, are also agents who at least have the illusion that they are in control of their own destinies. And against that background, certain concepts are essential. I have suggested elsewhere (Hinde, 1979) that the concepts of perception, expectancy, goal direction, emotions/feeling, values and norms, etc. must be of pivotal importance. These are all also susceptible to operational definition.

Some such list of concepts would seem to be pivotal to a theory of interpersonal relationships. In the building of a concise theory, inter-relations between the six specified could be described, and the list perhaps reduced. For example, goal directedness often implies expectancy, and norms are related to values and thus to reward.

Many of the concepts met in studies of interpersonal relationships are clearly related to these pivotal ones. For instance, the pivotal concept of value is related to reward, cost, profit, dependency, equality, equity, justice, altruism, and status; and emotion is related to distress, anger and perhaps to cognitive dissonance, balance and consensual validation. In some of these cases, the relations between concepts imply "schemata of cognitive representations" — thus justice implies a comparison of values, and dissonance a comparison of attitudes and/or beliefs.

3a Higher-level descriptive concepts Many concepts which refer to individual characteristics depend on one or more of these pivotal concepts. For example "attitude" and "personality" depend upon the individual's perceptions, expectancies, values, etc.

3b Higher-level explanatory concepts Some of the concepts used in theories of interpersonal interactions or relationships depend on pivotal concepts. That of the "ideal self", for instance, clearly depends on concepts of values, goal direction, norms, and so on. "Role identity", used to refer to a person's imaginative view of himself as the occupant of a particular social position (McCall, 1970), will necessarily involve all six of the concepts listed above as pivotal.

The building of a science of interpersonal relationships will depend on attempts to relate the concepts used by research workers operating from within the frameworks of different disciplines, and at different levels of analysis. An obvious example is the term "role". Used by anthropologists to refer to behaviour, rights or duties associated with a particular position in society (e.g. Linton, 1936; Newcomb, 1952), its use is extended by social psychologists and becomes related to that of "norms" characteristic of a particular subculture (e.g. Araji, 1977; Tajfel, 1978), and even to norms that are almost idiosyncratic (e.g. Teevan, 1972). That might not matter too much, were it not for the additional fact that roles are used both to refer to causes of action, as when we say that an individual attempts to fulfill his or her role, and to consequences of action, as when we discuss the role of the navigator in an aircraft's crew (Hinde, 1978a). If we are concerned with the anthropologists' "roles" that are common to a society, the sort of consequences we focus on are liable to be very different from those with which the social psychologists' "roles" of more limited generality are concerned. Nevertheless, there may (or may not) be close similarities in the ways in which the roles operate in influencing the behaviour of individuals.

Integration is equally necessary between concepts used at different levels of analysis. While concepts such as "ideal self", "role identity" and "definition of the situation" may provide a useful and indeed necessary shorthand, in the long run it will be essential to relate them to pivotal concepts in a more or less precise fashion. Furthermore, it will be necessary to specify how far, if at all, such concepts imply emergent properties not associated with the concepts in terms of which they are defined.

To plead for integration is of course easy, but implementation is a matter of great difficulty. My aim has been to call attention to the diversity of approaches at present in the field. The most urgent task is not to prove one approach or paradigm right and another wrong, inadequate or irrelevant. Rather we must strive to specify how far they overlap, how far they are dealing with the same phenomenon at different levels of analysis, or different aspects of the same phenomenon at the same level of analysis, and can therefore be integrated.

Of course integration is not merely a matter of theory. At a practical level, studies that bridge the different approaches to relationships, and that link the study of relationships to other branches of psychology, are urgently needed. Some studies of aspects of the dialectic between societal norms and relationships are already to be found (e.g. Araji, 1977), and there seems no reason why the dialectic between personality and relationships should not also come under scrutiny. For example, studies of the marital relationship as the partners undergo the experience of becoming parents are of the greatest interest (e.g. Cowan *et al.*, 1978).

Conclusion

The main aims of this chapter have been to emphasize the need for a science of interpersonal relationships, and to argue that such a science will need a descriptive base. Along the way, however, have emerged the shadowy outlines of the structure that such a science might have. There must be an agreed data language, able to cope with the phenomena of action, interaction and relationship in both their behavioural and affective/cognitive aspects. There must also be principles, concerned with the dynamics of interpersonal relationships, derived from a number of different areas of current knowledge. These principles may employ explanatory concepts not in the data language. Such concepts will be concerned with diverse aspects of data at several levels of complexity: inter-relating of concepts will be essential.

CHAPTER 2
Studying Personal Relationships

Barry McCarthy

In an article written some years ago Wright (1969) summed up what he saw as the outcome of the previous decade's work in attraction and interpersonal relationships·

> More than a decade of vigorous research in interpersonal attraction has left us with numerous pieces of information, an indeterminate amount of misinformation, and little conceptual grasp of any kind of dyadic relationship such as friendship, engagement, marriage or roommate preference (p.295).

A reading of the most recent general review of research in personal relationships (Huston and Levinger, 1978) might lead the pessimistic to conclude that little has changed for the better since Wright's article was written: it is hard to deny that the accumulation of knowledge in the area has been uneven both in breadth and in quality; old and tedious controversies have lingered fruitlessly on; ambitious theoretical models have not been matched by operational developments; and all in spite of a great increase in popularity of research in personal relationships during the 1970s.

It is the present writer's view that, whilst such a gloomy assessment is not entirely justified, it is strategically preferable to the note of bland optimism that characterises many introductory surveys of social psychology generally, and of interpersonal attraction in particular. Scientific study of personal relationships will never be an easy or a routine undertaking: the phenomena are

23

too complex and variable for simple theoretical notions like social exchange or reinforcement/affect to have much more than a general heuristic function, and the actual gathering of data is fraught with various perils for both researcher and participants. It is entirely possible that there are insuperable barriers to the establishment of those general laws that are the ultimate goal of the scientific enterprise.

The aim of the present chapter is to examine the state of the art in personal relationships research with a view to highlighting the strengths and weaknesses of each of the main approaches currently in use, and to suggest some areas where improvement and advance may be possible. Theoretical developments will not be a central theme, though obviously references to theoretical and conceptual problems will be necessary from time to time. I had better make my own predilections clear from the outset: over a number of years I have attempted to apply experimental or quasi-experimental methodology to the study of friendship; I am still convinced that such an approach has considerable value, but experience has also persuaded me that methodological pluralism is the only road, albeit a winding one, to general progress in the study of personal relationships.

Problems of Research in Personal Relationships

It is appropriate at the outset to confront squarely the major problems facing the researcher in this area. There are three general conceptual issues to be resolved, or at least acknowledged, before ever a questionnaire layout is designed, or a subject recruited: namely, imprecision in definition of terms; intrinsic diversity and variability of relationships; and possible effects of societal norms upon the research enterprise. Subsequently, a number of more specific problem areas will be examined.

Definitions   ✓

Several writers have noted, with more or less dismay, the imprecision and lack of consensus with which basic terms in the attraction and relationships literature are used (Berscheid and Walster, 1978; Huston, 1974; Marlowe and Gergen, 1969; Rodin, 1978): there is considerable disagreement on the theoretical and operational definitions of concepts such as attraction, love, friendship, intimacy and so on. Essentially it seems to be a chicken-and-egg problem: if more were known about relationships such discord would be less likely, but the absence of theoretical or at least operational consensus impedes the acquisition of such knowledge. At the very least it behoves all investigators to be very explicit, to the point of redundancy, in specifying what exactly they *themselves* mean by the various terms used; only in this way can direct comparisons of diverse empirical findings and of theoretical models be facilitated and progress made toward eventual agreement on terminology.

Diversity ✓

A second general issue, not unrelated to the first, concerns the great variety of forms in which personal relationships may occur. Historical forces affect relationships as much as any other aspect of social life; this point has been made for social psychology in general by Gergen (1973), and illustrated in the area of personal relationships by Gadlin, in a review of the changing role of interpersonal intimacy in American society from colonial times up to the present (Gadlin, 1977). The "facts" sought by the deterministic social researcher may not be stable over time, as relationships change in form, in function and in salience from one historical period to the next in conjunction with general changes in economic, political and ethical systems. From this perspective social psychology becomes a branch of history rather than a discipline in pursuit of trans-historically valid laws of human behaviour. Even if a researcher eschews such speculation and fixes his or her sights firmly on the present, there is abundant evidence of great cross-cultural and even intracultural differences in the ways that personal relationships such as friendship and marriage are conceived of, regulated and inter-related with one another (Boissevain, 1974; Kerckhoff, 1974; Rosenblatt, 1974).

Such variations constitute both a constraint upon and a challenge to the study of personal relationships: a constraint upon the external validity of any particular set of data, and on the applicability of any theoretical model based on attributes of a specific culture or subculture; a challenge in the fascinating and sobering variety and complexity that even a brief survey of the cross-cultural literature reveals. As Rosenblatt (1974) demonstrates, most data on personal relationships in non-Western, non-industrial societies come from the accounts of ethnographers; though capable of yielding rich and insightful information in the hands of a skilled and articulate observer, ethnography is deficient in precision and quantification of measurement and liable to a variety of distortions. A diversion of some quantitative research effort away from the well-trodden paths of the white/middle-class/young/student milieu towards other, so far neglected, groups (even within Western society) might greatly extend and enliven our understanding of the diverse facets and functions of human affectional relationships.

An aspect of relationship variability that has begun to receive a good share of theoretical attention is the question of changes over time in the processes and foci of a single relationship. "Stage" or "filter" models have been proposed which promise to extend our understanding of relationship development (Duck, 1973; Levinger and Snoek, 1972; Lewis, 1973; Murstein, 1971). As yet, however, substantial supporting evidence for any of these models is lacking; whether this is because the models themselves are premature and formulated on an inadequate descriptive data base (Huston and Levinger, 1978) or because methodology is so far inadequate to test their predictions, is a question we may be able to address more confidently by the end of the present chapter.

Societal norms ∕

Cultural, subcultural and historical variations exist not merely in the entities being studied — the relationships themselves — but also in how investigators conceptualise them. Personal relationships are highly meaningful and salient features of most societies, and accordingly societies tend to evolve norms of propriety regarding eligibility for, and activities permissible in, various kinds of relationships. It is reasonable to propose that researchers, who presumably share many of their own culture's normative assumptions, are influenced by these norms in a variety of ways (Raush, 1977): in their choices of relationships for study; of terminology; of measurement devices; of hypotheses to test; and of interpretations to place on the eventual data. Societal definitions of marriage and family as proper and desirable relationships, and their corresponding legal and religious institutionalization may make it exceedingly difficult for a researcher to conceptualize the dissolution of such relationships in other than negative terms (Pearson, 1974).

On a more subtle level, the ideology of individualism subscribed to by most of Western society is likely to direct the investigator unconsciously to search for "the" determinants of relationships in the individual attitudes, values, needs and traits of the participants (Sampson, 1978); an investigator espousing a collectivist ideology might equally one-sidedly direct his or her enquiry towards socioeconomic or group-process determinants of the very same relationships.

Finally, in another context Berscheid and Walster (1978) have outlined the difficulties encountered by researchers in the USA in obtaining financial support for research in romantic/sexual attraction; complex public attitudes toward such relationships as sacred, mysterious or improper may have been a major factor in deterring many researchers from tackling such issues. As far as general public opinion is concerned, the researcher in personal relationships is (at least for the forseeable future) in an unenviable position: if he or she reports data consistent with public prejudices the enterprise is labelled trivial or a waste of time; if, however, the findings conflict with these prejudices, they are ignored, ridiculed or condemned (see Thorngate, 1976).

Other problems ✓

In addition to the three general problems already discussed, the investigator of personal relationships is likely to encounter a range of more specific pitfalls once the research project commences; these may conveniently be grouped under three headings: rapport, ethical issues, and cognitive limitations.

Frequently the researcher is interested in obtaining information of a private or intimate nature from participants in relationships; this has implications both for the social skill and for the ethical sensitivity of the investigator. As Armistead (1974) points out, the only reasonably reliable way of obtaining personal information voluntarily from subjects is to establish rapport with them; the researcher must literally become a confidant of the subject or of the participant dyad, if only for a short time and under admittedly rather special circumstances. This requires interpersonal skill and sensitivity of a fairly high order; one wonders how many would-be investigators are possessed of such gifts.

Ethical constraints upon the researcher in personal relationships are, rightly, quite severe; relationships are important to almost all participants and must not knowingly be endangered by research procedures. Assuming that the recruitment procedure is itself ethically acceptable in that participants have a *genuine* choice about whether or not to take part, the selection of method has further ethical implications. The most important point to make is that there are no techniques free of potential pitfalls: even the most apparently bland questionnaire may provoke anxiety or self-doubt in some respondents; likewise, the generally innocuous role-playing technique may on occasion produce extreme stress in participants (e.g. Zimbardo *et al.*, 1973) or induce actions which may have subsequent repercussions upon the relationship. Systematic behavioural observation entails risks of invading subjects' privacy; and experimental deception, which has been employed in a number of recent studies of personal relationships, is clearly a procedure to be employed with great caution.

In the absence of guaranteed ethically pure procedures it is, in the present writer's view, important that the widest possible array of research techniques be at the disposal of responsible investigators in this area; observational, experimental, questionnaire/interview and role playing procedures may provide valuable alternative perspectives (Olson, 1977) and none can be lightly dispensed with if an accurate and detailed understanding of personal relationships is to be achieved.

Finally, it appears to be a central fact of human psychology that we are limited in our capacities to attend to, to process and to recall information; selectivity in handling available information is evidently an unavoidable limitation on human functioning. In the research situation this limitation applies obviously to both subject and investigator. Nisbett and Wilson (1977) argue that subjects' reports of mental processes, in particular of cognitions influencing their own behaviour, are generally inaccurate and that this inaccuracy is greater the less obvious is the mental event as a cause of behaviour, and the longer the lapse of time between event and report. Since many of the questions researchers ask in the area of personal relationships concern participants' motivational and other cognitive/affective responses on occasions in the past, the implications of the Nisbett and Wilson thesis for the ways in which we go about our research activities are profound.

There are other problems associated with cognitive functioning that need to be faced: from a number of studies of attribution processes (e.g. Jones and Nisbett, 1971) it is possible that systematic distortions exist in the ways that people perceive the causes of their own versus others' behaviour; in general, it is suggested that one tends to see the sources of one's own behaviour in the environment, but those of others' behaviour in the attributes of the persons themselves. This general bias is surely as applicable to the judgements of the researcher, observing others' relationships, as it is to the self-reports of participants in those relationships (Kelley, 1977). Levinger (1977a) notes a difference in perspective between subject and researcher, which may enhance actor–observer differences in attribution: the subject sees events over time, in diverse situations, whilst the researcher sees behaviour in a restricted set of circumstances but over a wide range of different persons and relationships. Armistead (1974), in advocating subjects' accounts of their own mental processes as the basic subject matter of social psychology, argues that subjects' distortions of their own cognitions are not likely to be as bad as the researcher's distortions of them; this may well be the case, though the answer surely lies in *both* subjects' and investigators' accounts being recorded, and compared.

Principal Research Approaches

We now proceed to a survey of the approaches to the study of personal relationships most widely employed by researchers, particularly in the past decade. Emphasis will be on the methods themselves, their apparent virtues and drawbacks; theoretical and substantive issues, which have been dealt with comprehensively in a recent review (Huston and Levinger, 1978) will here be referred to only in passing. Three broad methodological categories are included: non-behavioural correlational designs, laboratory studies, and role playing; for convenience of exposition the first category is subdivided into simple, single-stage correlational designs and more complex, multistage approaches. In the following section I shall briefly examine the ways in which relationship data are actually collected, principally by self report attitude scales, sociometric devices, relationship descriptions, behavioural observation and self disclosure measures.

Simple correlational designs

Simple or single-stage correlational studies continue to constitute the most numerous category of research in personal relationships. The prototypical study involves the researcher in obtaining measures of some aspect of the relationship (for example, interpersonal affect, commitment, marital satisfaction) on the one hand, and of some sociodemographic, personality or other attributes of participants on the other, and calculating the nature and extent of the relationship between the two. Potential examples are abundant, and I shall be highly selective. Cattell and Nesselroade (1967) compared couples, classified as either maritally stable or unstable, for their degree of personality similarity on the 16PF questionnaire; other studies of the relationship between attitudinal or personality similarity and success of or satisfaction with a relationship include Dion and Dion (1975); Duck and Allison (1978); Murstein (1973); Stewart and Rubin (1976); Wright and Crawford (1971). Other researchers have examined the relationship between relationship measures and complementarity of needs (Lipetz et al., 1970; Wagner, 1975); physical attractiveness (Murstein and Christy, 1976; Price and Vandenberg, 1979); or environmental/demographic indices such as residential propinquity, race or social class similarity (Athanasiou and Yoshioka, 1973; Nahemow and Lawton, 1975; Segal, 1974). Several investigations have focused on individual participants in relationships, exploring associations between (for example) dispositional jealousy, interaction style, or exchange orientation and success in relationships (Bringle and Evenbeck, 1979; McCarthy, 1978; Milardo and Murstein, 1979). A growing tendency to include measures of a wide variety of attributes in a single study is discernible (e.g. Bentler and Newcomb, 1979; Dion and Dion, 1975; Kandel, 1978; Segal, 1974). Most data on interpersonal relationships in cultures other than the Western take the form of simple correlations, for example between freedom of choice of spouse within a culture and importance of sex as a source of attraction (see Rosenblatt, 1974).

That such investigations can be of considerable value and interest is not in question; however, limitations on the conclusions that can be drawn from such findings are severe, and there are a number of pitfalls peculiar to the use of correlational designs. For accurate estimation of a population correlation it is essential that the sample used correspond as fully as possible to the range of scores on the various indices to be found within the population in question; highly misleading conclusions may be drawn from restricted samples, and such unrepresentative samples are not scarce in social research. Wright (1968), in a review of the similarity–complementarity issue, pointed to two methodological problems attaching to correlational designs: first, using a multi-interval or multicategory index of one variable (usually an attitudinal or personality score) and a crude, dichotomous measure of the other (e.g. satisfaction–dissatisfaction) can result in a correlation based entirely on extreme scores; the second problem concerns the distortions that may be introduced when dyadic indices are used (i.e. scores of both members of a dyad combined into a single score, usually a "difference" score). These issues have not yet been satisfactorily resolved, and accordingly caution is indicated both in designing and in evaluating any correlational study.

Yet another snare in the correlational undergrowth surrounds the choice of a baseline against which to compare an obtained correlation; this applies particularly to investigations of hypothesized similarity or complementarity of attributes. In brief, ought correlations between scores of actual pairs be compared with those from randomly matched pairs within the subject pool, or with the correlation strictly predicted under the null hypothesis, namely, zero? Examples of both approaches are to be found in the literature (see Murstein, 1976 for a discussion of this issue) and a case can be made for each, but conclusions may obviously differ depending on which criterion is chosen, and the implications for comparison of outcomes from different studies is not always appreciated.

The two major limitations on interpretation of correlational data are directionality and the third variable or "spuriousness" problem. As is well known, the mere fact of a positive correlation between A and B does not permit the inference that A caused B; it is equally possible (though perhaps not equally *plausible*) that B may be the cause of A. Not all simple correlational studies are subject to the directionality problem; in particular those including a demographic or environmental variable may escape, for instance a study by Segal (1974) in which residential propinquity was positively correlated with friendship choice among police cadets; room occupancy had been allocated (prior to the cadets' arrival) in alphabetical order. One can be sure in this case that friendship did not cause propinquity, and the logical conclusion might be that propinquity (or propinquity-derived processes like frequency of interaction) determined friendship choice. But is such a conclusion entirely justified? What if alphabetical order of names were related to ethnic or racial origin, which thus determined both propinquity *and* attraction? One has, in this case, a rather implausible alternative explanation, but nevertheless an example of the celebrated third variable problem (Neale and Liebert, 1973); freedom from directionality in no way guarantees freedom from spuriousness.

A more appropriate example of the third variable in action is the likely confounding of similarity (of attitudes, social class, etc.) with propinquity in many simple correlational studies (Berscheid and Walster, 1978). As a review by Kerckhoff (1974) demonstrates, in most cultures a normative sorting process ensures that we tend to encounter — at school, at play, in adult work and social activities — a preponderance of persons similar to ourselves in race, social class, age, intelligence and also (probably) in attitudes, values and personality. Under these circumstances, one could only be confident that choices of similar others really constituted similarity-preference if subjects were also provided with an equivalent set of dissimilar others with whom to interact. In correlational studies this requirement is rarely if ever likely to have been met.

The above example highlights a particular drawback of the simple correlational approach to personal relationship: the lack of a temporal dimension. This is particularly salient when one considers that much recent theoretical work on long-term relationships has adopted some version of a developmental stage or filtering approach to acquaintance (e.g. Duck, 1973; Levinger and Snoek, 1972; Murstein 1971). By combining participants into a single group many simple correlational studies may have obscured theoretically significant differences between subgroups at different stages of relationship. In any event, the predictions of the stage theorists can be adequately tested only by a methodology that differentiates between stages, however defined operationally.

Correlation: More complex approaches

On a number of grounds, both theoretical and intuitive, multi-stage correlational studies are more satisfying than the simpler version; a substantial number of recent investigations come under this general heading, which includes both cross-sectional and longitudinal approaches. Cross-sectional studies involve selection of two or more groups of persons to represent different presumed stages or phases of relationship; essentially the same variables are measured for each group and two (or more, as appropriate) sets of correlations calculated. Measurements of the characteristics of both mutually exclusive samples may be done more or less contemporaneously, and the main aim is the comparison and/or contrasting of the degree of association between variables for the different subgroups. For example, Duck (1973) compared newly acquainted and established pairs of same sex friends on both the California·Psychological Inventory (CPI) and the Reptest, whilst Bailey, Finney and Helm (1975) compared short- and long-acquaintance friends on actual and perceived similarity of intelligence. Although such studies obviously provide data on a broader basis than those of single-stage investigations, and permit cautious comparisons to be made, nevertheless interpretation of cross-sectional data is a perilous business. Any claim that the relationship between variables observed at Stage 1 is either a prelude to or a determinant of the relationship observed at Stage 2 is unjustified; there is no guarantee that the particular dyads studied at Stage 1 would ever have persisted into the kind of friendship or other association obtaining at so-called Stage 2. There may be many differences between the two groups of subjects quite apart from the differences in the variables that are of interest, and though an investigator may attempt to match subjects on some of these potentially influential factors, he or she cannot hope to match on all of them.

Longitudinal studies afford the investigator the opportunity of following progress of specific relationships over time, taking measures of the variables of interest at appropriate intervals. The aim, obviously, is to record changes in these variables and in the relationships between them and hopefully to specify or to suggest causes of such changes. The variety or longitudinal investigations of personal relationships is considerable. Some take pre-acquaintance measures, and then measure these variables, among others, again on successive occasions in the course of the study; this is perhaps the fullest development to date of the longitudinal approach, and examples include Newcomb's (1961) famous rooming-house study over eight weeks, Taylor's (1968) 13-week investigation of social penetration among roommate pairs, and a two-year longitudinal study of students' dating relationships by Hill et al. (1976). Other examples of the general technique do not include pre-acquaintance data but do take at least two successive sets of measures of relationships in progress (e.g. Bentler and Newcomb, 1979; Curry and Emerson, 1970; Doherty and Secord, 1971; Duck and Craig, 1978; Lewis, 1973).

A third group of studies may also at a stretch be considered longitudinal, as they comprise pre-acquaintance measurement and subsequent data collection on a single occasion during the actual course of the relationship; such investigations include Duck and Spencer (1972); Mann (1971); and Sindberg et al. (1972). In the Duck and Spencer (1972) study, for example, subjects were administered the Reptest on first acquaintance, and six months later friendship pairs within the pool were identified sociometrically; friendship pairs were then compared with "nominal" pairs on Reptest scores.

Finally, there is a small group of studies in which groups are constructed by the researcher in accordance with some principle of interest such as similarity of personalities, and observed at intervals thereafter. Such studies tend to involve laboratory discussion groups which meet at regular intervals (e.g. Hoffman and Maier, 1966; Hogan and Mankin, 1970) and it is debatable whether their results are directly relevant to the study of voluntary personal relationship; nevertheless, the part played by role-based, essentially non-voluntary encounters in the development of affectively-based, personal relationships is surely worth investigating and this may be a feasible means of doing so.

It seems generally agreed among reviewers of research in personal relationships that longitudinal studies are A Good Thing and to be encouraged (e.g. Huston and Levinger, 1978; Newcomb, 1978), and I am fully in accord with that sentiment. However, the problems are severe, and often overlooked in the initial planning of such an investigation. A misapprehension frequently encountered among undergraduate students of personal relationships is that a properly conducted longitudinal study, complete with pre-acquaintance measures, more or less takes care of the problems of causal ambiguity that characterize simpler correlational designs. Such, alas, is not the case. Directionality is admittedly not normally a serious problem in such designs: an event at Time 2 is unlikely, on the face of it, to be the cause of a phenomenon observed at Time 1; nevertheless, the spectre of the third variable looms as large here as in any other kind of correlational study. Some unmeasured factor, say social class membership again, may be a powerful determinant of pre-acquaintance scores (e.g. in attitudes) and through the propinquity factor may also affect later relationship choice. Of course, attitude similarity *may* have played an important part in the development of attraction, but one cannot be sure of that just on the basis of preacquaintance similarity correlating with later choice.

Attempts at identifying and eliminating third variable effects, for instance through cross-lagged panel analysis, partial correlation, and time series analyses have not been conspicuously successful; the investigator is left with a decision among alternative explanations of varying plausibility, and the technique has not yet been developed that can make that decision for him. Interpretation of a significant difference in cross-lagged correlations, for example, is far from straightforward, although in principle such a difference should indicate freedom from spuriousness (Kenny, 1975). It is also possible that cross-lagged analysis is inappropriate for data from relationships undergoing rapid change, as this may violate one of the assumptions on which the technique is based, namely stability of underlying causal processes.

The problem of intervening events can be a serious matter for the longitudinal researcher. In effect, any employment of the approach means facing a tactical dilemma: in order to ensure as far as possible that all significant relationship events are monitored, measures should be taken at frequent intervals; on the other hand, the more frequently measurement of variables is undertaken the greater is the risk of subjects' responses being affected by repeated testing. The problem of intervening events is particularly salient where subjects are undergoing rapid biological or lifestyle changes, but any event in society at large or (more likely) in the participants' immediate milieu may affect the future course of a relationship. Effects of such events may well be impossible to assess anyway, but the chances of doing so diminish greatly the longer the time interval is between their occurrence and the collection of data. There are, of course, economic and other practical limitations on the frequency of observation of a relationship; in most cases one can only hope that unassessed intervening events have not been operative in the interval. Some studies, but only a minority, have attempted to assess any effects of repeated measurement by incorporating control groups (e.g. Curry and Emerson, 1970; Taylor, 1968): these groups' responses are obtained at the first and last stage of measurement, but not at any of the intervening periods; their data are then compared with those from subjects who have participated in the full series of data collection sessions in order to assess possible effects of testing. Not all longitudinal investigations are amenable to such an arrangement, in particular those with only two successive assessment points.

A final serious problem that may afflict longitudinal research concerns loss of subjects over time; this is well-nigh inevitable in all but the most short-term and tightly controlled project. A recent study of marital success and failure by Bentler and Newcomb (1979) reported follow-up data (after four years) from only 77 couples out of an original sample of 162; this is not an unusual drop-out rate. The main pitfall lies not in the loss itself but in the possibility that the attrition is not random, and that the sample at later stages of the study is significantly different in some unmeasured way or ways from the group that began the investigation, thus putting in question any comparison of the data at various stages.

In spite of the many pitfalls and perils associated with longitudinal research in personal relationships, stimulating and theoretically useful data can be obtained, and at least tentative conclusions drawn. An excellent example of the potential of longitudinal investigation is a study by Driscoll *et al.* (1972) in which the relationship between parental interference and feelings of romantic love was studied by both longitudinal and cross-sectional methodologies and attempts were made to eliminate the more implausible alternative explanations of the correlations obtained.

Laboratory studies

Although laboratory experimentation is the methodological mainstay of researchers in interpersonal attraction and impression formation (Anderson,

1971; Byrne, 1971) such studies, normally involving encounters with fictitious strangers in conditions of highly restricted availability of information,
are unlikely to provide data generalizable to long-term relationships. A
number of studies within the "fictitious stranger" paradigm assess the desirability of the stranger as a future partner (e.g. Grush and Yehl, 1979); but
apart from a study by Byrne *et al.* (1970), incorporating a rather short time-
lag, evidence is so far lacking to link such expressed preferences with subsequent participation in an actual relationship.

   True experiments, in which all independent variables are manipulated by
the experimenter under conditions of random assignment of subjects and
tight control of extraneous factors, are scarcely ever feasible in the personal
relationships area. However, a growing number of investigators has begun
to conduct laboratory based research involving acquainted individuals in
structured interaction situations; in a few cases manipulations of certain
variables of interest have been included, with random assignment to treatment conditions. Each of these categories of investigation merits detailed
examination.

   To the first group belongs a set of studies which are essentially correlational, though normally with live performance scores of various kinds
rather than self report data as the variable which is to be correlated with the
relationship factor. An early study by Back and Bogdonoff (1964) compared
groups of friends with non-friends on an autonomic index of stress (level of
free fatty acids in bloodstream) following an anxiety-arousing experience,
and found lower stress levels among friends than among groups of strangers.
Rubin (1970) had dating couples whose members were assessed as "strong"
or "weak" on his Love Scale observed from behind a one-way vision screen
during a brief discussion session; more mutual gazing was recorded in the
"strong" love couples. In a similar study by Russo (1975) pairs of primary-
school children were observed from concealment while they conversed on a
topic of their choice; eye contact was analysed as a function of sex, grade,
interpersonal distance and friendship status (friends vs non-friends).
Chapman, Foot and their co-workers have observed a variety of behaviours
of children with friends and non-friends in both free play and laboratory
settings (Chapman *et al.*, 1979; Foot *et al.*, 1979). Other aspects of behaviour
studied as a function of close relationships among subjects include speed of
learning of nonsense syllables (Lott *et al.*, 1970); perceptual distortion (Dion
and Dion, 1976); self disclosure (Morton, 1978; Won-Doornink, 1979) and
other aspects of interpersonal communication, such as conflict resolution
(Gottman *et al.*, 1978; Raush *et al.*, 1974).

   The second category of laboratory investigations is comprised of studies in
which correlational (i.e. relationship) and manipulated factors are combined, usually under conditions of deception or, at least, non-disclosure on

the part of the researcher. McCarthy and Duck (1976; 1979a,b) in a series of studies examined attitudinal and attributional responses to manipulated attitude agreement or disagreement of same-sex friends at different temporal stages of acquaintance; the initial study was closely modelled on the Byrne (1971) "bogus stranger" design (McCarthy and Duck, 1976). Employing a not-dissimilar methodology Derlega *et al.* (1976) induced subjects to disclose either intimate or non-intimate material to a close friend, in an investigation of disclosure reciprocity. Albert and Kessler (1978) compared verbal behaviours of friends and non-friend pairs during telephone conversations under either "structured" or "unstructured" instructions, whilst Peplau (1976) assigned dating couples to either a competitive or a cooperative task, and analysed the performances of the female members in terms of the scores obtained earlier on questionnaire measures of sex role attitudes and fear of success. Finally, Rutter and Stephenson (1979) recorded discussions among pairs of subjects on videotape and compared pairs of friends and non-friends, operating under either cooperative or competitive instructions, on indices of looking and eye contact. Several investigators have manipulated variables of interest in the context of real relationships, but without requiring actual interaction between partners: Regan *et al.* (1974) had subjects attribute an altruistic act, reputedly recently performed by a liked or disliked acquaintance, to one of a set of alternative motives. A similar procedure was employed by Seligman *et al.* (cited in Regan, 1978) to investigate the effects of enhancing the salience of either extrinsic or intrinsic bases for subjects' romantic relationships on subsequent liking and love ratings of the partner.

Of the two categories of laboratory studies the "mixed" or semi-experimental design has a clear advantage over the merely correlational, in that random assignment to conditions minimises any unwanted selection factors — the old problem of relationship groups differing on other variables than that which the researcher wishes to study. However, experimental manipulation of partners in a relationship has ethical implications (which also, however, are inherent in non-manipulative but covert observation studies), and furthermore is not always easy to achieve. An additional difficulty arises from the fact that any experimental treatments are usually complex: there is always the possibility that some detail of the treatment, irrelevant to the theoretical argument, is a source of alternative explanations of the effects obtained. This is, of course, a general problem in social psychological experimentation, but it may be more acute in the present case where laboratory events are interpreted by participants against a memorial background of many other shared experiences.

There are other pitfalls and limitations associated with laboratory studies of relationships: such studies, particularly those involving experimental manipulations, are virtually restricted to the cross-sectional mode; it is unlikely to be possible (on both ethical and practical grounds) to repeat a deception with the same group of subjects at a later time. Where such manipulations are not employed it should in principle be possible to conduct a longitudinal series of observations, but so far no such investigations have appeared in the literature.

In selecting participant groups on a continuous variable (such as duration of acquaintance) a decision must be taken, in effect, between splitting the subject pool at the median (or quartile point, or whatever) or using extreme groups. In general, the use of extreme groups always entails a risk of overestimating the real significance of any findings obtained, especially where the majority of individuals in the real world are likely to fall on intermediate regions of the continuum; on the other hand a median split may fail to reveal genuine differences, particularly if sample size is small.

These shortcomings and problems aside, however, it is clear that laboratory observation of behaviour in relationships is a promising addition to the investigator's repertoire. Advances in the technology of vision- and sound-recording are helping to solve the problems of observing complex ongoing behaviours by providing a full record of interactions for later analysis. The ingenuity of investigators, always tempered by ethical caution, can be expected to produce much useful data during the next few years.

Role-playing studies

The general issue of role playing as a research technique in social psychology has been a very lively one during the last decade or so (e.g. Cooper, 1976; Forward et al., 1976; Freedman, 1969; Geller, 1978; Miller, 1972; Mixon, 1974). The present treatment will confine itself to the implications for the study of personal relationships, where so far the number of investigations which employ such techniques is quite small; nevertheless, a wide range of roles in both actual and hypothetical relationships has been explored in recent studies.

A dimension on which role-playing methods have been dichotomized by a number of recent writers (e.g. Forward et al., 1976; Geller, 1978; Mixon, 1974) is that of passive/uninvolved vs active/involved role playing; there are a few studies in the personal relationships area from each of these categories. Passive role-playing is exemplified well in a study by Richey et al. (1972) in which subjects were given hypothetical positive or negative information about a liked or a disliked acquaintance, which was either consistent or inconsistent with their (the subjects') prior knowledge; subjects were asked to imagine the effect of this information on their evaluation of the acquaintance's character. Miller and Rivenbark (1970) gave participants a questionnaire describing eight hypothetical interaction situations, ranging from a

first encounter to marriage choice, and asked them to estimate the importance of physical attractiveness of the other as a determinant of their own
behaviour in each situation. Other studies which have employed individuals
in passive role playing of acquaintance or relationship interactions include
Kleinke *et al.* (1974) and Smith and Campbell (1973).

Among studies requiring more active involvement by participants, Keiser
and Altman (1978) asked students to actively play parts of "good friends" or
"casual acquaintances" discussing either intimate or superficial topics; the
interactions were videotaped and verbal and non-verbal behaviour scored for
immediacy, relaxation, and other indicators of emotional state. McCarthy
and Duck (1979b) asked pairs of subjects who were either short-term or long-
established friends to role play face-to-face agreement or disagreement about
a hypothetical issue with moral/ethical and pragmatic implications; subsequently they rated each other and the relationship on a number of scales.
Using a similar methodology, Raush *et al.* (1974) investigated aspects of
interpersonal conflict in married couples.

There are two clear advantages possessed by role-playing techniques over
manipulative laboratory studies: first, the range of situations and behaviours
that can be operationalized is enormously wide; secondly, the ethical problem is generally far less severe. However, neither of these advantages is
absolute, particularly if active or involved role playing is the method of
choice. If participant involvement is desired it may be necessary to provide a
full range of props, indeed almost a full stage set, in order to encourage
involvement; not every participant is capable of an intense performance in a
bare research room with no more than a table, a chair and the researcher
smiling encouragingly from the corner (see Geller, 1978). It is also the case
that involved role playing can be highly stressful even though participants are
not deceived and are provided with detailed information about the aims of
the study from the beginning (e.g. Zimbardo *et al.*, 1973).

The disadvantages of role playing seem to be three-fold. First, as already
mentioned, involvement is not always attainable by every participant; one is
then left with the question of how untypical of people in general are those
who do readily achieve involvement. Widespread use of involved role playing
may yield a psychology of exhibitionists' personal relationships. The remaining problems are relevant to all kinds of role playing (not just the involved
version) and to internal rather than to external validity of findings. These
problems, noted by Aronson and Carlsmith (1968) and Freedman (1969),
remain unresolved to the present: namely, socially desirable responding and
participants' lack of insight into their own motives, response tendencies and
other mental states.

It seems likely that in many situations role players, aware of the focus
of the researcher's attention, will exhibit behaviours and report affective

responses calculated (either consciously or otherwise) to present themselves in as favourable a light as possible. There is evidence that role players, as compared with deceived experimental subjects, behave more responsibly, altruistically and cooperatively (Miller, 1972; Willis and Willis, 1970). Researcher–participant rapport may mitigate this tendency somewhat, as may intense participant involvement, but self-presentation by role players remains a likely occurrence in many circumstances. Forward *et al.* (1976), in their defence of role-playing methodology, freely admit the likelihood of such an outcome, but make the case (not very convincingly in the present writer's view) that conscious self-presentation rather than spontaneous behaviour ought to be the main object of researchers' attention.

The problem of participants' lack of insight is an even more serious issue. It is likely that we are often unaware of how we would respond to a novel event; if so, role-playing performance could hardly be taken as a firm basis for prediction in the (real) future. There is convincing evidence (e.g. Nisbett and Wilson, 1977) that we cannot recall accurately mental events even after quite a brief lapse of time; under these circumstances role playing of past occurrences must also be of dubious validity, particularly where affective and cognitive, rather than merely behavioural events are being portrayed. Cooper (1976) claims that role playing results tend to resemble those of deception experiments only when the outcome is *obvious*; the findings of a comparative study by McCarthy and Duck (1979b) tend to support such a conclusion, as the counter-intuitive interaction effect between agreement/disagreement and duration of acquaintance observed under experimental conditions was not present in the results of the role-playing version.

Direct comparison of experimental and role-playing methods raises a number of epistemological issues. Both approaches are merely simulations of the "real" world (Geller, 1978); to dismiss out of hand role-playing data where they conflict with those from deception experiments is hardly justifiable, in view of the fact that experimental results have been attacked hard and often as unrepresentative of social reality. At present one can choose between the methods only on the grounds of relative plausibility of their separate claims; in this context a useful distinction may be made between the *hypothesis generation* and *hypothesis testing* phases of research. Role playing, with its great flexibility and imaginative scope, possesses considerable advantages as an exploratory tool, and personal relationships are but one of many areas of social psychology where creative, counter-normative and assumption-challenging ideas are sorely needed. In terms of hypothesis testing, however, the shortcomings of role-playing bear down most heavily and one feels little confidence in the findings of the great majority of such studies, particularly where hypothetical rather than actual relationships are the object of study.

Measuring Relationship Variables

Up to this point attention has been focused mainly on those aspects of studies
to do with the determinants and correlates of personal relationships; it is
now time to turn towards the attributes of relationships themselves, and
their measurement. Several writers (e.g. Levinger, 1972; Wright, 1969)
have commented upon the apparent neglect by researchers of the "dependent
variable" side of interpersonal attraction and of relationships in particular; a
neglect which seems to go hand in hand with confusion as to how these
variables are to be conceptualised. We shall briefly consider four general
approaches to relationship measurement: self-report attitudinal measures
(rating scales, sociometric questionnaires, etc.); measures of meaning and
function of relationships; self-disclosure; and behavioural indices.

Attitudinal measures

These constitute by far the most popular category of response measure in
personal relationships research (as indeed they do also in laboratory studies
of attraction to strangers). Subjects are asked to rate their partner on an
ordinal or interval scale in terms of liking, enjoyment of the other's company, adjustment, similarity to self, perceived liking of self, or any of a
variety of dimensions which it is hoped will tap the nature and extent of interpersonal affect and beliefs within the relationship (e.g. Driscoll et al., 1972;
Lott et al., 1970; Rubin, 1970; Wagner, 1975). Closely related conceptually
and methodologically are measures of satisfaction with the relationship per
se (e.g. Levinger and Breedlove, 1966; Lipetz et al., 1970) or estimates of likelihood of the relationship persisting (e.g. McCarthy and Duck, 1979a,b). In
the majority of cases the scales are administered in the form of a printed
booklet, which the subject completes without close supervision; in a few
studies face-to-face interviews are conducted (e.g. Levinger and Breedlove,
1966). Sociometric questionnaires are essentially similar in use, but are
usually both more crude (in that subjects are asked to nominate individuals
rather than rate them) and more context specific (in that nomination is for
particular kinds of activity or relationship); use of these instruments is very
widespread (e.g. Nahemow and Lawton, 1975; Chapman et al., 1979; Segal,
1974).

It is easy to see why attitude scales and sociometric questionnaires have
remained the major tool of researchers in personal relationships: they are
quick and convenient to construct, to administer and to analyse; they have
few ethical drawbacks, and are expected and accepted by respondents. But

do they adequately perform their main function, of providing valid and meaningful data on personal relationships? There seem to be several grounds for doubt, particularly with regard to rating scales. Such questionnaires are readily fakeable; where the questions being asked concern intimate, controversial or embarrassing issues the incidence of deliberate lying by respondents is likely to be high, even where the researcher has taken pains to develop rapport. Several writers have commented that the attitude–behaviour relationship, often taken for granted when questionnaires are administered, is unlikely to be any more clearcut in personal relationships than in other areas of social life (Jones, 1973; Rodin, 1978); at the very least it is likely that the predominance of self-report scales has contributed to an over-emphasis on participants' attitudes, values and personality attributes as determinants and correlates of relationship initiation, development and dissolution.

Measures of meaning and function of relationships

In relatively recent years several investigators have begun independently to examine in a systematic fashion what people mean by friendship, love, marriage, etc. in terms of the needs these relationships actually do or should fulfil, the rewards they actually do or should entail, and the differential role requirements of various types of relationships. In general, the aim is to establish the perceptions held by members of a given population with regard to their own relationships and/or to relationships in the abstract. Several of these studies have involved collection of a great deal of data from each of a relatively small number of respondents, usually in lengthy face-to-face discussions (e.g. Bernard, 1972); others have used large numbers of subjects responding to written questionnaires, the data from which are then subjected to some form of multivariate or factor analysis in the hope of discovering "basic" dimensions of meaning on which we differentiate the various types of social relationship in which we engage. Many of the questions asked, and the dimensions identified, have to do with behaviours. with roles, shared activities, the everyday utilities of close relationships. La Gaipa and his colleagues have conducted a number of detailed investigations of friendship rewards and expectancies since the late 1960s, culminating in the development and validation of a Friendship Inventory (La Gaipa, 1977b). Wish *et al.* (1976) had subjects rate 20 of their own interpersonal relationships and 25 hypothetical role-relationships on numerous bipolar scales; multivariate analysis revealed four dimensions (friendly–hostile, equal–unequal, intense–superficial, and informal–formal). Weiss and Lowenthal (1975) content-analysed some 1700 descriptive statements about friends provided by over 200 respondents of various ages, and found some sex differences in friendship

definition but no age differences. Among other studies in this general category are those by Rands and Levinger (1979) and Wright (1969).

Self-disclosure

Since the pioneering work in the 1960s by Jourard (1964) and by Altman,
Taylor and their associates (Altman and Taylor, 1973; Taylor, 1968), studies
of self-disclosure in the context of interpersonal attraction and personal
relationships have proliferated, and there is no sign as yet of any decline in
interest. The majority of studies come under the heading of inter-stranger
encounters or acquaintance exercises, and tend to take the form either of
deception experiments in which the subject is approached by an experimental
confederate (e.g. Derlega *et al*. 1973) or of role playing in a getting-to-know-
you type of setting (e.g. Davis, 1978). The relevance of such studies to the
issue of self-disclosure in ongoing relationships is not yet clear; however,
Derlega *et al*. (1976) found that self-disclosure in friendship pairs did *not*
reflect the patterns in experimental "stranger pairs". A number of other
studies have dealt with self-disclosure within existing relationships (e.g.
Morton, 1978; Panyard, 1973; Rubin and Shenker, 1978; Won-Doornink,
1979). Findings are varied and interesting, with some convergence of
evidence that reciprocity of disclosure tends to decline with intimacy, and
that degree of mutuality of disclosure is often overestimated by respondents.
In most studies questionnaire measures of self-disclosure have been taken,
but a few investigators have begun to analyse aspects of disclosure from
videotapes of interactions between friends or marital partners, e.g. Morton
(1978); Won-Doornink (1979).

Many of the self-disclosure data may tell us more about what participants
think they disclose (or think they *should* disclose) than about actual disclosure; the tendency towards analysis of actual disclosure sequences is thus a
welcome one. A perennial problem for self-disclosure researchers is to decide
what types of items are, in fact, seen as intimate or superficial by the participants; there are likely to be considerable cross-cultural as well as social class
and interdyadic differences in definition. Altman and Taylor's (1966) list
of intimacy-scaled topics has been widely used, but it is likely to yield misleading results in cultures other than that of the US student milieu; even within
that group it is possibly out of date. At least one recent researcher (Won-
Doornink, 1979) has felt is necessary to construct her own intimacy scale for
use with her (Korean) subjects; it is an undertaking that may be inescapable if
meaningful self-disclosure research is to be extended.

Behavioural measures

The behavioural approach to the study of relationships is still very much the Cinderella of the methodological family, as noted by Jones (1973). Whilst observations of behaviour have been a feature of studies in affiliation for some time (see Mehrabian and Ksionzky, 1974), very few investigators have attempted to examine actual behaviours in the context of ongoing relationships. However, at least three recent studies have employed measures of looking and eye contact as a function of friendship (Foot *et al.*, 1979; Russo, 1975; Rutter and Stephenson, 1979) to complement Rubin's earlier study of dating couples (1970), whilst other investigations which include measurement of verbal, perceptual or learning behaviours relevant to personal relationships are cited above. The number, however, remains small and such measures seem virtually confined to laboratory studies of relationships.

An important development in recent investigations is a growing tendency to incorporate measures in a variety of modalities within a single study. Olson (1977) reviewed five studies of family power in which both behavioural and self report data were obtained; large and consistent differences were found between results obtained on the two types of instrument. Chapman, Foot and their colleagues similarly found large discrepancies between sociometric nomination of "friends" among primary school children and various behavioural indices of friendship (Chapman *et al.*, 1979; Foot *et al.*, 1979). Other studies that have employed measures of behaviour as well as self reports and/or reports by third persons include Brown and Woodridge (1973); Gottman *et al.* (1978); and Rubin (1970). Widespread evidence of lack of association between relationship measures is disturbing, and underlines the desirability of obtaining as many behavioural data as possible to complement and if necessary correct the picture of relationships constructed from paper-and-pencil indices.

Perspectives and Priorities

Out of social psychology's more recent episodes of self-examination a kind of consensus seems to be emerging with regard to the objectives and means of enquiry into the social aspects of human life (Elms, 1975; McGuire, 1973; Smith, 1978): namely, that there are two complementary perspectives on the task; those of Causal and Interpretative understanding, respectively (Smith, 1978). The former perspective is traditionally from a standpoint *outside* the individual or group under study; the latter perspective is from *within* the social actor's own experience. Significantly, recent discussions of the problems of conceptualizing and investigating close personal relationships have arrived at a similar dichotomy of behavioural and experiential approaches. Olson (1977) distinguishes between *outsider* and *insider* perspectives on personal relationships: each is seen as focusing on a different kind of reality, and a grasp of both the objective and subjective realities of interpersonal intimacy are judged to be essential to a full understanding of such relationships. Examples of both approaches have appeared in preceding sections of this chapter, but on both behavioural and experiential fronts it is clear that there is much room for development, necessitating perhaps some changes in research priorities.

Observation of on-going behaviours, is, as has been demonstrated, still relatively rare in research in personal relationships. Behaviours most amenable to observation and recording are those in more or less structured, laboratory settings; this type of study is, however, open to criticism for disembedding relationships from their social contexts (Gergen, 1978). It is likely that only a proportion of typical relationship exchanges can be successfully reconstructed in the laboratory, whether under manipulative or role playing regimes; however, among those that can be simulated there may be a number of quite important classes of interaction.

Where observation of actual behaviour is impossible, behavioural self report is worth considering as a substitute (Olson, 1977); though a few examples have been cited above this is an approach so far under-used in research in personal relationships. Behavioural self-report involves obtaining subjects' accounts of overt actions relevant to the relationship; cognitive distortions are likely to be less of a problem than in reports of affective or cognitive phenomena, and the fact that many behavioural self-reports are potentially capable of being checked may mitigate tendencies to give socially desirable responses. In the struggle to obtain a fuller idea of what participants actually *do*, behavioural self-report is a worthwhile instrument.

The experiential/interpretative approach to personal relationships aims at providing information in terms of the perceptions, judgements and feelings of participants. In this context the traditional rating-scale approach may be seen as too restrictive and even distorting; standardized questions and rating-dimensions are unlikely to be flexible enough to catch the nuances of individual experience. What appears to be required is a much greater recourse than at present to unstructured, free descriptions by participants, obtained as soon as possible after the occurrence of relevant events. Such an approach can be adapted to the face-to-face interview setting or can be employed (as in the case of diaries) by participants going about their everyday lives (e.g. Harvey *et al.*, 1978). A recently developed technique for sampling the contents of consciousness which is applicable to subjects engaged in their normal daily activities has been described by Hurlburt (1979): the method simply involves auditory signals randomly emitted by means of an inconspicuous device — in appearance rather like a hearing-aid — to subjects who then record what they were thinking or doing when the signal sounded. This method may have applications in sampling not only relationship experiences but also relationship behaviours.

Several writers have recently pointed to the fact that personal relationships may be studied from a number of orientations; this is an issue distinct from the insider-outsider dimension already discussed. From this viewpoint a relationship is not a specific, fixed entity but rather a phenomenon which can be observed and evaluated from a number of alternative positions. Raush (1977) identifies the *personal, dyadic* and *societal* orientations as frames through which both outside observers and participants may view a relationship; these orientations are rarely congruent, and investigating the disjunctions between them can be a fruitful research approach. Raush (1977) cites conflict between norms of propriety and individual desires as an example of personal/societal orientation disjunction; conflict between individual needs for autonomy and forces toward dyadic intimacy constitute an example of personal/dyadic disjunction. A similar approach is taken by Levinger (1977a), who distinguishes between individual, pair unit, social group and societal perspectives.

The tendency among researchers up to the present has been to study personal relationships from one standpoint or another, but rarely from more than one orientation in a single investigation; this selectivity has no doubt been accentuated by the appropriation of particular orientations to the various disciplines within the area. Thus, social psychologists have laid claim to the individual/personal and dyadic, sociologists to the societal; investigation of group or social network aspects has largely gone by default (but see Boissevain, 1974; Verbrugge, 1979). It is encouraging, therefore, to note the (still small) number of investigators that are beginning to investigate individual, dyadic and larger group variables within a single study (e.g. Driscoll *et al.*, 1972; Nahemow and Lawton, 1975).

A pattern of discrepancies is evident between theoretical ambition and methodological performance, as well as between the size of the empirical data base and the elaborateness of the theoretical structures built thereon. To put it simply, we are attempting to run theoretically when we are methodologically capable of little more than a plodding walk. The problem is a complex one: we have a number of quite detailed theories of relationship development (e.g. Duck, 1973; Lewis, 1973; Murstein, 1971) but have not adequately tested many of the main tenets of these theories; it is possible in any case that such theories are seriously deficient simply because they have developed on too small and too ambiguous a basis of descriptive data, and have consequently relied upon dubious "commonsense" assumptions about relationships. I would strongly endorse Elms' (1975) call for a behavioural census: a programme of accumulation of fundamental data, using every available legitimate method, to go hand in hand with development of a more integrated and conceptually relevant methodology for testing hypotheses about relationships.

Not one of the methods discussed in the present chapter is free of serious limitations, either on the uses to which it may be put or on the conclusions that may be drawn from the data obtained. Even with maximal combination of methodologies and measurement techniques (and this is still a relatively unusual research strategy) there are important questions that cannot at present, and perhaps may never, be satisfactorily answered. Attempting to study systematically the aggregate of phenomena we call personal relationships is to test the scientific approach to the limits of its capacity; and accordingly, frequent disappointment is the inevitable lot of the researcher in this area. In spite of these limitations, however, I value the knowledge generated by systematic investigation more highly than the confident pronouncements of those, often in eminent positions, who know it all already.

CHAPTER 3
Interpersonal Relationships and Social Context

G. M. Andreyeva and L. J. Gozman

That social psychology has long ignored social context is by now an accepted criticism of the field. Numerous suggestions have been made about the origins of this asocial orientation and about ways of changing it (e.g. see Gilmour and Duck, 1980). Undoubtedly one of the significant factors has been the basic incorporation of the laboratory approach as essential to the "scientific" image of social psychology; and the selection and simplification of factors consequent upon this has meant that fundamentally important determinants of sociopsychological phenomena have been dismissed as inessential or discarded from theoretical formulation, or at best noted in parentheses as simply a common denominator for a given subject population. For example, research on group effectiveness has disregarded the content of group activity, and hence the problems of leadership have been approached in a way that disregards the traditions and laws — the larger social background — of a particular society.

A similar state of affairs applies to research in interpersonal relations, which is nearly always carried out without due consideration for the natural conditions of human activity. This situation manifests itself in a number of ways, for example in the choice of variables for study, and the restricted focus on individual, "temperamental", or "personality" characteristics.

47

But no matter how important such parameters are, the analysis of interpersonal relationships remains insubstantial if the social characteristics and
backgrounds of the actors are left out.

It would be unfair to say that in present investigations these two classes of
variables (i.e. social characteristics and social background) are completely
disregarded; but group activity tends to be presented through procedure, not
content characteristics (for instance, in description of such group activities as
competition and cooperation), and this, we shall argue, leads to an underestimation of the important qualitative differences in the content of interpersonal relations. Thus on the one hand, the obvious difference between old
friends and, say, customer–seller relations is left unrevealed in the usual style
of empirical research: while on the other hand we ignore the difference in
colouring that the same *sort* of relation can acquire in the context of different
culture and types of society. A society of a given kind creates the conditions
for any sort of interpersonal relationship and so cannot be disregarded as
"exterior" to the study of relationships.

In this context, focusing on so-called "ecological factors" alone (like
spatial closeness, availability of communication between interpersonal relations members, and so on) seems methodologically unjustified. These factors
play a leading part at the early stages of acquaintance; but in the matter of
stable, long-term relationships, the "exterior conditions" can no longer be
reduced to ecological factors. In reality people interacting with each other
belong to a definite type of society with in-built stereotypes and norms of
behaviour. In other words, relationships develop within a definite social context, the importance of which is still, in practice, disregarded when it comes to
investigations of interpersonal relations.

In all likelihood this disregard of social context along with reluctance to
analyse the content characteristics of mutual activity in groups is (inten-
tionally or unintentionally) linked with the general behaviouristic approach
that features in many studies in this field, irrespective of the investigator's
particular theoretical outlook. This behaviouristic orientation reveals itself
not only in terminology but also, and more importantly, in an approach to
science which emphasises the attempt to establish causal inter-relationships
between variables. The prevalence of that approach leads to the study of a
phenomenon in isolation and it brings about a situation where much interesting work is actually left uncompleted, since many authors consider their
goals have been reached as soon as they have answered the question "how?".
They never bother to ask "why?" or "what for?" — questions that, in our
opinion, are the most important ones for any scientific research.

An Alternative Approach to Interpersonal Relationships

One alternative that we propose to a traditional approach in the study of interpersonal relations is consideration of interpersonal relations from the viewpoint of the *activity principle*, elaborated in much Soviet psychology (Leontiev, 1977), which regards the activity of the person as being the prime focus of psychological concerns and views this activity as being socially determined. Although the principle is most often employed in general psychology, it has some important implications for social psychology in general and the study of interpersonal relationships in particular. *First*, the basic orientation of social psychology should be towards real-life (and not laboratory) social groups, since they alone participate in a living system of relations within a definite type of society. Such groups do not need to be artificially included into the social context, since they already exist within it. *Secondly*, the study of relationships as they exist within groups should pay due regard to the reciprocal activities that involve all members of the group. It should also clarify how mutual group activity can itself determine interpersonal relationships. Such principles also tie in with a more general argument that regards the historical development within social psychology of separate psychological and sociological strands as unfortunate and which urges the value of attempting to unify or relate the two traditions in current work (e.g. see Backman, 1980).

Within the scope of the present chapter it will be possible only to focus on one aspect of interpersonal relations — that is, its emotional regulation — to exemplify the approach being advocated. This topic gives rise to a cluster of problems which can be interpreted in terms of attraction, a traditional subject in social psychology. Here also earlier criticisms apply: research has separated the phenomenon from its social context and focused on individual variables that, however important, do not tell the whole story. Indeed in some cases, the ambiguity of empirical data suggests that such variables are not necessarily the most relevant ones. For example, cross-cultural research shows that the influence of the attraction characteristics that are usually subjected to analysis is different within different cultures, i.e. they work through other variables. In studies which have shown the importance of the type of communication, peculiarities of social intercourse, etc., the investigators have concentrated on variables that are almost completely accounted for in terms of the participants in the interpersonal relations. These variables are sometimes chosen at random and as such they have no causal connection with the wider situation in which these relations actually develop. For instance, the hostile or friendly attitude of the experimenter's partner to the subject in Aronson's experiments (Aronson, 1972) or altruistic versus egotistical reaction in works on altruism (Hornstein, 1976) are defined within the experimental design alone and, while they have some degree of validity, they are not connected, as in real life, with the whole system of external social parameters.

At first sight, therefore, it would seem more natural to investigate attraction with regard to the other phenomena of emotional life and try to elucidate its specific character as compared to these other emotions — in which case interpersonal attraction evolves into a problem of general psychology. Without denying the validity of such an approach and while being fully aware of its heuristic value, one can offer another seemingly less evident but nevertheless important analytic perspective which would take into account the interpersonal character of attraction that originates from, and is actualized in, the real process of social intercourse. In other words we propose the analysis of the phenomenon within a wider group and social context, not least because one can hypothesize that the study of attraction in isolation from the social environment and group activity which influence people's relations is responsible in part for the ambiguity of many results and the relative lack of structure evident in much empirical research.

Before getting down to the essence of the proposed method, we shall analyse some of the results so far accumulated both by "sociological" and "psychological" branches of social psychology.

A Sociological Perspective on Personal Relationships

The so-called "sociological" approach in the context of social psychology has long traditions of research into emotional relationships. The contribution of this trend to the understanding of attraction is considerable and it perhaps exceeds that of the psychologically orientated research. At least until recent times there were representatives of this tradition who could give well-founded practical recommendations aimed at stabilizing interpersonal relationships, particularly family relationships. The researches based upon this approach do not question the interconnections between attraction and social context but presume them — and this, in our opinion, accounts for their fruitful results. It also provides them with quite a satisfactory explanation of the role of emotional relations in the society as well as the mechanism for the formation of cultural differences.

Good examples are to be found in a number of studies within this tradition. In the article "Love: the position of a social anthropologist", Sydney Greenfield (1973) analyses the function of love under the conditions of modern American society. He starts from the widespread opinion that the USA is highly pragmatically orientated. "Our standards of success, worth, prestige and dignity are, for the most part, material standards. *Things* are important to us and much of our social life is spent in producing and accumulating these valued material objects'' (Greenfield, 1973, p.41). Analysing both the production activity and the social activity of Americans, Greenfield shows that they are either directly or indirectly conditioned by material needs. This also applies to that part of the population that is excluded from the sphere of material production, like housewives, etc. By taking care of her husband, cooking and keeping the house, a woman contributes to the productive activity of her husband and so the whole existence of the family can be explained within the picture of a pragmatically orientated society.

This does not mean, however, that love in American society is an epiphenomenon and as such is irrelevant. The author argues that, if the functioning of a formed family is part of a rational economic pattern, then the act of marriage itself (at least for a man) is economically unprofitable because from that time onwards the man is expected to support his wife and children. That is why getting married cannot simply be determined by the same economic laws as other aspects of an individual's social life. According to Greenfield (1973) an alternative system of motives and other laws begins to act in that case. The cause of marriage (at least the main cause) according to the majority of sociopsychological and sociological research is love. If in society love were not such a widespread and generally accepted phenomenon, the institution of marriage, which is vitally important for the normal functioning of the society, could be ruined. Hence, Greenfield arrives at the conclusion that in order to maintain the stability of an American society based on material values, its members should, at a certain period of their lives, subscribe to a rather contradictory system of values, the predominant position in which belongs to love. (Though Greenfield's analysis focuses on American society, it has nevertheless, more general theoretical value.)

The mechanism of attraction that function in society cannot be thoroughly understood if we confine ourselves to the study of one isolated culture, and here cross-cultural comparisons are indispensable. Until lately they were mainly devoted to the role of attraction in family formation and function. It turned out, however, that within many societies love is excluded as a basic reason for marriage-making and in some societies emotional relations between future wife and husband are considered highly undesirable (Murstein, 1974, 1977). The data at our disposal make it possible to link the role of emotional, ''impractical'' factors with other aspects of life of the society under study, though initially they relate to the free choice of a conjugal partner. In the societies where a husband either is chosen by parents (in keeping with their perception of an advantageous versus disadvantageous marriage) or is to be picked out of very restricted social circles, according to the social status and the interests of the clan — in such societies emotional attraction between partners is of no importance in marriage. The influence of love is also diminished by economic pressures underlying many marriages as well as the economic dependence of partners on each other (Gozman, 1974).

In the case where young people, being socially and economically unfettered, are free to make their own choice, the dominant feature of relationships becomes their emotional characteristics (Khartchev, 1964; Murstein, 1977). Research in this area thus tends to draw the conclusion that one of the functions of love is to give a complementary orientation in the choice of a partner when all the other, more concrete, ways of mate-selection are lacking — a function of love that can be called *compensatory*. This conclusion seems intuitively plausible and is supported by the opinion of many authors that emotions in general play a compensatory role, compensating for deficits of information (Simonov, 1971). Nevertheless, we offer another way of interpreting the data in question: the increasing role of love in the face of a lack of economic and other forms of compulsion can mean that only under these more favourable conditions can the ability to establish emotional contacts with others be realized. This explanation corresponds to the concept of love elaborated within the framework of humanistic psychology distinct from the above-mentioned sociological position and appeals to the individual rather than group processes.

By this we arrive at a conclusion that love is a multifunctional rather than unifunctional phenomenon and the whole set, as well as the relative values, of its functions, are connected with different aspects of social life. Moreover, within different societies one can develop different hierarchies of love functions.

The influence of such universal parameters, as for example, free choice in mate selection on the emotional relations of the couple, is still unresolved. Rosenblatt (1974) points out two means by which these characteristics may be connected. First of all, there are norms and expectations, which underlie the individual's behaviour. They determine whether contact with this or that person is seen as rewarding or undesirable; whether initial interaction can or cannot grow beyond mere dating. Secondly, there is the question of opportunity for interaction: in order to have a real free hand in the choice a lack of constraint is not enough in itself; one should also have an adequate number of encounters with potential partners. The society may either facilitate or forbid such contacts, and cultures with a restriction on freedom of choice either limit or prohibit certain sorts of contacts. Wide freedom of choice on the other hand turns out to be connected with the free availability of such contacts. For example, in Soviet society not only are meetings between young men and women unrestricted, but also there are some traditional arrangements aimed at encouraging acquaintance, such as dances, joint recreation, etc.

The mechanisms that are considered by Rosenblatt, by no means exhaust the diversity of links between social context and attraction. They display, however, both the strengths and weaknesses of the analysis of attraction in a sociologically orientated social psychology. If the positive aspect of this approach is bound up with the possibility of materialistic interpretations of the phenomena in question, then the negative one refers to the fact that the object of analysis is society as a whole, a group, or a somewhat abstract statistically average individual. Attraction is not simply a sociological, but also a psychological phenomenon, but even when sociological aspects of attraction have been pretty thoroughly studied in cross-cultural research, the psychological features of attraction have hardly ever been subjected to analysis — the sociological mechanisms of attraction are studied separately from the psychological ones. Thus, instead of solving the problem of social context influence on attraction between individuals, a similar, but not identical problem is posed: that is, some social parameters are being related to average parameters of attraction-phenomena that are devoid of any psychological content.

The sociologically orientated social–psychological analysis makes it clear that the lack of wide interaction between peers in, say, a small African village diminishes the prevailing role of love in marriage. This conclusion, however, is also true for villages in general and not just for one particular village. But it cannot necessarily be applied at the level of a real couple from a real settlement, who can fall in love and get married in disregard of any statistical laws.

One cay say that citizens of a large city have more chances of getting married through love than provincials but this fact does not exclude rational and prejudiced marriages of the city dwellers. Thus, the "cultural context of attraction" turns out to be an exterior situation and either contributes to or prevents the interaction, but does not influence the *content* of the process in specific cases.

A Social – Psychological Perspective

The real issue for social psychology to solve is whether the social context of attraction can be an "interior" situation. In other words, does it directly influence the feelings of people? Do people's feelings towards each other depend on the society they live in? Getting back to the example of an African young couple falling in love: do their feelings differ in essence and intensity from those that bind a young couple belonging to quite a different culture?

The most reliable answers to the question could be gained through *direct experimental examination.* Unfortunately, the present level of developmental psychology prevents us from carrying out such a study. Comparative measurement of emotional intensity within different cultures and subcultures is a problem that is, as yet, unsolved. Verbal methods, apart from inherent shortcomings, are extremely difficult to apply to other cultures. As for non-verbal methods, these measure things that are not connected with emotions directly, but are mediated through other variables. That is why, even if a given index is adequate for a definite community it is extremely difficult to predict the degree of its validity for another group. The galvanic skin response (GSR) index, for example, one of the most widely used indicators of emotional excitation, is affected by sex, age, ethnic group of a subject, etc. in ways that are not precisely known, so that the use of psychophysiological indicators in cross-cultural research of attraction is not practically possible. As far as we know no adequate methods for such research have yet been elaborated, which means we have to search for an alternative, non-experimental way of solving the problem.

In this direction the *content-analysis of various philosophical and artistic works* from or belonging to different cultures is, presumably, fruitful. Here, universality of human feelings is the first thing to catch the eye: the patterns of relations are common either for all or at least for the majority of cultures. The fact that one nation can understand the literature of another supports this view.

It is not impossible, however, that similarity occurs speciously through, firstly: the reciprocal influences of cultures or, secondly: through universal laws of historical development. Kon's (1974) brilliant historical–psychological analysis of friendship carried out in the USSR, witnesses to the fact that it is too early to jump to a conclusion that the content of emotional relationships is entirely independent of social context. Kon has pointed out that even in ancient times friendship had emerged as a highly institutional relationship. The choice of a friend was far from being free: it was actually determined by various economic and political considerations, such as the interests of the clan, etc. Thus, taking into account Kon's findings, we reach the conclusion of a relatively weak emotional colouring of ancient people's friendship as compared to friendship of our days.

In Kon's other paper (1977) data are cited which present an attitude to children in the Middle Ages which is markedly different to that of the twentieth century. This amounted not so much to a system of paedagogical control that differed radically from ours, as to a whole attitude towards children, which was far less intimate and was more formal than ours. These data, however, do not provide final answers for the problems under discussion. They only indicate that the content and the psychological meaning of friendship in ancient times differed from what we imply by them now and it remains possible that a deeply personal, intimate feeling, coinciding in its content with modern friendly feelings, might also have existed earlier. Pre- sumably, these sorts of feelings were, comparatively, of little social value, or not so widespread as nowadays and because of this they drew little, if any, attention from philosophers and artists. Thus, such methods of research as content-analysis and historical-psychological analysis cannot by themselves confirm whether social context really influences attraction.

The third possible approach, in our opinion, lies in *theoretical and conceptual analysis of the attraction phenomenon itself*, with the application of results, gained by psychological-social psychology; that is, considering the connection of attraction and social context from the perspective of social psychology where it coincides with the psychology of personality. It is necessary to clarify first of all whether the social psychology of attraction gives any grounds for confirming the validity or falsity of an hypothesis that places attraction in its social context: and if the hypothesis is to be confirmed, one should try to elucidate the mechanisms of this connection. As was mentioned above, direct comparisons between attraction and social context parameters have not yet been drawn. For this reason, some indirect, often ambiguous, data have to be taken into consideration here.

There is an accumulation of paradoxical results in the social psychology of attraction. The most intriguing ones lie in the fact that there is apparently almost no connection between the stable personal traits of the subject of attraction (measured by the tests in common use) on the one hand, and the intensity and content of the feeling itself on the other hand. In experimental research carried out by American psychologists, correlation of attraction with such qualities as authoritarianism, dogmatism, and other dimensions has not proved significant (Gubennesch and Hunt, 1971; Byrne and Griffitt, 1973). An exception here is self-esteem, the level of which influences attraction greatly and often unexpectedly (Stroebe, 1977).

These results derive, on the whole, from the laboratory study of attraction. The analysis of attraction in a naturalistic situation leads, however, to analogous conclusions. Dean (1961) comparing young men's and young women's level of romanticism (characterized by their readiness to participate in emotionally charged interaction) with the level of emotional maturity, measured by standard scales, arrived at the conclusion that there is interdependence of these two variables. The data obtained by some Soviet investigators may be interpreted likewise: for instance, results of work by the present authors demonstrate a weak connection between orientation towards a given style of communication and personality traits measured by the HSPQ (Gozman, 1974). Although research has identified certain other important conceptual inclarities (Duck and Craig, 1978), in part, the lack of positive results can be accounted for by the imperfection of the methods used for measuring personality traits. Taking the F-scale as an example, Gubennesch and Hunt (1971) showed that question-by-question analysis of personality tests could contribute more to the understanding of attraction than the use of integral global indexes. The authors discovered that 13 question out of 26 are closely connected with interpersonal perception and the index of authoritarianism that is thus acquired actually has a greater impact on evaluation of other people than the F-scale index calculated as a whole.

However, methodological faults alone cannot account for the fact that the relationship between two people appeared to be independent of the characteristics of the subjects of this relationship. In order to explain this finding either a large amount of data has to be treated as artefactual, or it is necessary to revise the present concept of attraction, and make the assumption that it is only feebly conditioned by the individuality of the subject who is involved in the communication process.

In social psychology, as well as in common-sense belief, the idea of the spontaneity and exclusive influence of inner determination of emotional relations is widespread. However, the data pointing to there being little or no connection between attraction and personal qualities lead us to believe that emotional relations are often externally determined. If the exterior determination of attraction is accepted as plausible, then the evidence of the impact of situational parameters on attraction (unexplained from the viewpoint that emotional relations are spontaneous) becomes clear. For example, Casler (1973) shows the role of conformity in the genesis of love. He claims, specifically, that at a certain period of an individual's life the norms of society prescribe that he should fall in love with another person of the opposite sex. But if this does not occur then the individual is exposed to all the pressures felt by someone subject to group influence who violates group norms. Hence, attraction is presumed to be not only determined by exterior influences but also normative in its essence, and the behaviour that accompanies it is, to a great extent, role behaviour.

The recognition of the normative character of attraction and, consequently, its direct connection with the social and group context, clarifies not only many scientific facts, but also a number of everyday-life observation, like the great increase in "romances" at secondary school.

In one and the same (mixed-sex) class almost all girls can simultaneously fall in love with classmates (and many of them with the same person). This occurs in spite of great individual differences between them, in terms of the level of emotional or intellectual maturity, etc. Their affection, with the behaviour and feelings accompanying it, is nothing but a conformity reaction, the urge to be in line with popular patterns.

Attraction as an Attitude

In those froms of attraction phenomenon that are studied experimentally, the role of the normative component is considerable — but taken by itself it can hardly account for the complex influence of the social context on attraction. If the possibility of direct social context effects on attraction is to be confirmed, then we are faced with the question of how the influence occurs. If we consider attraction as a particular attitude towards another person and accept for present purposes a three-component model of attitudes, some assumptions about the mechanism of social context influence on the components of attraction can be suggested. In this case, too, the suggested approach is based on the studies carried out earlier within the framework of different research orientations. One of our main objectives is to prove that our adopted approach has definite premises within a tradition which on the whole, does not subscribe to the necessity of investigation of attraction within social context. A number of data, gathered within the framework of this tradition do, however, contradict it and, consequently, compel us to search for another explanatory principle.

Let us consider from this angle the affective component of attraction, basing our discussion on a two-component model of emotions (Schachter and Singer, 1962) which implies that emotions can appear only under the simultaneous influence of two factors: physiological arousal and the presence of cues for the subject to interpret it in terms of emotions, i.e. only when definite cognitive and linguistic constructions, as well as bodily sensations, operate. E. Walster (1971) conducted a series of investigations in which both factors were independently varied. Analysing the phenomenology of love, Walster observed, among other things, that love is often preceded by, or combined with, negative experiences like fear, grief over the loss of the beloved, etc. This connection is even retained in the etymology of words denoting strong emotions. Thus, the word "passion" denotes both the "feeling of love" and "suffering" (currently, however, the second meaning is seldom used). Walster accounts for this by the fact that unpleasant (e.g. dangerous) events, no less than pleasant experiences, lead to a high level of physiological excitement which is later interpreted as a feeling of love.

Given, then, the two-component model of emotions, we can proceed to the analysis of the influence of social context upon the affective component of attraction. To begin with, many influences on physiological excitement are regulated by society, i.e. excitement-causing stimuli and situations are either sanctioned or prohibited. For example, many countries have laws aimed at the non-proliferation of drugs. Many communities condemn the use of artificial stimulants and the creation of situations which lead to an unusually high level of excitation in a great number of people, for example, some pop-music concerts. The spread of non-pharmacological excitation stimuli, such as erotic stimuli, is also regulated either by laws or by traditions in each particular community. It might be expected, however, that the influence of society over this component of attraction tends to be rather limited and indirect.

Another, and more straightforward, way of determining the affective component of attraction by social means lies first in a social definition of the "set" of feeling, and secondly in building up some rules of operation with the set. This set, together with the rules of its use, is dictated by art, mass media, etc. Through these channels the society influences every individual and thus determines the content of his emotional attitudes. It is the mechanism of artistic influence that becomes here of particular importance: art both promotes the expansion of the emotional set and also gives the rules for its use. Through a process of identification by the reader or the spectator with the main character it becomes possible for him to adopt the hero's viewpoint or to accept his models of the surrounding world and share his ideas on the ways of solving his collisions with the world. Apart from this, identification enables a person to share the character's feelings, i.e. if we apply the two-component model, to learn to interpret his own emotional states. Here we can therefore distinguish two aspects of art influence. First, it not only induces changes of cognitive structure, which would readily be reversed by other influences, but it also effects the expansion of emotional set or a new way of using it, which is a more stable acquisition and which does not disappear under the influence of new information. Secondly, and more importantly, a real artist creates a character whose feelings and sufferings, shared by the reader or the spectator, express the extraordinary vision of the author. Endowing his hero with such feelings, the artist, being a highly sensitive person, thus provides his contemporaries and later generations with patterns of feelings and emotional reactions towards other people, that are much more universal and free from circumstantial characteristics of communi-cation than cognitive schemes. That is why the best works of art enable us to learn to feel with greater intensity and vigour.

The actual examination of this mechanism, however, has not yet been experimentally carried out, though we have some indirect data testifying to its existence. These are, first of all, the results of some cross-cultural studies demonstrating the connections between emotions and the presence of corres-ponding linguistic constructions. At least one tribe, the Manu of New Guinea, is known not to have the word "love" in their vocabulary, and the members of that tribe never establish the corresponding emotional relations with each other (Kon, 1977). In Soviet literature, the data on the deter-mination of emotional relationships with others by cognitive structures are given in Luria's (1974) book "On the Historical Development of Cognitive Processes". Also, similar conclusions could be drawn from the analysis of subcultural, particularly sex differences, for example from the fact that women are more romantic than men. An attempt to explain this inclination by physiological differences alone, is highly unsatisfactory. On the contrary, a number of data point to the fact that sex differences in human relationships are caused, first and foremost, by social rather than biological factors. Berscheid and Walster (1974) among other things, explain the differences in the level of romanticism by the so-called double sexual standard according to which men are "allowed" to have premarital and extramarital liaisons while women are not.

Finally, another indirect testimony of the social influence on the affective component of attraction lies in the recognition by many psychologists of the direct connection between the richness of emotions and the variety of corresponding linguistic constructions. For example, the adherents of sensitivity training consider the enlargement of the active vocabulary of emotions on the part of members of T-groups as a proof of the efficiency of these groups. The enlarging of this vocabulary is believed to be connected with an expansion of the emotional range. But the subject of the vocabulary is society or culture and, hence, it is the parameters of wide social context that form the general foundation on which the individual differences are later built up.

Thus, a number of data and assumptions contained in traditional studies of attraction can be used as a basis for showing the impact of social context on the affective component of attraction. Similarly, the same researches can provide data for conclusions about the influence of social context on the other components of attraction.

The mechanism of wide social-context influence on the two other components of attraction-as-an-attitude, namely the cognitive and conative components, is much simpler than that described above. The cognitive component of attraction is the knowledge of another person as the concrete manifestation of knowledge of "people in general". The process of this concretizing may be complicated and ambiguous, yet one can assert that both the subject's own ideas of human nature, and general attribution processes will influence his perception of another person. But views on the nature of man, on the most probable causes of his behaviour, and on human motives are to a great extent engendered by society. Patterns of behaviour and motivations sponsored by society are spread through the channels of mass media, included in educational systems, and conveyed by art and folklore.

Again, direct experimental data are lacking, and we must use information gathered within other frames of reference (Subbotsky, 1972). For instance, some indirect data point to the straightforward connection between ideas of positive personal characteristics and behaviour appropriate to all people on

the one hand, and the degree of benevolence toward a given individual
on the other. These results were obtained from experiments on altruistic
behaviour. In one of them (Hornstein, 1976) some of the subjects, listening to the radio, were informed of an altruistic deed while some were told
of an egotistical action allegedly performed by a certain person on that
day. After that, the subjects participated in a "prisoner's dilemma" experiment. The subjects who received the more favourable information more
frequently demonstrated cooperativeness in the situation of real communication.

    Naturally, these as well as other results cannot be considered as direct
proofs of social-context influences on the cognitive component of attraction. A more relevant test, as in the previous case, would derive through
cross-cultural and subcultural comparisons. Such researches, however, have
not been done until recently and we can therefore only make indirect use of
some results of cross-cultural research, devoted to other problems (e.g.
Staub, 1974).

    The impact of social context on the last (conative) component of attrac-
tion takes place in two ways. To begin with, the communication habits
acquired by a subject are set up not only by the direct environment but also
by wider culture. This can be shown by means of the classical Bandura
experiment on the impact of imitation on aggressive behaviour; by
Berkowitz's work demonstrating the increase of the subject's aggressiveness
in the presence of aggressive tools in this perceptual field and also some
researches on the impact of mass media (TV particularly) on the behaviour
of the subject. All these investigations were carried out within the framework of a behaviouristic set of assumptions and consequently their results
are interpreted from these theoretical positions. Social context parameters
— namely, patterns of behaviour, other people's reactions, etc. — are considered to characterize only some extrinsic factors of a person and not
his/her personality as such. This approach, however, does not clarify why a
subject takes only one pattern of behaviour for his/her very own while
rejecting some others. In all likelihood, another theoretical pattern is necessary to understand the mechanism through which the parameters of social
context influence the inner content of the attraction process (as well as interpersonal relations in general).

    All this brings us to the conclusion that the logical development
of attraction research leads a whole group of investigators to the idea
of its connection with social context. But the mechanism of this influence
is not yet sufficiently clear — nor, indeed, is the concept of "social
context".

Group Context, Activity and Attraction

Further advances in the investigation of the social determination of inter-personal relationships can only be based on a signally different theoretical approach. The core of this approach would involve accepting the concept of a subject who not only may be seen as capable of resisting circumstances, but also may be construed as being capable of creating them and also of actively reproducing them. In our opinion this solution to the problem was proposed by Marx on the philosophical level and realized on the psychological level in the principle of activity. According to this principle the main psychological characteristic of a subject is his activity and this activity is socially deter-mined. Thus, application of the activity principle to the system of socio-psychological knowledge would mean the interpretation of a group as the subject of activity, which would mean the consideration of all group processes through group activity. In Soviet literature the hypothesis that a system of interpersonal relations in a group also depends on group activity was put forward by Petrovsky (1973). We have suggested that elaboration of this approach in the context of social perception phenomena would be directly relevant to the investigation of attraction, and, among other things, to the elucidation of its connection with social context.

To begin with, some general typology of attraction phenomena, with regard to the group members' distribution, should be built up (cf. Hinde, 1979). We distinguish between at least two different types of attraction in this regard: (a) attraction between the members of one and the same group; (b) attraction between the members of different social groups (Andreyeva, 1974).

Let us consider the situation where both members of the pair belong to one group. The group can influence attraction in the pair first by defining the structure and content of communication; secondly, by influencing self-conscious characteristics of its members, which in its turn influences attrac-tion. Evidently, mutual group activity is connected with the first type of influence. In the research of Soviet social psychologists it has been con-vincingly shown that the parameters of group activity significantly serve to define the final result of the interpersonal perception process. For example, in a series of studies Bodalev (1970) demonstrated that group members show better memory for the member characteristics which are important for successful group activity. In a number of studies under the direction of the present authors it was shown that such variables as the time of group activity, and the level of the group members' involvement in this activity (namely, the acceptance of the aims and values of these activities), are also important. Though these variables become more obvious in other processes (for instance in causal attribution), they are also valid for attraction.

To refer back to the three-component analysis of attraction, one can observe the influence of group activity on each component. To take the affective component of attraction as an example, we may say that group activity influences it primarily by providing the general emotional background. The group context determines an individual's mood greatly, which, in its turn, influences the inclination to feel attracted to another person. In the group, also, self esteem is developed and this is one of the most important determinants of attraction.

This process of group-context influence on attraction takes place even when individuals belong to different groups: but in that case, it is rather the influence on the *cognitive* components that becomes evident. Attraction depends on many within- and between-group components and also on the general characteristics of society, in connection with perception of another person as a member of another group, who has to a certain extent, internalized the group characteristics. The laws of interpersonal attraction depend in this case on the degree of subject's *propensity* to a stereotypic perception of the other group members, and on the content of the stereotypes used. If, for example, the object of attraction belongs to the group towards which a negative attitude has been already formed in the subject, the evaluation of the object would most likely be negative. This is confirmed by numerous Soviet and other investigations. One should stress, however, that the disposition to the stereotyping of the perception of another group's members is bound up not only with the personal traits of a perceiver, but also with the characteristics of the society as a whole. For example, in a racially unprejudiced community, membership of another race would not influence attraction, whereas belonging to another race would be very salient in communities with race discrimination. Presumably, in societies with more humanistic attitudes, where good and bad characteristics are not associated with specific sociodemographic groups, the influence of such stereotypes would be less.

Attraction between members of different groups is also determined by the kind of relations — cooperative or competitive — established between them. In general, competition tends to promote hostility, while cooperation leads to more positive affect. Of course, it is impossible to avoid all competition between groups in any society, but the traditions and laws of a society will greatly influence the relative number of cooperative versus competitive interactions between groups (and the character of that competition).

V.S. Ageyev's research (carried out under the guidance of one of the present authors — Andreyeva) has studied the ways in which one group's perception of the other group is conditioned by the content of the mutual activity. In the situation where group activities are aimed at reaching those goals that are socially valid for members, the degree of in-group favouritism and out-group hostility was considerably reduced. Though this research does not, strictly speaking, belong to the study of interpersonal attraction it does indirectly confirm the idea of mutual-activity influence (in our case, not in-group, but between-group) on the conative component of attraction.

Let us now consider the contrary influence of attraction on group activity. The basically important problem of attraction functions, traditionally explained at the individual level, may also be considered at the group level. If this is done then the problem of the functional role of interpersonal attraction turns into the old, but still unresolved, issue of the influence of emotional relations between group members on different parameters of the group's activity.

The results of empirical research in this field have been analysed by R.S. Veisman (1977). Veisman argues that the ambiguity of data indicates the operation of a hidden third variable, which conditions the influence of two other variables (namely, interpersonal relations and group efficiency) on each other. The level of group development (i.e. the degree of sharing by group members of the mutual values and objectives) is suggested as such a hidden variable. Together with the introduction of such a variable, one can suggest a more elaborate analysis of the concepts used in the studies of group efficiency. Here, the meaning usually attributed to the notion of efficiency does not appear to be adequate for specifically *psychological* studies of group activity. It often happens that this concept is reduced to the "successful performance" by the group of a certain task, irrespective of group members' attitude towards it and of the role which it (and the activity of fulfilling it) plays in the wider context of group functioning.

This approach seems to be sufficiently justified only when the group members are strongly and positively motivated towards the performance of this task. In many cases, however, especially when it comes to studying real groups, there is only doubtful justification for the assumption that such motivation exists: the group may have negative attitudes to its activities, or treat them as unimportant, for instance.

It is the underestimation of the motivational element that sometimes brings the research to deadlock. From these positions, for example, it would be difficult to account for the low efficiency demonstrated by some highly cohesive groups. The point is that the goals of the group, as they are understood by the group members, can considerably diverge from externally imposed goals and it is the latter which are usually taken into account by experimenters. It would be more in accordance with psychological research to understand efficiency in terms similar to success in the achievement of the goals that the group members have accepted themselves, satisfaction of the group members with their mutual activity, and communication and stability of the group in the face of destabilizing influences.

If we consider group efficiency from this angle, its interpersonal origins become apparent and then it becomes tenable to argue that interpersonal attraction positively influences the efficiency of group activity, and thus one of its functions is to promote successful group interaction. In attraction studies there are a number of results which support this hypothesis. For example, in many investigations a connection has been established between attraction and inclination to help a person who is the object of attraction. Intensification of attraction leads to increase in altruistic acts; and altruism and helping on the other hand promote increase in mutual attraction between members of an interaction. The data in hand are not sufficient to decide if there is a causal–sequential connection between the two variables (altruism and attraction) or merely a correlation accounted for by the impact of a latent variable. Nevertheless, existence of a positive relationship between attraction on the one hand, and altruism on the other, may be regarded as firmly established.

Some experimental findings also bear witness to the fact that people involved in attraction relations tend to evaluate each other more highly compared with those who are strangers to each other or even acquainted but still not mutually sympathetic (Lott and Lott, 1972). On a verbal level this process manifests itself in a benevolent style of communication and in positive presentation of partners in talks with other people. All this promotes, firstly, a psychologically beneficial atmosphere within the group and, secondly, which is especially important in a situation of an intergroup conflict, the group looks cohesive in the eyes of outsiders.

Psychological comfort and confidence in the positive attitudes of other group members are not only important for their own sake. Only when this condition exists can there be a situation where outspoken disagreement with another person's position not only fails to diminish sympathy towards that person but may even increase it. Thus it follows, that the members of a group which is characterized by a high level of attraction may argue and criticize each other without any fear of negative effects on their relationships. This helps to establish and preserve the creative atmosphere in the group.

Attraction also influences conformity and imitation levels. Both of these phenomena become stronger when a person, highly attractive for a subject, is chosen for a model. If we consider these results in combination with the data that bear witness to the facilitating impact of attraction towards a learner on the learning process, it becomes obvious that attraction facilitates both the new member's entrance to the group, promoting a quicker acquisition of the necessary skills and lore, and also the transmission of experience from one group member to another. The processes of mutual instruction and information exchange in groups with high levels of attraction are also smoother because of a positive connection between attraction and level of communication: the higher the attraction between two people, the more often they get involved in communication or at least try to do so (Lott and Lott, 1972).

The evidence of great precision of interpersonal perception in the case of high degrees of attraction between the members of communicating networks also presents interest. In some situations, especially stressful ones, this may be extremely useful both for the essential activity of the group as a whole and for each of its members. We must add that there is direct evidence of the fact that the presence of individuals who are attractive to the person can help the latter to cope with stress.

Let us again turn to the characteristics of groups with a high total attraction index. In such groups, the level of mutual assistance is high, the relationships between the members are characterized by benevolence, which at the same time does not stop criticism and the exchange of differing viewpoints. The group members identify themselves with the group and share group objectives. If we start analysing these and a number of other facts from the point of view of Petrovsky's (1973) theory of group activity, it turns out that attraction between group members promotes the development of the group itself and its evolution into a genuine collective. This interdependence, unexpected at first glance, becomes clear if we bear in mind that attraction as well as interpersonal relationships, as a whole, are conditioned by the group activity which, consequently, remains the most significant influence on the level of group development. On the empirical level the coincidence of group development determinants and attraction determinants manifests itself, for example, in the fact that similarity of attitudes (which serves as an indicator of group cohesiveness) is at the same time one of the most important correlatives of attraction (Byrne and Griffitt, 1973).

Other results drawn from investigations of interpersonal attraction and showing the influence of emotional relations on group activity could be given. But, in our opinion, the data so far presented are enough to support the conclusion that consideration of the results of empirical investigations of attraction from the viewpoint of the activity principle shows the positive influence of attraction on the efficiency of group activity — and also prompts us to put forward a proposition about the connection between attraction and level of group development.

Summary and Conclusions

All this brings us to the following conclusions. Interpersonal attraction research, undertaken in the frames of reference of different theoretical social psychological approaches has accumulated a considerable body of factual material which enables us to approach the formulation of an hypothesis about the connection of this mostly "personal" component of interpersonal relations with social context. The very formulation of the hypothesis, however, and especially its experimental testing, demands turning to another explanatory model which differs markedly from behaviouristic conceptual schemes. This explanatory model can be based on the activity principle. Applying this principle to the concrete phenomenon under study results in the demonstration of the influence of mutual group activity, representing "social context" on attraction. At the same time, the activity principle provides an analysis of the reverse influence of attraction on the parameters of mutual group activity. Such an approach seems fruitful for a deeper understanding of the mechanism of interaction with social context not only of attraction, but of other group processes as well. It thus opens the wider perspective of a genuine reconstruction of socio-psychological knowledge, or at least that part of it which is connected with interpersonal relations research. Naturally the testing of the proposed theoretical approach implies a wide panorama of new experimental studies.

CHAPTER 4

A Systems Approach to Personal Relationships

John J. La Gaipa

Social psychologists are becoming more and more sensitive to the meta-physical assumptions and epistemological issues underlying their work, and the study of personal relationships cannot stay neutral in this time of conflict. This chapter presents a new way of thinking about personal relations in terms of a systems approach: this includes, but goes beyond, the idea that the whole is more than the sum of its parts and has a number of metaphysical and epistemological implications. In a systems approach, the parts of a system cannot be identified except with reference to the whole which functions as a whole by virtue of the interdependence of its parts, and is called a system. From a different angle, systems theory is a "method" designed to study complex situations so that the largest possible number of interdependent factors can be included in the analysis.

Evidently a systems approach will have considerable application to the study of personal relationships and will be able to expand the theoretical approach by extending the present narrow range of issues in current research. Too often have personal relationships studies focused attention on single dyadic relationships and on the behaviours that occur in them whilst disregarding the nexus of other relationships to which individuals are exposed. Such other networks of relationships affect the individual through cultural norms, for instance, or as part of socialization. They can also offer specialized support systems (e.g. family and kinship) as well as providing an important set of alternative relationships that not only may be as significant as the particular one that the researcher has chosen to focus upon experimentally but also may be important moderators of his behaviour in it. This chapter will therefore expound a systems-based approach to personal relationships both by looking at a three-dimensional model for understanding relationships and by reference to the various real life contexts and systems in which they take place.

General Properties of Systems Models

There are a number of competing systems theories. The particular one emphasized in this chapter is called "holistic structuralism" and I have drawn quite heavily on Overton's (1975) description of this perspective. Structuralism is a general method or approach used for understanding and explaining phenomena; it is interdisciplinary, and as such is a content-free method. The hallmark of this approach is a commitment to go beyond the observational level and to construct models to represent the underlying organization assumed to be involved in the phenomenon under study. The major task thus involves the definition of organized systems and the reciprocal interactions among such systems which produce changes in them.

In a holistic structuralist programme, the first requirement is to decide on the specific activity or functions of the phenomenon that are to be examined. The second requirement is the rational discovery of the particular organization of the activity which means that the investigator seeks to establish some kind of conceptual representation of what is being studied. This construction, or model building, involves the identification of the relevant elements; placing them into their inter-relations or system; and specifying the form of the inter-relationships. A structure, then, is imposed on the phenomenon by the construction of a model, and this in itself facilitates understanding, as the model is useful in examining the relationship between the parts and the whole, or the subsystems and the total system.

To adopt a holistic structural approach to personal relations involves making a number of commitments to metaphysical positions and a particular world-view. Structuralism is more than simply a procedure that calls for the need for conceptual models (an idea that is not unique to structuralism); rather, structuralism is defined in terms of a commitment to a critical-idealistic philosophical tradition instead of to a rational-empirical position. Assumptions are therefore made regarding the primacy of holism over elementarism; emergence over reductionism; organized complexity instead of simple complexity. Commitments are also made to function or activity instead of substance, to a dialectic causation and change, and essentially to an organismic world-view instead of a mechanistic world-view.

A mechanistic world-view, on the one hand, favours the "analytic ideal" of science: understanding proceeds by breaking down the object or event into its simple elements which are then related in unidirectional and linear causal sequences. Essentially, the search for explanation by a non-structuralist approach is in terms of antecedent conditions: order is reducible to the identification of antecedent conditions. A structural approach, on the other hand, looks for a different kind of order — an order that arises from the conceptualization of the phenomenon, and such conceptual representation obviously cannot be reduced to antecedent conditions. Usually such work involves *levels of conceptualization* and such hierarchic notions of reality are important to the structuralist in his search for explanation, which is sought by looking at higher levels of reality instead of moving down to lower levels in the process of reducing or breaking down the phenomenon under study. This is not to imply that structuralists limit understanding to higher-order levels. Some "middle-of-the-road structuralists" suggest working back and forth between analysis and synthesis.

A dialectic perspective is another important characteristic of a holistic structural approach (cf. Wozniak, 1975). The dialectic image of man sees him as engaged in activities designed to resolve internal and external contradictions. Man is seen as an active rather than as a passive agent, as changing and changeable, as seeking out disequilibrium rather than equilibrium. Contradictions within a dialectic framework reflect bipolarities in nature that mutually presuppose one another — one cannot exist with the other. The resolution of contradictions leads to change, and growth occurs when conflicts are resolved by the synthesis of dimensional demands (Riegel, 1976). Such dialectics exist in the interpersonal world because this world is governed by many contradictory forces and many of the dilemmas in personal relationships reflect this.

A problem sometimes raised regarding the structural position is whether or not the "form" or "structure" or "organization" can be defined in terms of reality — the empirical world. The answer here is that the term "social structure" has nothing to do with empirical reality but with models which are built up after it (cf. Kelvin, 1970). The form or structure, then, is defined in terms of knowledge, not as a thing of the physical world. To argue that structures are properties of physical reality would be contrary to a holistic structuralism which posits that structure is *more* than the elements of the object and their relationships. Activity and functions have priority over substance.

The greatest difficulty with the systems approach arises out of the fact that everything cannot be said or looked at simultaneously. A structural model is useful for providing a frame of reference that focuses the perception of the scientist who is observing social phenomena but in using a holistic-structural approach, it is important to be careful in selecting one's observation point and in deciding which of the concepts will be used to order one's observation. In choosing the parts, observability must be the criterion since it is necessary to remain as close as possible to the empirical level in defining structure. In choosing relational concepts, therefore, we should be careful to employ ideas that are easily checked against empirical reality — it is an easy mistake to invent abstractions that can be manipulated logically, but have no basis in common sense.

A Three-dimensional Systems Model for Relationships

Given this general background, we can now begin to explore the application of a systems approach to personal relationships. The first step is to note that the concept of hierarchical levels (discussed above) has an immediate and obvious relevance here. Personal relationships can be seen to be influenced at the cultural–normative level, or the behavioural level, or at the psychological level, and these constitute the first dimension that shall be considered below. However, this is too simple on its own and I shall borrow Levinger's (1977a) notion of a matrix to describe the underlying structure of personal relationships. Two more dimensions are thus added to the "levels perspective" to create a three-dimensional model, these two being a "support systems dimension" (including such social structures as the family, kin, friends and neighbours) and a "psychosocial resources dimension" (including the psychosocial contributuion that other people can make to a person, such as identity needs, affect, expressivity, sociability, and instrumental service). These dimensions are represented in Fig. 1. Such a three- dimensional matrix (Fig. 1) would permit the observer to visualize a larger set of combinations of variables, but always, of course, within the larger organization of the "total system". Insofar as the "total system" is an open system, it is possible to move back and forth from analysis at the interface of two or more points, as well as synthesis in looking at any interface within the larger context.

The usefulness of this three-dimensional model can be assessed in a number of ways. Does the model help to integrate existing, rather disparate findings from different disciplines such as psychology, sociology, and anthropology? Does the model contribute to a greater understanding of the complexity of personal relationships within a larger contex? Does the model help to locate areas where research is needed, and does the model generate questions leading to such research? This chapter can only begin to address

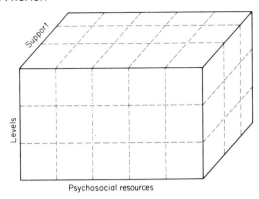

FIG. 1   Three-dimensional model for structural analysis of personal relationships.

some of these issues and accordingly I shall present little more than a skeleton, with a few attempts to "flesh out" some of the bones and ligaments.

Levels

The systems concepts of holism, interdependency, and hierarchical organizations are often used in terms of a so-called *levels perspective* which is based on certain assumptions about the nature of human reality. Human reality consists of a number of superimposed levels, each of which is conceptually distinct and "causally" autonomous. Most theorists posit four levels of reality, ranked as follows: the cultural, social, psychological and biological (Levinger, 1977a; Raush, 1977). The explanation of relationships and causes is interpreted as impossible to advance by reducing one level to the explanatory context of the level below. Instead, explanation is sought in terms of higher levels of abstraction: the higher the reality level, the more integrative the role and the more causally significant.

More specifically, Riegel (1976) has proposed a levels perspective that highlights the notion of dialectics. The four interdependent dimensions are (1) inner–biological; (2) individual–psychological; (3) cultural–sociological; and (4) outer–physical. A dialectic approach is concerned with the "inner" dialectics (the first two dimensions) and the "outer" dialectics (the last two dimensions). Dialectic psychology, then, deals with conflicts between "inner" and "outer" dialectics, and conflicts which create asynchronies within or between any two of the four dimensions. Conflict resolution occurs by synchronizing the dimensions or when synthesis takes place.

Braiker and Kelley (1979) have developed a multilevel model of the interdependence of close relationships that makes a major contribution to systems thinking. The three levels of interdependence occur in personal characteristics/attitudes; norms and roles; and specific behaviours at the lowest level.

Two individuals in a close relationship are said to be mutually dependent and the very nature of this interdependence is a factor in conflict. It is also noted that two persons may be interdependent on different levels.

A minimum of three levels is necessary for the conceptual framework outlined in this chapter to approach personal relationships. The *cultural-normative*, the highest level, deals with the norms, roles, social rules, expectations and ideals that affect personal relationships. These are essentially acquired during the process of socialization, and have some constraining properties. The second level is the *interpersonal behavioural* level of analysis of personal relationships. This level includes various kinds of interpersonal events, particularly in face-to-face groups. Braiker and Kelley (1979) treat this level as the lowest one, and include here specific behaviours, such as occur during conflict, e.g. nagging, temper displays, withdrawals or sulking. The third level, of course, is the *individual-psychological* level — essentially, the intra-individual dimensions. Much of what will be presented in the main body of this chapter are descriptions of interpersonal behaviours in different contexts. Hence, at this point we will limit the discussion of levels in this section to cultural-normative and individual-psychological levels.

The cultural-normative level

Support systems, such as the family and friendships, are constantly subject to extrasystem inputs such as norms, values, and rules. These instructional inputs serve to define intrasystem allocation of behaviours and patterning of performance but adjustments and adaptations in interactional patterns are necessary, particularly within the family, to accommodate to these influences. A major task of the family, as the socializing agent, is to enact and resolve instructions issuing from the value structure of the larger community. The demand structure of the culturally normative system contributes to conflict-ridden interactions in the family, e.g. when the parents seek to motivate the children into performances that are incongruent with the child's biological proclivities. Such problems as over-conformity, over-compliance, and negative sanctions arise when the adaptive functions of the family are inadequate. Some family systems try to reduce internal conflicts by increasing the rigidity of the system boundaries, i.e. inducing members into a "closed" family system and remaining impervious to external demands. This is one way to avoid strain, but whereas the family is thereby maintained as a system, such procedures may be dysfunctional and inappropriate for family members in adapting to other social systems.

Conformity to normative expectations is not always a simple matter. Problems arise when such instructions are too diverse or incongruent, particularly when members of the family have to adapt to normative value requirements that are mutually contradictory or poorly integrated (Lennard and Bernstein, 1969). Role obligations are often idealized and overdemanding, ambivalent, contradictory, inconsistent, or conflicting. Indeed, norms, values and roles do not specify concrete behaviour; they are more or less general rules or guides, and do not contain sufficient "information" to specify the detailed operation of the system or to "map" more than a small part of the variety of the environment or possible alternatives. For example, in modern British society, kinship is not a strong structural feature of middle-class society and this creates some problems in maintaining smooth kin relationships since the rules of obligation and behaviour towards kin are not clear-cut. There are vague sets of social expectations which create problems of choice and decision (Firth *et al.*, 1971) but it is necessary for obligations and responsibilities to be assessed in terms of personal judgement instead of formal rules. The lack of clear guides for action in this case can generate some strain and tension in kinship relationship. Diffuse and ambiguous social rules, however, can have the opposite effect in maintaining system viability. A mechanism has been identified in Japanese society (and elsewhere) whereby uncertainty as to who is in debt acts to facilitate kin ties. Attempts to discharge debts to kin are made difficult by the indeterminancy in debt repayment which acts as an inhibitor of repayment and hence strengthens indebtedness. Diffuse social rules, then, can operate to support the kin structure (Johnson, 1977).

Friendship, however, differs from other such systems in that a long enduring gap between ideal and real behaviour can hardly exist: when friends cease to do those things expected of friends, the relationship breaks down (Babchuk, 1965). Perhaps, this is why ideal postulates about human relations are commonly put into the notion of friendship rather than other primary relations: friendship ideals can exist even in the relative absence of close friendships in society since, unlike kinship, there is less day-by-day monitoring and reality testing of friendship ideals. Moreover, when a disparity is observed the specific relationship can be questioned instead of the ideals: for example, loyalty is still cherished, even though many friends are not loyal. In social contexts characterized by suspicion and distrust, however, friendships are unlikely to operate effectively as adaptive mechanisms for coping with psychological or social atomism. Under such cultural–normative conditions, friendships may be idealized, but the underlying cynicism contributes to the instability of the relationship; conflicts develop between high expectations placed on friendship and the "image of man" as basically untrustworthy; feelings of distrust toward people in general may limit success in relationships; once high-intensity friendships are attained, frequent scenes of jealousy and frustration occur and friendship is transformed to enmity. Such things are often reported by social anthropologists studying peasant, tribal, and socially atomistic societies where the kinship boundaries are generally quite rigid (Gilmore, 1975). Boundary-maintaining mechanisms have their source in fears and anxieties rather than exclusiveness of function. A fairly typical anthropological observation was reported by Banfield (1958) in a study of a southern Italian village where friends were viewed as luxuries that the Montenegressi felt they could not afford — friends and neighbours were not only potentially costly but dangerous as well.

High friendship expectations also have to be considered in terms of the capacity of individuals to meet the demands of others, since such cultural–normative expectations can be a source of tension insofar as the demands go beyond the performance capabilities of an individual. There are a number of different ways of handling such disparity between cultural–normative expectations and the behavioural manifestations. The avoidance of close, intimate relationships, of course, is perhaps the most common way to deal with such disparities. Ideals can survive in the absence of any intensive relationships and reality testing can be minimized by the actual choice of friends. For example Thai villagers are characterized by mutual suspicion and a belief that the interpersonal world is untrustworthy, so friendships are sought among participants that are geographically separated. This physical separation enables the Thai villagers to maintain fantasy friends — whose loyalties are never tested (Honigman, 1978).

The individual-psychological level

This level of analysis focuses attention on intra-individual psychological states and processes. What is emphasized here depends to a large extent on the particular psychological orientation of the investigator — psycho-analytic, behavioural, existential, or cognitive. The preferred orientation, of course, has considerable impact on the choice of concepts — for example, respectively, anxiety, self-reinforcement, fulfillment, information process-ing. Braiker and Kelley (1979) use a personality trait approach as a key concept in describing the psychological level in their multilevel model of interdependence since the personality — as a system — is one way to account for the interdependence at this level. The choice of concepts is important in that it influences the kind of interpretations that are made regarding the nature of interdependence and the nature of the conflicts at the psychological level of analysis.

A consideration in the selection of key concepts is: what is the person trying to explain in the social world? The "image of man" that is of interest here is of one who is looking for a "good match" between his psychosocial requirements and the availability of support systems. From a phenome-nological perspective, the important focal points are those "organizing tendencies" within the individual that are involved in the perception and interpretation of interpersonal events related to social exchange and personal relationships in general. The individual has to integrate information regarding his own psychosocial deficiencies with information on existing or potential human delivery systems. It is not sufficient, however, to know that there are some social rules to guide him. Such rules are often incomplete, and represent just one source and kind of information: we know very little about the requirements for this kind of cognitive task but it has serious behavioural consequences regarding the strategies used to satisfy one's psychosocial needs.

We are thus brought to the point in the argument that indicates the value of adopting a cognitive psychological orientation here, and one way of looking at cognitive structure is to conceptualize it as memory; it is a storehouse of past experiences. On the other hand, cognitive structure can be looked at in terms of "anticipation" where cognitive structure provides a guide to future experiences. Cognitive structure can be analysed, then, as an effect of past experience (memory), a cause of future experience (anticipation), and a context within which the present is meaningful. But what determines what a person has stored in his memory, and the kind of expectancies that he has? There is some "organizing principle" involved here and the notion of an implicit psychological resource theory may be of some relevance since the notion of interdependence is also applicable at the psychological level of analysis. Conceptual schemes are necessary to understand what the individual is perceiving and experiencing when faced with some of the decisions and actions required for obtaining resources via the appropriate support system.

A major function of cognitive structure is the construction of a social reality that helps the individual to establish competence in the interpersonal world. A basic assumption of implicit psychology is that human beings act as psychologists in constructing theories about social reality: implicit theories are like formal theory in that the same motive is involved — understanding, prediction, and control. Implicit theories, like formal theories, consist of a set of concepts and a set of relations linking the concepts: for example, Wegner and Vallacher (1977) have made explicit a number of implicit theories: in addition to the well-known implicit personality theories, other implicit theories concern abnormal, motivational, and social relations.

An "implicit resource theory" is posited here as a cognitive structure of possible high relevance to interpersonal effectance. Such an implicit theory could be conceptualized as internal representations of the concepts and their inter-relations, making up the three-dimensional model described herein. A person's implicit resource theory, then, is the social reality that has been constructed to contain concepts relating to support systems, the psychological

resources, and relationships between them. The organizing principles underlying implicit resource theory have yet to be established, but perhaps there is
some correspondence with the levels analysis described here. *Psychologically*, implicit resource theory includes cognitive orientations towards people
— "image of man" — and towards others, such as, family, friends, and
neighbours. *Behaviourally*, implicit resource theory might include notions
about means–ends relations and strategies for obtaining needed resources. At
a more *normative* level, the implicit resource theory might contain references
to the social rules and evaluative criteria including notions of justice and reciprocity (La Gaipa, 1977a). A whole series of propositions, then, about the
social world might be generated by relating concepts from one level of analysis to the next.

In developing and testing an implicit resource model, the individual faces
again some of the same tasks as a theorist. It is necessary to establish the functional relationships among a set of variables: Which relationships are linear
or non-linear? Which are the intervening variables? Which are the main
effects and interactive effects? This is not to imply that such statistical questions are made explicit, but a careful examination of "everyday" conversation indicates that such problems are implicit as people try to make sense
out of their social world.

Cognitive arousal and tension occur when an implicit resource theory is
not working properly — when the theory provides a poor fit with the data.
Cognitive arousal is also influenced by the perceived form of the relationship:
non-linear relationships may generate higher levels of arousal than linear
relationships since it is more difficult to make predictions when more than
two points are needed. It would follow that a socially incompetent person is
likely to be an individual with an implicit resource theory that generates poor
predictions and that provides him with limited understanding and control of
his social environment.

Psychosocial resources

It is a truism that personal relations are designed to achieve certain goals, and
that failure to do so may lead to disruption or termination. There is some
reluctance among social scientists to develop lists of needs and goals since
there are many lists already available. However, the present argument
requires such a list, although a systems approach would use the term
"taxonomy" rather than list. Such a taxonomy would call attention (a) to
characteristics of the "need" or "goal" which influence the quality of the
relationship, and particularly, (b) to the nature of the interconnections
among the dimensions. An important factor in developing my list was that it
should be fairly comprehensive and still be applicable to enough primary

groups to permit comparisons. (Thus, sexual needs were left out because of their limited application to same-sex friends, and to neighbours of either sex.) In developing a taxonomy of psychosocial resources, my thinking has been influenced by the categories developed by Bennis *et al.* (1964): emotional-expressive; confirmatory; change-influence; and instrumental. Foa (1971) also has developed a resource class taxonomy that includes love, services, goods, money, information, and status, whereas my own research has identified such friendship dimensions as positive regard, helping, authenticity, empathy, self-disclosure, strength of character, and similarity (La Gaipa, 1977b). The specific categories described below, however, are more congruent with a resource theory in marriage that has gained fairly wide acceptance among family theorists (cf Safilios-Rothschild, 1976).

Accordingly, my taxonomy of goals, needs and relevant resources, is:

1. *Identity* — search for self-confirmation; self-evaluation (beliefs about self-worth) and self-definition (maintenance and validation of identity).
2. *Affective* — affection, love — loving and being loved; feeling needed and needing the other.
3. *Expressive* — understanding, emotional support and intimate disclosure.
4. *Sociability* — companionship, conversation, leisure, common interests.
5. *Instrumental aid* — psychological, economic, and material serivices.

The present approach suggests that personal relationships are influenced not only by these needs individually but also by the structural relationships between each of them and the other psychosocial dimensions. Unfortunately, the structure of the relationships among such resource classes has received very little attention although an important contribution in this area was made by Foa (1971) who developed a circularly ordered taxonomy of six resource classes plotted along the two dimensions of particularism and concreteness. There are nevertheless other organizing principles yet to be identified and one possible way to visualize the underlying structure of the five resource classes described above would be to locate them within a Maslow-type triangle. A rather arbitrary ordering would place instrumental aid at the base, followed by sociability, affect, expressive, and identity needs. The dimensions, then, would be arranged upwards impersonal to personal. Intuitively, it would seem that the direction of causation is likely to be upwards more often than downwards.

We are not too concerned here with the "giving" and "receiving" of similar or different resources. Rather, the focus is on the problems — especially the contradictions — that arise from conflict between content dimensions as they are related to possibly inherent features of relationships; to essential conditions for need fulfillment; and to any constraints resulting from system maintenance issues. But equally it is the case that in order to understand adequately the functioning of a specific support system, it is necessary to examine the nature of the pattern of the need dimensions in terms of other systems parameters. These parameters include the following.

(1) *Interdependence* An implication here is that changes along one psychosocial resource dimension have consequences along the same and other dimensions: thus, behaviour along such a dimension as instrumental aid is likely to affect behaviour along the dimension of sociability. At a more psychological level, also, the organizing tendencies that are characteristic of the individual organism make an impact on such interdependency.

(2) *Dialectics* This notion sensitizes us to the possible contradictions within a given resource class, and to conflicts across dimensions. The resource classes are viewed as having a conflict potential as such; moreover, there is a potential source of tension as a function of the characteristics of the goal states in interaction with one another. There is a patterning effect, then, within the system that results from interactions — and this is not discernible merely from isolated information regarding a specific goal state.

(3) *Task characteristics* Each of the content dimensions makes certain task demands on the individual or social system that make it difficult to "give" or "receive". The tasks are sometimes complex, ambiguous, and even contradictory in nature so that it is often difficult to measure progress towards goal-directed activity, or to know precisely when a goal has been reached. For example, how can one specify when an individual has found his "identity"? How much emotional support is adequate? There are few guides available, particularly for the higher-level resource types.

(4) *System capacity* Whether two or more resource demands are excessive depends on the multiple effects of the specific resources and the psychological capacities of the parties involved. Functional overload on a system may be a product of cultural demands, such as in "companionship marriage".

Over and above the tensions and conflicts created within such patterns, there are other dilemmas created for the individual because of other relationships within the system. We can consider four of them here: expressive needs vs identity needs; expressive vs sociability; expressive vs instrumental; and systems viability and expressive needs. It is important to recognize that such dilemmas are not products of individual parts of the system but result from the interconnections and conflicts of different parts of the system. Clearly, unless one takes a systems-based view of personal relationships, such an important point is unlikely to come to light.

The expressive vs identity dilemma

From a psychological point of view, an essential condition for validating one's identity is the availability of a "significant other" with whom one can exchange and interpret the kind of ego-relevant information necessary for this task. A spouse if often chosen as the significant other, but this choice is not without its problems. Berger and Kellner (1972) see a potential conflict area here: the stability of marriage as a system demands a fairly high rate of interaction, but personal identity requires periods of privacy for reflection. The requirements for fostering stability in a marriage may thus conflict with the conditions needed for privacy, or expressive needs may be satisfied but at the expense of personal growth. As a second example, intimacy is sometimes used as a substitute for self-acceptance and self-respect: thus, two people may establish a relationship to provide each party with the emotional support that each needs but a problem arises when each person seeks appropriate but inaccurate flattery as a means of maintaining a satisfactory ego identity (Glazer-Malbin, 1975).

The interdependency of psychosocial resources, then, permits individuals to substitute one resource for another, but not without some loss. This interdependency can also have negative effects in limiting the capacity of the individual when coping mechanisms in one area have harmful effects on a different area: for example, the desire to provide emotional support to another person may be difficult to express if that individual has been trained to flee from intimacy and conditioned to protect autonomy by fending off closeness (Glazer-Malbin, 1975).

The expressive vs sociability dilemma

It is not uncommon to find adult males who cannot express much warmth or provide emotional support to the males in their peer group. One possible explanation is that male sociability plays a major role here (Mussen, 1962). During adolescence male sociability is related to male role training and performance such that sociability is engendered by the need to cope with common male role requirements rather than for friendship. Competition is learned early and has an inhibiting effect on male-male relationships; other men are viewed as not too reliable as friends. Male sociability, however, is not a medium that facilitates personal growth or the development of social skills essential for establishing and maintaining an intimate relationship. The training for a competitive role, then, constrains the acquisition of some of the skills important in friendship.

Douvan and Adelson (1966) offer a psychoanalytic interpretation of conflict between these two psychosocial dimensions: the focus on sociability in the American culture is seen as a way of coping with anxieties generated in the realm of intimacy. "Adult friendship is often no more than a mutual flight from boredom — a pact against isolation, with an amendment against intimacy" (Douvan and Adelson, 1966, p. 178). These authors view this preoccupation with sociability as also having damaging effects on personal identity since, for example, things crucial to personal integration (such as a person's history, or his value system) are often excluded from interaction. The superficiality of such relationships does not provide the context essential for success in a search for identity.

The expressive vs instrumental dilemma

The functional relationships between instrumental service and the other psychosocial dimensions is a critical problem in kinship, friendship, and even in trying to be a "good neighbour". In kinship, instrumental aid is expected, and there are varying obligatory pressures depending on the strength of the tie. In friendship, the role of instrumental aid is somewhat contradictory and considerably more complicated. The "giving" of instrumental aid should be spontaneous, but failure to reciprocate will eventually lead to the disruption of the relationship: short-term "balancing of accounts" is discouraged because of the economic overtones, but long-term imbalance generally leads to the termination of the relationship (see La Gaipa, 1977a).

Based on an extensive review of the anthropological literature, Cohen (1961) concluded that instrumental aid, particularly economic assistance, is the primary function of friendship: friendship is often part of man's "survival kit". Cohen posits that instrumental aid does give rise to emotional support, thus seeing these two dimensions in a causal relationship, but friendship ideology in American society keeps economics and friendship as separate entities. However, the relationship between expressive and instrumental functions varies with the sociocultural context. The Japanese tend to exchange instrumental values and expressive values simultaneously, and as their relationship becomes more and more intrinsically satisfying to one another, they become more and more useful to each other (Befu, 1977).

There are some contradictory elements in the relationship between normative expectations and friendship performance since friendship must be sentimental in inspiration, but instrumental aid cannot be ignored: there is no way to demonstrate one's sentiments other than through those actions which speak plainer than words. Instrumental aid, then, serves an important function regarding the validation of affect (Young and Wilmott, 1957). Nevertheless, there are limits beyond which increase in instrumental aid does not increase affect levels since instrumental aid can create a dependency state, and the resulting subordination of one person to another may affect the quality of the relationship. This is a problem, for example, with the aged as they become more and more dependent on their children and experience a shift in roles: when actual aid eventually becomes the central fact of the relationship, there often is a significant decrease in the affectional and enjoyable aspects of the relationship (Glasser and Glasser, 1962). Excessive service, apparently, has side-effects that interfere with the conditions necessary for the free expression of sociability and intimacy.

Changes in family structure have been found to be associated with changes in the relationship between instrumental and non-instrumental functions, whilst tensions have been associated with the inequitable distribution of resources, particularly regarding the inheritance of property. This has been an important feature in peasant societies, and is not uncommon in modern, western society. Latterly, however, the surrender of instrumental functions to other institutions has reduced some of the tensions between siblings, insofar as economic survival has become less and less dependent on the family. For instance, studies on the Japanese family in Hawaii over three generations have noted a shift in resource type with decreases in economic interdependence such that there has been greater equalization among siblings, and an increase in expressive and sociability functions. The decrease in instrumental aid is thus related to increases in kin solidarity (Johnson, 1977).

Systems viability and expressive needs

Identity creation depends on intimate coversation, but this is not always possible in many marriages. Marriage is — as Berger and Kellner (1972) admit — a precarious relationship and it may well be that whole areas of conversation have to be avoided in order that the marriage may continue to exist. Confiding behaviour may actually place a strain on the marital structure and self-disclosure may have dysfunctional effects on dyadic systems (Askham, 1976), or unfavourable information about oneself, whilst relevant to identity formation, may nevertheless be threatening to the dyadic unit. This notion was aptly expressed in a cartoon series "The Lockhorns" by Bill Hoest. The husband commented to the marriage counsellor "If we were really to communicate, it would probably drive us further apart."

Support systems

Support consists of any action or behaviour that functions to assist the person in meeting his personal goals or in dealing with the demands of any particular situation. Support may be tangible in the form of assistance, or it may be intangible in the form of personal warmth, love, or emotional support. Support, then, consists of social, emotional, and instrumental services which are defined by the giver or the receiver as necessary or at least helpful in maintaining his style of life. A support system is essentially the delivery system for the giving and receiving of different supports. There is a reciprocal element in support systems in that the direction of flow is two-way, and the dependence that the individual can place on the support system (that is, the reliability of its outputs) relies heavily on the inputs that the individual makes to other person's interlocking support systems. An individual is likely to experience tension and strain if he has problems in the ready mobilization of resources, and the disparity between an individual's needs and the availability of resources is manifested in such psychological states as anxiety, agitation and insomnia (Tolsdorf, 1976).

Support systems differ in a number of ways. Thus, whilst the permanence of kinship is one of its essential characteristics, friendships, by way of contrast, lack that constancy and "inevitability" which distinguishes relations in the nuclear family. Equally, friendships are characterized by a spontaneity that is often missing in kinship and some people find it difficult to be comfortable with relatives in that they feel some constraints on their desire to be authentic, to "be themselves". Authenticity is more likely to be evident when there is an exchange of full information relating to one's identity, but such information increases one's vulnerability (Kelvin, 1977; La Gaipa, 1979). Because of the permanent nature of kinship, identity-relevant information needs to be handled with discretion and identity needs, then, may interfere with kin sociability.

An essential condition for friendship is equality of status. For instance, there is a near taboo on personal friendship among deckmen in the Norwegian merchant marine since there are few relationships of equality between men. The top positions are only reached from the bottom, and they can be, in theory, reached by everyone so that there is competition at all levels, and this precludes the development of close friendships (Brian, 1977). In kinship there is always superordination and subordination and this inequality among kin is most pronounced when the participants are in some form of economic interdependency. A major source of tension in many societies relates to the inheritance of property and the division of property is a primary cause of disruption of kin relationships. Brian (1977) has observed that in the African tribe of Bangwa, when a man is dying, he calls his friends, not his relatives: the latter are interested in his death since the property a Bangwa leaves behind is considerable. Indeed, a friend may often have to fight off greedy relatives because there is a general scramble for his property even before the corpse is cold in its grave.

As an institution, there are many more obligations and constraints associated with the family than with friendships but there is often some ambivalence associated with these obligations. Field studies by social

anthropologists often contain reports that friends will point to their relationship as freed from kinship constraints, and that friendship operates as a
"safety valve" with regard to kinship (Parkin, 1978). Important considerations here involve the fact that friendships are based on free choice, they are
voluntary and achieved rather than ascribed; and friendships are not usually
embedded in intense social networks, i.e. friendships generally lack the high
level of interconnectedness characteristic of the extended family system.

Systems maintenance

The viability of a marriage depends on the effectiveness of the coping
mechanisms in dealing with boundary problems. A commonly used technique to maintain system identity is to promote the notion of exclusiveness of
function: this is implied in the maxim that "the family that plays together,
stays together". Alternative systems for the satisfaction of psychosocial
needs, such as friendship, are often discouraged and no other social relation
is judged important enough to allow competition with the interpersonal
demands made by the husband or wife (Lopata, 1975). That men enjoy themselves and express themselves among men is fought "tooth and nail" by
many wives as an encroachment on an all-exclusive marital relation by
relationships independent of the spouse (Babchuk, 1965). In one study less
than half of the married couples had a single primary friend i.e. who was a
friend of one person but was not also a friend of the spouse (Brian, 1977).

Unit friendships are the social norm in modern, middle-class, urban
society: two couples get together to form one friendship unit such that most
of the activities occur at the same time. But, only rarely do all the participants
experience the same quality of friendship — seldom are both parties equally
close. Intimate conversations are also less common in unit friendships: the
women do tend to confide in each other somewhat more than the men, but
women are much less likely than men to exchange confidences with the
opposite-sex member. This form of friendship, then, may be beneficial to the
marital unit but dysfunctional to the individual systems.

Women's friendships have received relatively little attention in the historical and anthropological literature (Seiden and Bart, 1975) and female friendships are often treated as a peripheral part of the social system, rather than in
their own right. Proponents of women's liberation are disturbed by conceptualization of women's friendships as a "prelude to marriage" or as providing support for the family structure and arguments have been made for a
non-biological sense of kin and the notion of friends as a "chosen" family
(Skolnick and Skolnick, 1974).

Sex differences do exist regarding the reliance on marriage as the vehicle
for the expression of intimacy needs, and because of the psychological and

social constraints on the male expression of intimacy, the wife is often the man's only confidante. Whereas men tend to satisfy their needs for intimacy largely within the marriage, a woman's closest confidante is most likely to be a woman friend, particularly when the free give-and-take of confidence is missing in marriage (Blau, 1973). Women who lack female friends have tended either to succumb to mental illness or distortions of a marital pattern or vicarious living through children (Seiden and Bart, 1975).

Normative expectations regarding friendship differ by social class. The notion of companionship marriage is largely a middle-class phenomenon, whilst extramarital friendships are subject to less constraints among working-class men. There are, also, some differences in the priority given to the resource types: the working-class friendship, particular for the males, relies more heavily on sociability than expressivity, probably because efforts to elicit emotional support conflict with the image of masculinity. Identity problems, then, place a limit on satisfactions in terms of emotional support and intimacy needs.

The situational context of the friendship is a major difference between social classes. Allan (1977) found that when working-class respondents get to know someone, it does not result in their interacting with that person in different settings, and that working-class friendships are situation-specific in that each relationship was seen as relevant only to a particular social structure. Middle-class respondents, on the other hand, emphasized the individuality of the friendship rather than the context of their interaction. There are also some class differences in the reliance on kin as friends, with the working-class respondents dependent on siblings of the same sex as their specific confidante for warmth and emotional support. Such kin relations, however, were not situation specific. It would seem, then, that siblings are often a substitute in the working class for the kind of friendships characteristic in the middle class.

Interdependence of kinship and friendship

There is no consensus as yet among social scientists regarding the relationship between kinship and friendship. In a classic study using a social network approach, Bott (1957) established the importance of residential proximity as a contributing factor to the interdependence of kin, friends and neighbours. This was found in a London borough characterized by high density, long established relationships and low mobility. Litwick and Szelenyi (1969) argue that in modern mobile society, primary groups have become functionally differentiated with kin, neighbourhood, and friends serving quite separate social functions, with relatively little overlap.

Babchuk (1965) reports that the contributions made by kin to the total resources seemed to be independent of the contributions made by friends. This interpretation was supported by the finding that interaction with kin did not quantitatively appear to be related to interaction with friends, and vice versa. Similarly, interviews on friendship and kinship suggest that the individuals kept the two categories of kin and friends as distinct, each being treated as having its own special quality, and one not being a substitute for the other (Firth *et al.*, 1971).

If a quantitative relationship exists between kinship and friendship, a change in one should be reflected in a change in the other — but this was not found by Booth (1972). A decline in kinship ties was not found to prompt an increase in friendship, but Booth did find that individuals satisfied with their kin support system were also likely to be satisfied with their friendship support system. Evidently, individuals rich in interpersonal resources in one area were apt to be rich in others and the persons that could turn to their kin for support also were the same ones who reported more close friends and group membership. Such a finding, of course, suggests the possible role of interpersonal skills as a mediating factor.

The significance of the sociocultural context is again evident in research done in Israel (Soen, 1975). In contrast to overseas studies, it was found that the frequency of social relations with friends was greater than with kinship group, which probably represents the highly mobile nature of Israeli society. What was highly significant within this cultural framework was the positive correlation between the intensity of kinship group and the intensity of ties to friends.

Any statistical analysis of the relationship between kinship and friendship is a difficult task since there are no measurement techniques useful for equating friends and kin along the same metric dimension. There is a further confounding of the quantitative and qualitative aspects of primary relationships and the problem is further complicated by the apparently low correlation between the amount of support received and satisfaction with the support.

The relationship between quantitative indices of friendship and mental health is thus still beyond the present state of the art. When individuals are asked to specify the number of close friends, the modal number is usually one or two, rarely over three, but despite the low numbers, respondents give the impression that they have sufficient primary-group resources at their disposal (Babchuk, 1965). Perhaps, two or three primary friends are all a person needs to remain personally well integrated; or possibly, different combinations of acquaintances, friends and kin provide adequate support. Babchuk notes that it is too early to tell what constitutes a pattern of primary relations sufficiently adequate to lead to a well-balanced and healthy existence.

Defining the boundaries

One approach to the analysis of the boundaries between friendship and kinship is in terms of the labels used to differentiate these two systems. In some societies the social norms do not clearly differentiate between kinship and friendship and many tribal societies have no term to distinguish "friend" from "kin"; people are classified either as "kin" or as "strangers" in these societies (Hendrix, 1975). Behaviour between particular kin may thus not necessarily be "kin behaviour" as usually understood; it could be friendship behaviour. In some cultures, friendship values may be the values of certain kin relationships (Paine, 1969).

The boundaries of friendship and kinship in western society are disintegrating, if they really ever existed: "A wife is her husband's best friend." (Kieffer, 1968). The use of kin terms to describe friends and friendship terms to describe kin is quite evident in both tribal and urban industrial societies as well where Lauman (1966) found that 15% of the persons named as friends are relatives. The terminological or definitional overlap signifies that certain kin are defined as having the characteristics which are said to be typical of friends, and vice versa. Paine (1969) speaks of the greater similarity between the meaning of kinship and friendship in American society than in many others and explains this as due to the fact that property rights are increasingly a matter beyond kinship in middle-class society. There is no opposition between the values of kinship and friendship since the family has ceased to lay an exclusive claim to the loyalities of individuals, and questions concerning property are becoming increasingly matters beyond kinship (Brian, 1977).

The specific labels may be less meaningful than the normative expectations differentiating kin and friend along different dimensions. Do individuals have expectations about their siblings which differ from those which they have about their friends? Are there any sex or age differences? Clark and La Gaipa (1979) attempted to answer such questions, using modified forms of the La Gaipa (1977b) friendship exectancy inventory, by administering the interpersonal relationship scales to 213 subjects aged 10-19 residing in a rural village in southern England. The same interpersonal values were used; one group responded in terms of same-sex or opposite-sex siblings, whereas the other group responded in terms of close friends.

Apparently, females do not make much of a distinction between their sisters and their close friends regarding positive regard, similarity and helping. However, females expect more from friends than from their sisters regarding such expressive values as authenticity, empathy and self-disclosure. By way of contrast, little distinction was made by males between brothers and friends. The main difference was that younger boys expect more help from brothers than friends, and older boys expect more similarity from friends than from their brothers. Somewhat surprisingly, few age differences were noted, and, in general, no dramatic differences were apparent in what was expected from friends and siblings. Siblings appear to be an important support system even in pre-adult years.

What concluding statement can be made regarding the interdependence of kinship and friendship? A "systems" interpretation of existing data would be that we cannot treat the interdependence of kinship and friendship apart from the specific dimensions involved and the social context in which interactions are taking place. Given a holistic–structural perspective, no other conclusion is logically possible.

Conclusions

An underlying theme in this chapter has been the dialectics between the cultural–normative and behaviour levels — the disparity between the "ideal" and the "real". Normative, ideational culture has no existence unless it is practised and influences behaviour and thinking; the actual behaviour and thought of men is not intelligible if it is separated from the social ideals which men have created or discovered for themselves and try to realize in their daily lives. A task of the social scientist, then, is to determine the extent to which there is agreement between theory and practice in any given culture; to make sense of such disparities in terms of the overall system; and to determine how individuals seek to resolve such disparities.

Another theme has been the pervasive quality of tension and conflict. From a systems point of view, tension is a normal, ever-present dynamic agent which, far from being "reduced" must be kept at an optimal level if the system is to remain viable (Buckley, 1967). Tension can exist within one sub-system or level and such tensions may have effects beneficial to the total or larger systems. Such tensions may be tolerated because they contribute to the greater stability of the total or increase the flexibility of the system in adapting to changing conditions. Tension-free systems, then, are unadaptive to changing conditions, if only because tension activates feedback mechanisms and hence provides information regarding dysfunctions in a system. Tensions result from disparities between the ideal and the real, normative constraints, behavioural interdependence, ambiguity of task requirements, interference with goal-directed behaviour, and from monitoring of self and/or other regarding level of resource competence.

For a system to work effectively, then, it must provide methods of limiting, controlling, or resolving conflicts (Radcliffe-Browne, 1962). System properties can have a major impact not only on the kind of conflict that occurs but also on the resolution of the conflict. The availability of conflict intervenors is an important consideration and in the area of personal relationships the extended family, with its interconnectedness and generalized form of exchange, is ideally suited for providing compensatory mechanisms. When a conflict occurs in the extended family, there are persons available to play a mediating role. This is not possible, of course, in the nuclear family which is relatively independent of the larger kinship group because of such factors as residential mobility. Neither is the intimate friendship likely to be able to draw on external conflict mediators, because such friends are usually not embedded in intense social networks. Larger social units, then, can generally tolerate more conflict and tension because of the availability of conflict-reducing mechanisms.

There are some methodological questions in the "levels" perspective that merit attention. A basic question centres around problem definition: What level of analysis is most appropriate for a given problem? Should causal priorities be established and assigned for any given level when two or more are involved? Is it premature to engage in synthesis before a problem has been really analysed, i.e. can we look at a problem from a two-dimensional perspective before understanding it at any one level?

There has been a heavy reliance on social anthropological data, mainly because such research has been concerned with the sociocultural context. Because of this, few of the reported findings were subjected to tests of significance and most of the findings or observations could not be replicated — the social context would not be the same. But when we try to study personal relationships in the laboratory — out of context — the results may be more reliable but often less meaningful. Strong interactions between the context and the behaviour when we leave the laboratory, can in fact reduce the validity of the propositions generated within the laboratory setting.

In conclusion, a systems framework can be applied toward a fuller understanding of Man. A systems approach permits the integration within a single framework of inter-related phenomena across levels as well as within a level: psychological, social and cultural factors can be treated as variables within a unitary systems analysis. Unfortunately, there is much resistance to a systems approach as most of us have been socialized to worship at the altar of the "analytic ideal". But, a holistic approach is not incompatible with alternation between synthesis and analysis, between parts and wholes. This is a mode of thought necessary to a holistic approach, since its basic postulate is that the whole is more than the sum of its parts, and this is as true of personal relationships as it is of any other system.

Summary

Structural analysis was used for locating and examining personal relationships within a three-dimensional conceptual framework: a levels perspective (level of analysis); structure (support systems such as family and friends) and function (psychosocial satisfactions). Interpersonal problems are viewed in terms of the interdependency and dialectic relationships existing within and between these three parameters. Tensions are viewed in terms of systems requirements (boundary and maintenance problems of the support systems), task demands (meeting psychosocial requirements that are often ambiguous and contradictory), cultural demands (normative constraints on personal choice), and cognitive demands (understanding, prediction and control needed to establish competence in the interpersonal world). The individual in his personal relationships is viewed as experiencing functional overload as a result of this demand structure.

CHAPTER 5
Analysis of Social Networks

Hubert Feger

In the analysis of personal relationships the social scientist ultimately needs a formal representation of the social structures that he observes and this chapter will show the contribution that social network analysis can make to the achievement of that goal. Social network analysis is an attempt to represent different types of personal relationships beyond the simple dyad and it concerns such things as representation of chains of communication, clique structure, popularity status and dominance hierarchies. A variety of techniques and methods can be used in this task which then facilitate the testing of models to explain the data that have been observed, and, as such, network analysis is a valuable addition to the methodological and theoretical armoury of the social scientist who is interested in personal relationships.

The formal representation and analysis of social relationships is, of course, a large area of research and there is space here only to discuss a very small part, with some examples taken from classic or interesting data. The goal of such work is a gain in understanding without loss of information through the mathematical techniques employed. For every theoretical or practical problem the method has to be specifically adapted so that social network analysis can operate in its ideal mode: that of model testing. However, there are general features of the approach which will be discussed first before we consider their application in specific cases.

Representation and Analysis of Social Relationships

There are two essential features to the analysis of social networks. First it is necessary to conceptualize the general nature of social relationships; and secondly, it is sometimes valuable to represent them graphically for more detailed analysis. To delimit our concerns here, I shall give an overview of the concepts involved, using the perspective of data theory (Coombs, 1964). We must first therefore differentiate between (1) observations; (2) their interpretation as data; (3) the analysis of the data by measurement models; and finally (4) the examination and testing of whether the model is adequate.

Some basic concepts of data analysis

In order to facilitate the interpretation of observations and the choice of a model to represent them it seems desirable to give a taxonomy of observations on social relations. But there is no well-known or even generally accepted taxonomy of this kind, and I can report only some taxonomic viewpoints which have proved useful. First, I have observations on social relations that are either *open* or *closed structures*. I define structures as "open", if there is no information on the social relation between at least two members of the structure, or if there is information that the social relation analysed (e.g. power, communication) is non-existent between at least two members. Thus the structure is not closed or open *per se*, but as a function of the kind of relation analysed. Secondly, I differentiate observations as either *qualitative* (quite often dichotomous, e.g. relation present/absent), or given in the form of categories which are at least *ordered* among themselves. Thirdly, I have to differentiate and consider the *kind* of social relations under study, e.g. contact, communication, liking, influence, which are most frequently analysed in social science. Fourthly, it is useful to contrast observations which *describe social behaviour* with judgements which *describe experiences* of social orientations, e.g. contact frequency versus statements of liking.

In the next step, observations are interpreted as data. There are several data theories, but I refer to the best-known one: Coombs, 1964. Figure 1 shows his model, describing the kinds of data, ". . . from which all psychological measurement arises".

Only a few examples are necessary to explain the application of this data theory to the interpretation of observations on social relations. Thus, Quadrant III-b interprets observations as proximity relations on pairs of points from one set: for example, observations on subjects as to who has contact with whom could be interpreted as Q III-b data. Quadrant III-a, on the

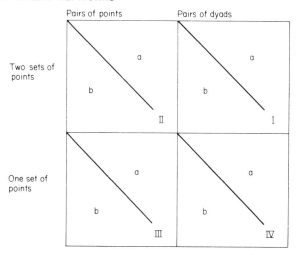

FIG. 1   The four quadrants, each with a = order- and b = proximity-relations, giving rise to eight kinds of data (after Coombs 1964, p.21).

other hand, assumes order relations, and so sociometric choices could be interpreted as being those kind of data. But if the same sociometric observations were analysed so as to retain the distinction between senders and receivers of social choices, then they could be interpreted as Quadrant II-a data because they then involve more than one set of points.

Having interpreted observations as data the next step would be to find a representation of them. The purposes of a representation might differ according to circumstances: e.g. to facilitate the inspection of the data; to reduce masses of data to what is considered the "relevant" information in the data; to achieve measurement of some aspects of the data through the representation by a measurement model (for example, because these measurements are needed for further analysis or because the fit of a measurement model leads to knowledge of the data structure which is valuable in itself). To achieve these purposes *structural rules and structural concepts* are helpful. A structural rule is a statement of a relationship R between elements, $a, b, c, \ldots$ of a social structure S, for example: For all elements, $a, b, c, \ldots$ of a structure S, and a relationship R denoted by $\rightarrow$ (indicating a social choice), then

$$a \rightarrow b \rightleftharpoons b \rightarrow a$$

which describes strict (qualitative) mutuality of social choices. A structural concept consists of at least one structural rule and some further qualifications which may be other rules, specifications of the validity of the rules, and so on. If, for example, the rule of strict mutuality is combined with the postulate that this rule should be valid for every pair of a trio of social elements, then we have defined the structural concept of an absolute clique (Luce and Perry, 1949).

Social networks and graph theory

Graph theory is a formal — mathematical — system well suited to analyse social networks (in this paper I shall not treat the analysis of social relations by means of an alternative method: multi-dimensional scaling method). The goal, of course, is always that of learning more about personal relationships, as will be demonstrated in examples presented in the next section.*

In the first step, application of graph theory leads merely to a graphic representation of the social network. Usually we want more. Thus in a second step we can use several concepts and results of graph theory to describe the network or parts of it with a few informative indices. In a third step we define formal operations on the graph either to condense the information on social relations by data reduction techniques or to see whether the data correspond to empirical laws, formulated as structural relations and concepts. We may do both in one procedure, and this procedure might be the application of a measurement model.

Some Examples of Social Network Analysis

The principles outlined above have a variety of possible applications to the analysis of social relationships, but space permits me to present only a few examples. I have therefore selected classic or specially interesting data which best illustrate the method in question in relation to a specific sort of problem.

Structures in a contact network

Homans (1950) reports observations by Davis *et al.* (1941) regarding which of 18 women participated in 14 activities. These recordings have been repeatedly analysed (e.g. by Phillips and Conviser, 1972; Breiger *et al.*, 1975; and Bonacich, 1977), but the methods are often unsatisfactorily intuitive, iterative, or probabilistic and lead to partially inconclusive results. If we interpret the observations as Q III-b data, some concepts of graph theory can be used to describe what Mayer (1975, p.10) has called "structural solidarity".

---

*Introductions to graph theory are given by Harary (1969) and, with special reference to the analysis of social relationships, by Felling (1974) and Mayer (1975).

The solidarity of a group has something to do with the density of relationships between group members. . . . Typically there exist one or more subgroups within which the relationship network is very dense relative to the density prevailing in the group as a whole.''

Graph theory has developed several concepts to describe this relative density, e.g. a ''component'' or a clique, of which many forms are defined. A quote from Harary (1969) may help us to understand these concepts:

'A *walk* of a graph G is an alternating sequence of points and lines . . . beginning and ending with points, in which each line is incident with the two points immediately preceding and following it. . . . It is a . . . *path* if all the points . . . are distinct'.

Thus a walk can often be interpreted as providing the basis for communication and influence. To continue with Harary: "A graph is *connected* if every pair of points is joined by a path. A maximal connected subgraph of G is called a component of G''.

It is not necessary to use a computer program to find that all pairs of women in Homans' data are connected by a path, if one defines two persons as being connected when they have contact by joining in the same activity. But since the graph cannot be divided into components, we have to look for a stronger structural concept. If we define a perfect clique as a maximal complete subgraph, in which every element is directly connected with every other member of that subgraph then, for Homans' data, we can find three perfect cliques that are large relative to the whole group and partially overlap. Their existence shows a strong tendency towards (qualitative) balance:

$$A \rightarrow B \text{ and } B \rightarrow C \Rightarrow A \rightarrow C$$

which can also be called transitivity of (qualitative) mutuality. With these data, however, the resolving power of the clique concept is not very high. I therefore introduce the concept of a *structurally equivalent position* (SEP),* which demands even more regularity in the data, and define: members of an SEP are those and only those elements between which the relation analysed (here = direct contact) exists and which have the same relations *to all elements* not being members of this SEP.

In other words: within an SEP, everybody knows everybody else, and all know the same persons outside. For the Homans data we can find a representation (Fig. 2) of five SEPs, one of which has only one member. It is always possible to find an SEP-structure, trivially with one member per position, but a solution like Fig. 2 has considerable social significance. One position *(a)* is central; all its members are in direct contact with all other women. The

---

*Algorithms for this and other concepts are available from the author.

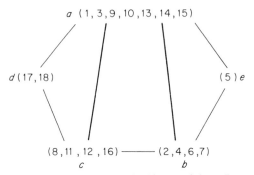

FIG. 2   Structurally equivalent positions for Homans' data. Every position is characterized by the numbers of its members. A line indicates direct contact between all
members of two positions

relationship between the three perfect cliques and the five SEPs is:

$$I = a + b + c$$
$$II = a + b + e$$
$$III = a + d + c$$

Thus, members of a central position are members in all perfect cliques. The
connectedness of the structure in Fig. 2 is almost invulnerable; one has to
remove at least two of the five positions to make it incoherent.

It might be argued that it is largely accidental that the SEP-concept
describes Homans' data so well. However, I have analysed several sets of
data and have found multiple membership in the same structurally equivalent
position in observations on: students participating voluntarily in a course on
behaviour therapy; sleeping groups of vervet monkeys observed at weekly
intervals (Struhsaker, 1965); groups of dolphins in Argentina's coastal
waters (Wuersig, 1979); and rifle clubs at their weekly meetings. This suggests
that the SEP-concept describes the data better than chance under these
conditions:

(a) the social relation analysed is one of mutual support so that there is a
    positive motivation to congregate (voluntarily);
(b) because other motives and distractions are operative as well, there
    should be repeated opportunity to come together so that the redun-
    dancy in the data allows the identification of a stable structure.

Order relations in networks: popularity

The sociometric choices collected by Hoehn and Seidel (1976) are reproduced
in Fig. 3 which can be interpreted as a directed graph with each arrow representing a desire for contact. A large number of indices can be computed (or

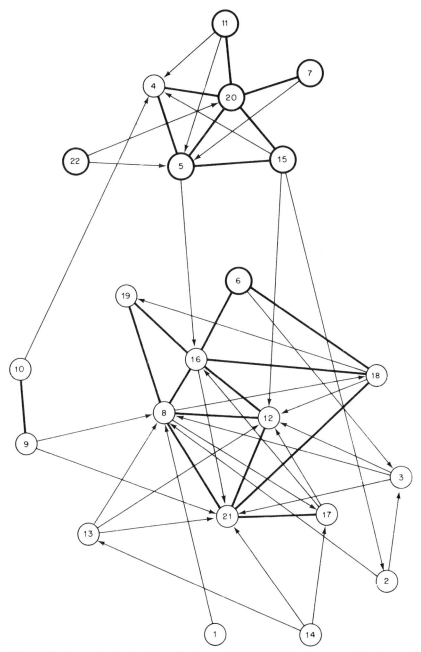

FIG. 3   Sociometric choices from Hoehn and Seidel (1976) drawn as a "sociogram",
i.e. as a directed graph.

statements tested) to characterize the network as a whole, or parts of it: the density, defined as the percentage of possible relations which actually exist; the degree of mutuality, defined as the (relative) number of reciprocated choices; the kind of reachability or connectedness (for definitions see, for example, Harary, 1969). These indices — and many more — may be used to compare the network at different points in time or with other networks. Several features of representations like Fig. 3 are not informative but completely arbitrary: that the representation is in two dimensions is a matter of convenience, as is the configuration chosen; and the distances between the points do not correspond to measurement based on a scaling model. In short, this kind of representation is not based on a model of social relations; it is a translation of observations into a formal system with no loss of information and no gain in understanding.

Sociometricians therefore usually go one step further and interpret the observations, quite often simultaneously, as Q III-a and Q III-b data. This can also be done in the example selected. Mutual sociometric choices are taken as a measure of proximity, and if all three pairs of a triplex of three elements show reciprocity that is sufficient to identify a clique. At the same time one looks for "stars" and "isolates" at the top or bottom of the popularity-status. This popularity status should not be confused with an influence- or power-status, the concept of which leads to several postulates that are meaningful for power-status (e.g. chains of indirect influences) but are at least doubtful for popularity status (for a systematic treatment of power-status see Felling, 1974 and Ziegler, 1972). Since the analysis of power networks by methods of graph theory has been throughly conducted by Felling, we shall turn to problems in the determining of popularity-status (PS).

Typically, PS is determined as the number of sociometric choices received by a subject. This operationalization does not distinguish between choosers i.e. every choice contributes an equal amount to PS. Clearly, however, there are occasions when a choice should be weighted more if it is a choice made by a highly respected group member than by an outsider; hence the following definition, which does not imply the substitutability of choosers: if A is chosen by $X_1 \ldots X_k$, and B is chosen by $X_1 \ldots X_{k+1}$, then B's status should be higher. Application of this definition leads to a representation of the data of Fig. 3 in Fig. 4.

Every path in Fig. 4 corresponds to a Guttman scale and thus provides a quantification on ordinal scale level without assuming substitutability of choices. The status-relationship is transitive, e.g. (6) is lower than (19) and (19) is lower than (21), so (6) is lower than (21). The subjects 1, 14 and 22 are assigned PS = 0 by definition. Subjects 3, 16 and 18 are not accounted for because they are neither higher nor lower by the above definition. Of the 12 Guttman scales in Fig. 4, only three have three elements. Thus, the quantifi-

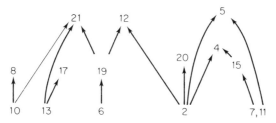

FIG. 4   Guttman scales of popularity status for data from Fig. 3.

cation is, on the whole, not very successful. My experience with observations of this kind suggests that this result is rather general and does not change if a self-choice ($X \rightarrow X$) is included in the set of choosers of every element. There seem to be several reasons for this result. First, a Guttman scale under these circumstances cannot be longer than the maximum number of choices given by the senders who serve as items for the quantification process. Secondly, mutual choices, which are quite frequent in this kind of observation, cannot be represented on the *same* Guttman scale. Thirdly, the existence of cliques is quite often equivalent with many choices to the in-group which do not contribute to status differentiation. The typical social structure as captured by sociometric choices — interpreted as order relation on pairs of points — is a *partially ordered set* or "poset". This is " . . . a set of elements, P, and a binary relationship ($\rightarrow$) which have the following properties: (a) Reflexivity: $x \rightarrow x$ for all $x \, \varepsilon \, P$,   (b) Antisymmetry: $x \rightarrow y$ and $y \rightarrow x$ implies $x = y$, (c) Transitivity: $x \rightarrow y$ and $y \rightarrow z$ implies $x \rightarrow z$" (Mayer, 1975, p. 51). so we have several people "on top", several at the bottom, quite a few not comparable to all others with respect to popularity. The frequency count operationalization of PS thus gives a wrong impression of the order-structure in human groups.

Things seem to be different in other parts of the animal kingdom. To illustrate the strength of the status definition given above I use observations from Waterhouse and Waterhouse (1976) on rhesus monkeys as transformed and given in Fig. 5.

Figure 5 gives the *power-status* defined, as in the previous example, by the number of the same animals dominated. So monkey (1) dominates all others, (2) dominates (3)–(19), (3) dominates (4)–(18) etc. The structure is described by 12 interwoven Guttman-scales, one with four steps, four with five steps, one with six steps, two with seven steps, two with eight steps, and two with nine steps, indicating a rather "deep" hierarchization. The structure also differs from that in Fig. 4, representing the pupils, in that there is an α-animal, dominating all others. The structure is not a tree, it is not a semilattice, because some pairs do not have only one individual to dominate both pair members (Mayer, 1975, p. 51), indicating that conflict is regulated from relatively "high above" in the hierarchy.

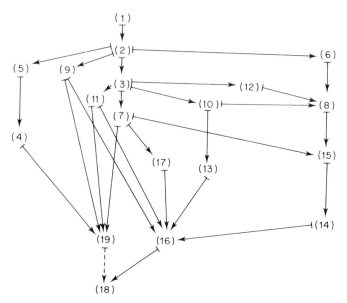

FIG. 5   Power status for data from Waterhouse and Waterhouse (1976). The arrows
represent the existence and direction of a dominance relationship.

Every status definition — and there are probably as many as definitions of
cliques and clusters — captures only one or a few aspects of the observations,
and leaves other information unused. And the properties of the structure, of
course, depend upon the status definition used. If, for example, we use the
apparently simplest status definition that A defeats B implies A → B, and that
a path from A over B to C implies A → B, B → C, and A → C, then the Waterhouse data and quite a few similar data lead to several difficulties. We may
observe loops, e.g.

$$(6) \longrightarrow (19) \longrightarrow (13)$$

which prevent the interpretation of path length as a measure of status difference. Or, quite often, we find irregularities such as this: (8) has a super-
ordinate = (7), some of whose superordinates = (4), (5) are not superordinates of (8). These *dominance range limitations* prevent a path representation (and could not occur with the Guttman-scale status definition given
above), unless an element is represented more than once.

Going back to popularity status, to be derived from sociometric judgements, it may be that asking merely for choices is not enough to obtain data
structures rich enough for status quantifications. So we turn to sociometric
rankings or ratings, from which we intend to use ordinal information only.
Then the problem is formally the well-known one of combining rank orders

of several subjects to get a common order. There are many solutions to this problem (Coombs, 1964). I illustrate mine, calling it *multiple unfolding analysis*, for observations collected by Bartram *et al.* (1978). They asked 29 pupils to rate their desire to cooperate with everyone else in their school class, on a five-point rating scale ranging from 1 = "like to cooperate very much" to 5 = "do not like at all". The data are interpreted as being Q II-a, because during the analysis, for the interpretation and the calculation of the popularity status we want to maintain the distinction between sender and receiver. By an algorithm (obtainable from the author) we obtain one or several multiple qualitative joint scales. The Bartram *et al.* data contain the structures given in Fig. 6. Every structure describes a subset of the group, agreeing in a specific way in their social judgements.

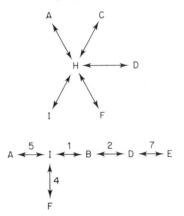

FIG. 6   Status structures contained in the data from Bartram *et al.* (1978).

All pairs of members of every subset show mutuality in their preferences for one another on at least ordinal scale level. From every point in the structure as a sender the sociometric rating given to any receiver is monotonally decreasing as a function of the number of points between sender and receiver. In a receiver-point all paths of judgements from all others end, containing in their length the information how large the difference in status is between every sender and this receiver. If a sender wants a short social distance to a receiver, he gives him a contribution to a high status. If there are several subsets with overlapping membership, a person may have different statuses in different groups — as is usually taken for granted. But within every subset there is agreement on the basis — one or more attributes — with regard to which social preferences are expressed.

To give an idea of possibilities for further quantification I report the conditional rank orders from the persons in the second structure in Fig. 6 as senders. The first structure does not lead to a quantitative multiple J-scale.

The rank orders are derived from the ratings in the original data and (   ) denotes a tie.

A: (B, D, F, I), E
B: I,D, (A, E, F)
D: (B, F, I) (A, E)
E: D, B, I, F, A
F: I, (A, B, D, E)
I: (B, D), (A, E, F)

From A's rank order we derive no useful information on the rank order of the distances.

From B: $BI < BD$
From D: $BD < DE$, $BD + BI < DE$, $BD + BI + FI < DE$, $FI < AI$
From E: $FI < AI$
From F: None
From I: $BI < AI$, $BI + BD < AI$, $BI < FI$, $BI + BD < FI$

These restrictions are compatible with the following solution (among others; scale level of higher-order metric):

$AI = 5$, $BI = 1$, $FI = 4$, $BD = 2$, $DE = 7$

The popularity status, computed as the sum of the length of all incoming paths, is:

$A = 43$, $B = I = 23$, $D = 27$, $E = 55$, $F = 39$

Chains of communication

Krueger (1973) asked 33 pupils (14–15-year-olds) to rate the frequency of speaking with all members of their school class. The results for the first ten Ss are given in Table 1.

Analysing this kind of data, one might start with the observation that there are usually centres of intense communication within the total social system, groups within groups. Numerous methods of clique- or cluster-analysis enable us to identify these regions of concentration. If we use the cluster analysis of Peay (1975) and symmetrize the data by assuming that the intensity within a pair is equal to the lowest intensity $X \rightarrow Y$ or $Y \rightarrow X$, then we obtain a dyad (B, C) on the highest level of intensity, and on the second highest level we observe (G, H), (D, I), (I, F) and a clique (B, C, F).

TABLE 1   Ratings of "speaking to . . ."-frequency. 1 = very often, 2 = often, 3 = medium, 4 = rarely, 5 = very rarely, 6 = never. Data from Kruger (1973, p.2).

		RECEIVER									
		A	B	C	D	E	F	G	H	I	J
SENDER	A	-	5	3	6	4	4	6	6	6	1
	B	3	-	1	3	2	2	3	4	3	3
	C	3	1	-	4	2	3	3	4	4	3
	D	4	3	3	-	3	3	5	4	2	2
	E	5	2	2	4	-	3	3	4	3	5
	F	4	3	3	3	3	-	2	4	2	3
	G	4	3	2	5	3	3	-	2	5	5
	H	5	4	3	5	3	4	2	-	5	5
	I	4	3	4	1	3	2	5	4	-	3
	J	3	3	3	3	5	2	6	5	3	-

Using procedures of Hubert and Schultz (1976) it is possible to test for the existence of cliques, i.e. whether relative to the variability of all distances those distances within a clique are significantly shorter than the distances to non-cliqual members (Feger, 1978). But we might feel that we do not describe the communication structure properly if we identify only the intensive spots; there should be linkages for streams of information in the whole system, at least, if the system — defined one way or the other — is still coherent. To identify those streams of information one could draw the network of all relations between elements that are stronger than a certain minimum, e.g. ≥ 2, and this leads to Fig. 7.

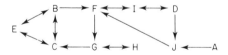

FIG. 7   Mutual and directed relations of frequent communication; data from Table 1.

The problems with this approach will be discussed by an example. In Fig. 7 a path from A to C via J, F and G is indicated. If information should go from A to C, it could certainly use this way, but considering that A → C is of medium frequency, it could also go directly from A to C. On the other hand, if the intensity of communication, starting from A, would montonally decrease over all the members of the path between A and C, then this path is a likely one. Our interest in such a path would be strengthened if at least a part of it were frequently used, and if not only were it a path between a pair of people, but between several members of the system, and having the monotonicity property for all elements of the path. We call such a path that passes information in all directions a communication chain (cc) and give it the following definition:

1. A chain contains at least three elements.
2. Members of a cc are neighbours if at least one relation between them ($X \to Y$ or $Y \to X$) is of minimum intensity.
3. For each element of the cc the intensity of the communication is a monotonally decreasing function of the distance (= number of intermediate elements) to all other elements.

For the data in Table 1 we find (with the help of an algorithm) these chains:

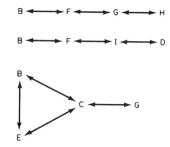

It is unlikely that such a structure would be found in purely random data: there is more than one chain, and the chains partly overlap, so that both seem quite natural. The subject B is apparently important for information exchange in this group, while A and J do not participate in the main streams of communication.

Every cc identifies all the members feeding into its mini-system with a fixed minimal intensity, though these members may not get information from the rest of the system in equal intensity. The analysis is possible for both open and closed structures. A *quantification* of the length of the distances between the elements is possible by scaling algorithms like Roskam's (1977) MNSTRUC. With this interval scale quantification one can calculate desirable network characteristics, e.g. the shortest way between two members, the time to reach all connected members from any given starting point, etc. Formally we define single-peaked intensity functions for every member of a cc, the peak being at this member, and the intensity monotonally decreasing along all paths originating at this member. A cc thus may be conceptualized as a joint scale of Coombs' unfolding theory. This joint scale is not necessarily one-dimensional; it is not multi-dimensional, since the network does not define a dimensional space, but is a multiple joint scale — thus a generalization of unfolding comparable to multiple scalogram analysis. To find cc's, the data have to show a high degree of quantitative mutuality, i.e. if $X \to Y = a$, then $Y \to X = a'$, where a' is a (positive) amount of intensity "similar" to a.

Concluding Remarks

I have thus attempted to show how network analysis is related to social science methodology in general, and that its goal is to represent different kinds of personal relations beyond the dyad. I have tried also to show the flexibility of this approach, although it was not possible within the constraints of this chapter to cover a number of very interesting topics such as bipartite and multiple graphs, probabilistic and personal networks, problems of inferential statistics in this context, and the logical relations between diverse structural rules and concepts. In my opinion, for every theoretical or practical problem the method has to be specifically adapted so that network analysis ideally is done as model testing.

Section II
Some Aspects and Examples
of Personal Relationships

CHAPTER 6

Sexual Relationships

D. P. J. Przybyla and Donn Byrne

Sexual behaviour is too often given an individual focus despite the fact that it is usually carried out in conjunction with others. It is necessary, therefore, to investigate sexual activity in terms of, and in the context of, personal relationships, and to consider not only the reciprocal interaction of sexual partners but also the psychological meaning that their relationship has for them. In this chapter we propose to develop the above perspective, in considering research on functioning within a range of same-sex and opposite-sex relationships, and to suggest, finally, an integrative developmental framework for the investigation of sexual relationships.

For the present purpose, the concept of a sexual relationship is considered similar to that of any interpersonal relationship in that it is subject to the same principles of interaction (Kirkendall and Libby, 1966). The expression of both its social and genital aspects can be demonstrated to be affected by physiological, psychological, and cultural factors (Byrne, 1977). Initiation and development are rooted in interactive personal requirements and societal specifications as to the fulfilment of these requirements (Levinger, 1977; Tripp, 1975). If positive feelings, psychological satisfaction, and a sense of achievement can be considered goals of sexual interaction, then one measure of the success of a sexual relationship is the extent to which these ends are consistently met. When the long-term consequences of sexual interaction are characterized for both partners by increased self-fulfilment, the enhancement of a satisfactory self-concept, and adequate interpersonal competence, normal and successful interpersonal behaviour can be inferred (Shope, 1975).

But the psychological meaning of sex for its participants and the effects of sexual behaviour on interpersonal relationships have not yet become central research issues (Peplau *et al.*, 1977). It is generally acknowledged that sexual relationships owe some of their development and functioning to freedom of choice on the part of those involved, to a goal or sense of purpose, and to some sense of predictability (Shope, 1975). Partners in a relationship expect to be able to predict the reactions of the other, and this relative predictability contributes to the continued existence of the relationship. Planning, in turn, is dependent upon predictability, and relationships are usually initiated and developed on the basis of planned satisfaction (Cox, 1978).

Therefore, issues such as the desisions made by the partners in a sexual relationship, their patterns of behaviour, and their specific goals beg investigation that does not focus solely on the attitudes and experiences of individuals but also on the interaction of partners and the recognition that any relationship is one of process having shared meaning and mutual needs. This general approach treats the sexual relationship as an autonomous and private one (Sprey, 1969). Considering the dyad as an independent unit does not disregard the influence of social factors, but serves as an alternative to traditional qualitative distinctions between a sexuality that is procreative and one that is not procreative, i.e. heterosexual versus homosexual, marital versus non-marital, and adult versus adolescent.

Functioning within Same-Sex Relationships

Psychological research on relationships typically has passed over homosexuals (Huston and Levinger, 1978). Most investigations into homosexuality have considered males, and most frequently relative to factors of aetiology and personal adjustment. Recently, however, empirical documentation of lesbian sexual interactions has offered a sense of direction (Peplau *et al.*, 1978).

Female relationships

Peplau *et al.* suggest the presence of two distinct value orientations that may influence lesbian relationships. The first, dyadic attachment, concerns an emphasis on establishing emotionally close and relatively secure love relationships. The second, personal autonomy, concerns an emphasis on independence and self-actualization that may lead to a questioning of traditional relationships.

Relative to the first orientation, lesbians (in contrast to homosexual males) have been depicted as emphasizing the emotional quality of love relationships. They apparently are less promiscuous and have longer-lasting exclusive relationships (Cory and LeRoy, 1963; Cotton, 1975). Peplau *et al.* suggest that, irrespective of sexual preference, females are still taught to value closeness and permanence in relationships that are based more on love and romance than on sex.

Relative to the second orientation, Abbott and Love (1972) indicate that lesbians, more than heterosexual females, develop qualities of strength, independence, and self-actualization because they are less afraid to do so. Their choice of same-sex partners demonstrates the rise of personal autonomy over socially prescribed role behaviours. Cassell (1977) suggests that females who become lesbians define themselves not in terms of their relationships, but in terms of their activity. If so, an emphasis on autonomy might engender less exclusive female relationships that are maintained only as long as they are personally satisfying.

Bearing in mind the suggested primary dimensions, evidence was found linking females' values concerning relationships to characteristics of their relationship. Those who endorsed attachment values of togetherness and security differed significantly from those who placed little emphasis on these values. An emphasis on attachment was associated with spending more time with the current sexual partner, reporting greater closeness and satisfaction with the relationship, expressing greater confidence that the relationship would continue, and worrying less that personal independence would create difficulties for the relationship. Females who endorsed autonomy and equality, having personal interests outside the relationship, and not emphasizing future commitment, differed significantly from those who gave less importance to these values. A strong emphasis on autonomy was associated with spending less time with the partner, being less willing to maintain the relationship at the expense of work or education, being more likely to have a sexually open relationship, and worrying about having an over-dependent partner.

The majority of females said their current relationship was extremely close and personally satisfying, and most reported power-sharing within the relationship. In addition to these areas of commonality, wide variations were found in their values regarding relationships and in reports about specific characteristics of their own ongoing relationships.

Male relationships

While comparable data with males do not exist, Jones and Bates (1978) have dealt with the problem of discrepancies in couple satisfaction. No relationships were found between the degree of discrepancy between the two partners' satisfaction scores and items presumed to be related to couple satisfaction and stability such as affection, appreciation, and lack of conflict. However, in contrast to male couples who described their relationship as moderately successful, highly successful couples reported greater appreciation of the partner and the couple as a unit, less conflict, and more feelings that could contribute to stability (such as positive feelings about love relationship and future plans as a couple).

In a similar vein, Dailey (1979) reported information concerning couple adjustment in heterosexual and homosexual pairing relationships. Of a small sample of male and female homosexual couples, married couples, and non-married heterosexual couples, the least consensus in adjustment within the relationship was reported by the homosexual couples. The author suggested that the homosexual tries to maintain a meaningful relationship in a social context which offers no support or sanction for the relationship, or even oppresses such expressions. The lack of external consensus about the viability of homosexual relationships may produce a lack of consensus in those couples with respect to matters of importance to the functioning of the relationship. Non-married heterosexual couples had slightly lowered consensus scores which may reflect a similar consequence. There is, however, more tolerance of the non-married heterosexual relationship than of the homosexual relationship in our society.

There are distinct problems in investigating the initiation and development of same-sex relationships, particularly when approached so as to examine the meaning of sex for its participants and the effects of sexual behaviour on interpersonal relationships. It has been noted previously that the sexual relationships of homosexual males tend to be brief. The modal form of sexual activity is one of frequent and impersonal sexual encounters. Even more enduring marriage-like couplings last an average of less than three years (Saghir and Robins, 1973). It should be noted, however, that despite general agreement about such a characteristic pattern existing among male homosexuals, modifying evidence has been reported by Bell (1978). He indicates, as has Sonneschein (1968) before him, that the impersonality and brevity of homosexual relationships is characteristic only of certain subgroups of men.

A socio-psychological perspective developed by Harry and DeVall (1978) indicates that there is a pattern of anonymous self-presentation among homosexual males. This anonymity forestalls the development of closer and more enduring relationships, for the development of such relationships would violate the norm. If a relationship of some commitment were to be developed, one of the partners would have to violate the norms and either offer information socially identifying himself or solicit it from the other individual. Perhaps related to this issue, the ability to adjust self-disclosure is considered critical in maintaining a sense of worth (Altman, 1975). Westin (1967) suggests that adjustment of self-boundaries contributes to a sense of personal control and independence.

Derlega and Chaikin (1977) indicate that sharing a secret with others may contribute to fostering and committing oneself to a personal identity, as well as identifying oneself with a select group. Kimmel (1978) and Warren (1977) demonstrate that the crisis of public identification as homosexual may be one of the most significant acts of his or her life. Thus disclosure and interaction commits the individual to a new identity.

Another principal contention of Harry and DeVall is that homosexual males have been socialized with condemnations of homosexuality that began in their pre-gay lives and continue through heterosexual associates. As a result, they hold negative attitudes towards each other and tend to interpret each other's faults in terms of popular stereotypes. This in turn can give rise to an unwillingness to commit oneself emotionally, as opposed to sexually, to another homosexual male and to the closeness of a loving relationship.

In contrast, as indicated earlier, the interpersonal behaviour of lesbians differs substantially from that of male homosexuals. Harry and DeVall suggest that lesbians do not internalize negative attitudes towards other lesbians as much as do gay males. Negative stereotypes differ not only in emotional intensity, but in their degree of salience. Although research indicates that both male and female homosexuals are intensely disapproved of by the public (MacDonald and Games, 1974), the authors suggest that the lesbian stereotype is less salient in the popular mind; lesbians are less a general concern than are gay males. In support, of this hypothesis , they cite both impressionistic and research evidence. Notable among their pieces of evidence are the frequency of references to male homosexuality in popular discourse and the anxiety that arises in the parents of a male child as opposed to a female child when the symptoms of potential homosexuality occur (Maccoby and Jacklin, 1974). When a negative label is not salient, individuals to whom the label would apply will not experience it regularly. As a result, they are not encouraged to focus on comparisons between themselves and convention, and do not strongly internalize the label.

While Harry and DeVall have demonstrated a relationship between attitudes towards other gay men and lack of interest in paired intimacy, they also found that emotional intimacy was unrelated to number of sex partners. Arguing against a necessary polarization of intimacy and promiscuity in behaviour, the authors note that the fact that a given person has sexual encounters with many other men does not necessarily imply he is not interested in intimacy. An interest in intimacy virtually requires that a person search for others with whom he may be intimate. Thus, a large number of sexual encounters may be an expression of a search for intimacy rather than an expression of lack of desire for it. The majority of their respondents indicated that they either had or wanted a "long-term lover," suggesting that some of their sexual encounters were expressions of that desire.

A comment on sex roles in homosexual relationships

The differences in intimacy, commitment, and duration of sexual relationships between male and female homosexual couples have been noted. It also has been noted (see Peplau *et al.*, 1978) that females, whether homosexual or heterosexual, are exposed in some degree to socialization pressures encouraging close dyadic attachments. Strom (cited in Peplau *et al.*, 1978) also contends that while the courtship behaviour of lesbians differs from that of homosexual males, it closely resembles that of heterosexual females.

Alternative roles have come to the forefront of male sexual activity. It has been suggested that the continuation of sexual relationships between homosexual males is limited because both partners were socialized as males. Hoffman (1968) claims that both males expect to be dominant and the solution to this conflict is not specified by society. Maccoby and Jacklin (1974) indicate that to the extent that a relationship is intimate or has the potential of becoming intimate, both parties will inhibit attempts to dominate. In male relationships, attempts at domination could easily lessen commitment to an intimate relationship. One might expect that commitment to specifications of masculine dominance would give rise to brief relationships or "an unwillingness to enter into relationships in which one's autonomy or dominance would be compromised" (Harry and DeVall, p. 53). Data gathered by these authors in fact indicate that a commitment to dominance is negatively related to a desire for emotional intimacy. It should be considered, however, that a successful, enduring relationship need not be intimate, as long as both partners derive psychological and physical satisfaction from their interaction. A sexual relationship does not always imply an intimate relationship.

Functioning within Opposite-sex Relationships

Heterosexual relationships other than marital and extramarital have been studied under the rubrics of adolescent, premarital, and non-marital interaction. The eventual application of this research seems to be directed toward plotting the development and effects of sexual interaction on the individual, rather than on dyadic functioning.

Sexual interaction outside marriage

While the generally perceived immorality of homosexuals has done little to encourage research into the morality of their sexual relationships (MacDonald and Games, 1974), this has not been the case with respect to non-marital sexual behaviour. Not surprisingly, such research has often dealt with proscriptions against sexual behaviour. In contrast, Jurich and Jurich (1974), have investigated individual's choices of whether to engage in sexual intercourse based on perceived quality of the relationship. They suggest that this requires a knowledge of reciprocity, an ability to experience subjectively the role of the other person in the relationship, and making a decision as to whether the relationship can be defined as a love relationship. As a result, several standards of affection would be possible. One might evaluate the relationship in terms of his or her partner and also in terms of the level of the relationship. Other standards might require more sophistication. For example, the decision as to whether to engage in intercourse differs not only with each person but according to circumstances. The decision ultimately rests upon the recognition by both partners in the relationship of the shared rights each has as an individual.

The authors go on to say that one standard is not more moral than another but that certain standards require a greater level of cognitive moral development. Although they are different in a systematic way, a sexual standard requiring a high level of cognitive moral development is not implicitly better than a standard requiring a low level of moral maturity. The latter might even be functional in specific environments. Therefore, "no value judgment should be placed upon this ordering of premarital sexual standards" (p.740).

D'Augelli and D'Augelli (1977) have suggested that interpersonal sexual behaviour is the result of a relationship-based decision-making process focusing on the morality of the contemplated pieces of behaviour and the implications of those pieces of behaviour for the relationship. In examining the association of moral reasoning to sexual standards, sexual philosophy, sex guilt, and sexual behaviour, they report that sexual involvement is a moral issue reflecting decisions about the self-defined quality of interpersonal relationship desired by the partners.

The individual's way of reasoning about interpersonal relationship underlies decision-making regarding the current and future quality of a person's interpersonal life. Relationship reasoning is involved at decision-making points in which the individual or dyad is confronted with choices as to the nature and quality of the relationship. These points concern change within the relationship, whether towards initiation, maintenance, enhancement, or dissolution. Decisions about sexual behaviour are related to this relationship development process as are other interpersonal resources.

A central assumption here is that qualitative differences exist in the way people evaluate relationship issues, particularly as applied to situations in which relationships of possible duration are involved. In such situations, behaviour consistent with long-term planning is more likely to be subject to cost and rewards analysis than is immediate behaviour.

Three levels of relationship reasoning are proposed. In Egotistic Reasoning, relationship reasoning is based on cost–reward analysis, with self as primary focal point. The individual views costs and rewards as coming not from the relationship, but from the partner. Decisions about what the individual will give are based upon predicted returns. Interpersonal interactions are seen as opportunities to give or to receive in reciprocal ways, with little or no conception of long-term interpersonal rewards. Each partner acts upon his or her own view of the relationship's norms with little reference to the partner's views, so that the optimal relationship is one which provides the most immediate benefits for the individual.

In Dyadic Reasoning, relationship decisions are based on the perceived expectations of the partner, consistent with role standards. The "other's" view of the relationship is of central importance to the individual's relationship decision-making. Reciprocity is based on role responsibilities, as is relationship change. Choices support the couple's socially defined conception of their relationship, sometimes to the detriment of personal rewards. By mutual agreement, locus of control for change within the relationship lies largely with the partner whose role responsibilities are perceived or are socially defined as including dominance and control. The optimal relationship is one which provides conditions for fulfilling the partner's expectations and facilitating one's role within the relationship.

Finally, in Interactive Reasoning, relationship decisions are based upon the couple's consensually developing conceptions of their relationship. The "couple's" conception of their relationship is open to change based on acknowledged responsibilities and norms, subject to changing needs and values. Their own conception of interaction is more critical to their behaviour than role-derived concepts. The locus of control lies with the dyad. Change results through a process of accurately sharing the other's point of view and examining the potential consequences of change for self, other, and the dyad. The optimal relationship is one which allows for the formation of dyad-specific norms.

While the authors can provide no empirical evidence on this point, they suggest that interpersonal reasoning can develop as involvement with another person increases. Partners may differ in terms of their maximal relationship reasoning. This point may provide an explanatory mechansim for intra-relationship advances. Differences between dyad members might facilitate the development of higher levels of reasoning in one member. A person cognitively operating at Interactive Reasoning might somehow encourage such reasoning in his or her partner. Unless rigid sex roles are operative, couples initially functioning at the Dyadic Reasoning level might be pushed toward Interactive Reasoning as a result of exposure to each other's preferences, values, etc.

Relating sexual behaviour and emotional intimacy

It has been traditional to investigate the links between sex and love in male-female research, perhaps because such links are not always immediately evident in relationships.

Kirkendall (1961) investigated the effects of the fondness the members of a couple had for one another on the meaning of sex in a relationship. Based on a continuum of affectional involvement, he showed that individual motivation and communication and the willingness of the males to assume responsibility for the consequences of sexual interactions, changed with degree of emotional involvement. At the deep affectional level there was more concern for developing communication that would result in understanding and insight towards the partner; motivation changed from a self-centred focus to a relationship-centred one; and the male increased in readiness to assume the responsibilities involved in the sexual relationship.

More recently, links between love and sex have been investigated by Peplau *et al.* (1977). These authors distinguish between couple interaction patterns as traditional, sexually moderate and sexually liberal. Their data demonstrate that for traditionals, emotional intimacy develops in the context of limited sexual activity. Sexual intercourse is strongly related to love but also importantly, to a permanent commitment, and a characteristic of this orientation is the belief that premarital sexual intercourse is immoral. For moderates, emotional intimacy guides sexual intimacy: as feelings of closeness increase, so too can sexual interaction. Moderates are orientated towards romanticism and emphasize closeness and love in their relationship. Liberals view sex as a legitimate dating goal. For them, sexual intimacy can be seen as a route to the development of emotional intimacy.

Peplau *et al.* used the timing of intercourse in the relationship as a rough index of the couple's orientation towards sex and love. Distinguishing between early-sex and later-sex couples, for the latter, emotional intimacy seems to precede sexual intimacy. Later-sex couples report first intercourse at a six-month period after they started "going together". Among early-sex couples, first coitus preceded "going together" by an average of one month. The authors suggest the impact of the sequencing of these two events on the couples' relationships.

> Both men and women in later-sex couples had higher scores on Rubin's (1970) love scale than did students in early-sex relationships. Later-sex students reported feeling significantly closer to their partner and knowing their partner better. A significantly higher proportion of later-sex students said they were "in love" with their partner (p.100).

The authors contend that the belief that love alone justifies sex may affect behaviour. Later-sex couples may delay coitus until their relationship is emotionally close. Also for later-sex couples, having had coitus may have heightened perceptions of love through a process of self-attribution: after having coitus, a person may then be motivated to investigate the rationale behind his or her behaviour. While members of early-sex couples might be likely to attribute their behaviour to sexual desire, later-sex couples might be apt to infer from their behaviour that they are in love.

Interestingly, no one pattern of emotional intimacy–sexual intimacy was more or less likely to foster satisfaction or permanence over a period of two years. Couples in early-sex, later-sex and abstinent patterns of relationships did not differ significantly in their overall satisfaction with their relationship. The most striking evidence that all the patterns examined could lead to committed relationships is found in follow-up data. No obvious correlation was found at all between whether a couple had early-sex, later-sex, or abstained, on the one hand, and their dating status two years after the initial testing, on the other hand. Individuals in each type of couple were equally likely to have broken up, continued dating, or married each other. There was no evidence that early sex inhibits the development of lasting commitments nor that a lasting relationship is necessarily facilitated by sexual abstinence or moderation.

Role concepts and heterosexual interaction

Sex roles have been suggested as influences on the bond between sexual interaction and the relationship. Kirkendall and Libby (1966), in discussing the work of Reiss, recount how adherence to a different standard for males and females leads to stereotyping of the individual's concept of his or her own role and that of the partner. What the individual may conceive of as freely chosen behaviour is intimately related to concepts rooted in the existing cultural pattern.

Relative to this issue, in 1959, Ehrmann investigated the association of premarital sexual behaviour and interpersonal relationships. Studying the progression of individuals through increasingly intense stages of intimacy as they moved towards or rejected intercourse, Ehrmann noted differences in the attitudes of males and females as affectional ties deepened. The degree of physical intimacy experienced or permissible among males was inversely related and among females directly related to the intensity of familiarity and affection in the male–female relationship. That is, while female sexual expression became more liberal with lovers than non-lovers, male sexual expression became more conservative.

Peplau *et al.* (1977), in contrast, focusing on individual attitudes, found that most sampled individuals, whether male or female, appeared liberal and egalitarian. Interestingly, however, individual and dyadic approaches to sexual activity can lead to different conclusions. When they examined the pattern of interaction in couples as opposed to their individual attitudes, they found clear evidence that traditional sex roles still bear significantly upon behaviour. "Permissive sex attitudes and increased frequency of premarital coitus have apparently not changed the basic script for sexual interaction in dating couples" (p.108).

The authors' argument is "that sexual role playing provides dating partners with a common standard to use in interpreting behavior and making inferences about a person's motives and dispositions. While some aspects of sexual role playing can be modified — how quickly the game is played, with how many different partners it is repeated, at what age the game is first begun — the basic form remains unchanged. A consequence is that male–female differences in sexual behavior are perpetuated despite changing attitudes about the value of traditional roles" (p.107).

Peplau *et al.* do report, however, that subjects in their study differ from the Ehrmann study in two ways. First, virtually all men in their sample seemed to exert positive control by initiating sex. Male interest in sex and willingness to suggest intercourse at some point in a premarital relationship are relatively constant factors in modern dating. Secondly, a smaller proportion of females today totally veto coitus or insist on a long-term relationship as a prerequisite for intercourse. "But in spite of these changes, traditional sexual role playing remains quite common among students in our sample. Males continue to exert positive control; they play the role of sexual initiator. This does not mean, of course, that females have no part in initiating sex. Females may indeed communicate, often subtly, that they are interested and willing. They continue to hold negative control, however; they can reject the man's advances or slow the pace of increasing sexual intimacy" (p.96).

Sexual interaction in marriage

Permanence remains implicit in marriage. Testing this permanence is an increasing emphasis on marriage as a relationship for emotional gratification of the spouses. Udry (1974) suggests that in marriage, equality of the sexes has come to mean that the relationship should be one of equals with similar goals and similar sources of gratification. The expectation is that each partner will find the same meanings and will derive the same rewards from the interaction.

This line of reasoning gives rise to the ideology that males and females are basically equal in most of their intellectual, emotional, and temperamental capacities, and notably in their sexual behaviour. Both, therefore, have equal rights to the enjoyment of sex and should derive equal enjoyment from it. Most pointedly, both sexes have the same kinds of desires — each initiates sexual activity as often as the other, each has passions which can reach the same intensity.

Whether or not this optimal dyad condition is operative in a marriage, the significance of sexual satisfaction in the success of marriage in general is noteworthy. Even though sexual adjustment ranks among the top problem areas both in successful and unsuccessful marriages, it is much less a problem among successfully functioning couples than among those having trouble (Mitchell *et al.*, 1962).

Sager (1976) paraphrases Abraham Lincoln: "Some couples who have good sex have a good total relationship all the time; all couples who have good sex have a good total relationship some of the time; but all the couples who have good sex do not have a good relationship all the time. Conversely, there are those who have a poor sexual relationship but who may have a good, loving relationship in other parameters of interaction." Sager goes on to say that the sexual aspects of the relationship of the couple often mirror their total relationship. The same power struggles, the same closeness or distance, the same demands, the same attitudes may prevail in sex as may generally prevail for the couple. Hunt (1974) offers support for such a notion by demonstrating a strong connection between sexual pleasure and marital success. He reports that a large majority of married men and women who found marital coitus very pleasurable during the preceding year rated their marriage emotionally as very close. In contrast, few of those who found marital coitus lacking in pleasure or actually unpleasant rated their marriage very close or even fairly close. Three out of five women and two out of five men who rated their marriage distant or not close found marital sex lacking in pleasure or actually unpleasant in the year prior to their response.

One can argue either that sexual pleasure is the cause of marital success or that sexual pleasure is a result of marital success. While sexual success tends to create emotional closeness, emotional closeness permits individuals to be sexually successful. There is no definite answer. It is likely that each phenomenon is both cause and effect in a reciprocal interaction. At any rate, Hunt's data do suggest the husbands and wives who share a pleasurable sexual relationship are much likelier to be emotionally close than those who do not.

But for many committed couples sex does not reflect a one-to-one similarity to their total relationship. Sex sometimes appears to be a special parameter of their interaction in which either or both may act differently from the way they usually act. There are couples who fight, disagree, struggle for power but continue to fulfill each other sexually as they are unable to do in other areas. Conversely, there are loving couples whose relationships are excellent, yet, sexually, they are not excited by each other.

Whether or not they are reflective of each other, the relationship between sexual adjustment and marital adjustment might be considered in the context of male and female sexuality. Most authors have acknowledged (e.g. Udry, 1974) that sexuality has traditionally been more fundamental to masculine than feminine personality organization and that "love comes to men in a sexual context, while sex comes to woment in a love context" (p.323). Research by Clark and Wallin (1965) has indicated that for each sex there is the same correlation between marital adjustment and sexual adjustment, but the main direction of causation is opposite for the two sexes. After examining data derived from the early years of marriage and from eighteen to twenty years of marriage, they concluded that for a man, the level of sexual adjustment has a causal effect on his marital adjustment with little reciprocal effect of general marital adjustment on his sex life. For a woman, the level of general marital satisfaction has an effect on the sexual adjustment with little reciprocal effect of the sexual adjustment on her general satisfaction with the marriage.

Rainwater (1964) suggests that where conjugal roles are highly segregated and marital interaction is built around a division of labour, as is characteristic of some lower working-class groups, a close and mutually satisfying sexual relationship is not likely to develop because partners do not as a matter of custom relate to one another in an emotionally intimate way. Rainwater also suggests that "a close sexual relationship has no particular social function in such a system since the role performances of husband and wife are organized on a separate basis, and no great contribution is made by a relationship in which they sharpen their ability for cooperation and mutual regulation" (p.463).

Sexual Interaction in the Elderly

Survival into old age has become increasingly commonplace. Despite concern over the fact and quality of this survival, information about sex in general and relationships in particular is meagre.

Botwinick (1978) gives several reasons for this. First, investigators tend to be uncomfortable with the concept of sexuality in older people, so they often exclude the elderly from their focus of investigation. Additionally, development through young adulthood for today's elderly people probably occurred in a period when open and frank discussion of one's sexual life was not normal behaviour. At this point in their lives, special circumstances would be required to foster openness and candour. Another reason why valid sexual information is difficult to obtain, particularly in regard to elderly men, is that some respondents are prone to exaggerate their actual sexual interest, reporting feats of virility, and making grandiose claims about their desires and capabilities in performance. Such behaviour stresses the importance of cross-validating responses within couples.

The extent to which the characteristic temperament of an ageing dyad is due to the effects of partner ageing as opposed to the length of the relationship itself is yet to be determined. Pineo (1969) indicates that as marriage continues through the lifespan, couple satisfaction decreases, subjects showing an increasing tendency to diverge in attitudes and behaviour, both sexual and non-sexual.

Masters and Johnson (1966, pp.263–265) reported that "the female partner may lose her stimulative effect as her every wish, interest, and expression become too well known. . ." Botwinick relates that the diminution of the stimulating effects of the marriage partner is attributable to factors such as the male's boredom with the repetition of the sexual act. In addition, as wives age, their physical appearances may have a negative effect on the potency of their husbands, or they may sexually repel their husbands because of personal habits, etc. (The male's appearance and personal habits certainly must bear on the female's behaviour in a similar way.) Masters and Johnson (1966, p.265) relate that "By their own admission, many of the women interviewed no longer showed concern for their husbands".

There is no denying that sexual activity is physically possible in the ageing. It has perhaps been less evident that interpersonal sexual expression should continue through the lifespan as an important form of positive affective reward. "All of us have been accustomed to associate sex and love exclusively with youth. Sexual activity of any kind on the part of older persons is rarely referred to except in derogatory terms" (Rubin, 1965, p.3).

Pfeiffer (1974) has acknowledged that sexual expression should be considered in the overall context of successful ageing. He demonstrates that successfully ageing persons are those who have made a decision to stay "in training" in the social, emotional, physical, and intellectual areas of their lives. Staying in training sexually may also help improve the quality of life in later years. For example, individuals who report their sexual desires in youth as very strong continue to report moderate desires in old age. Those who report their early desires as moderate or weak report themselves without sexual feelings in old age (Newman and Nichols, 1960).

Within the heterosexual marriage, it appears that the husband controls the frequency of sexual intercourse in old age. Pfeiffer, *et al.* (1972) found that elderly males and females in their samples who had stopped having intercourse reported the responsibility for stopping as being the husband's.

Ageing appears to bring somewhat less dramatic changes for homosexuals than for heterosexuals. Francher and Henkin (1973) note that developmentally, the major life crisis for their homosexual male subjects did not occur with ageing but during that period in which they had to adjust to their sexual orientation. They also suggest that the dominant early life crisis may effect their pattern of ageing (and parenthetically, their functioning within a relationship), typically having been less involved in the developmental changes and crises within families that affect the patterns of ageing for heterosexual males.

In the homosexual dyad, Weinberg and Williams (1974) relate that older respondents report less frequent sex compared to younger respondents but indicate that while sexual behaviour became less frequent in the lives of males as they grew older, it remained important. Homosexual partners felt it more satisfying in age than in youth. Kimmel (1978) reports a respondent's comment: "less accent on the genitals, more on the total person now". Perhaps male homosexual relationships can become more successful with ageing because secrecy and anonymous self-presentation become less important.

"The value and pleasure of a surviving function, be it vision or sex, ought to be appreciated and used" (as well as researched) " to the limit of individual prudence" (Botwinick, 1978, p.59).

Integrating Research Approaches: A Developmental Framework for the Investigation of Sexual Relationships

A wide variety of observations, research findings, opinions, and conclusions about many aspects of sexual relationships have been reported here. The challenge now lies in discovering how, or whether, these diverse elements possibly can be brought together into some kind of meaningful pattern. We

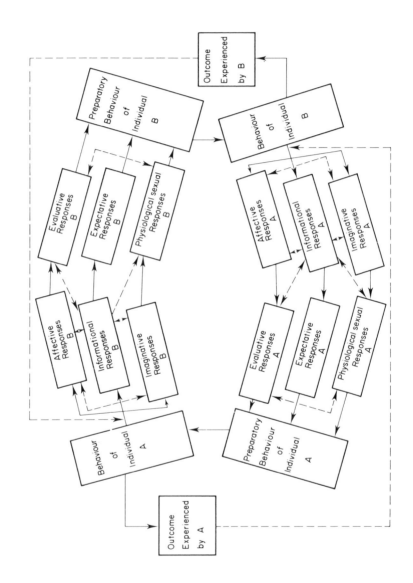

FIG. 1   The interactive behaviour sequence.

will present a brief version of one such way to organize and think about the development of human sexual relationships, with no presumption that this represents a complete and polished theory. In the presented form, it is a preliminary step and one that may prove helpful in our attempts to understand this rather central and rather complex aspect of human behaviour.

The interactive behaviour sequence

To present a psychological theory of the development of a sexual relationship, it is helpful to begin with a depiction of the model as in Fig. 1. This way of organizing this development grew from repeated attempts at making overall sense out of research findings in sexual behaviour in the areas of social and personality psychology (Byrne, 1977; Byrne and Byrne, 1977; Byrne and Kelley, 1981).

Each enclosed box in the figure represents a basic theoretical construct and each solid arrow represents a proposed antecedent–consequent relationship between variables. The dotted arrows represent secondary relationships and also indicate the way in which various aspects of the system are interdependent.

On the left of the figure is the primary external determinant of relationship behaviour, the potential sexual partner.

The six central variables involve internal processes that mediate the effects of external stimulation and that also can inititate behaviour. Affective responses involve momentary positive and negative feelings (such as joy and disgust). Evaluative responses are based initially on such feelings, but they consist of more long-lasting attitudinal dispositions (such as the judgement that one likes homosexual anal intercourse but dislikes sadism). Informational responses consist of beliefs that may be true, untrue, or untestable (such as the belief that males need sex more than do females). Expectancies are based on beliefs and refer to probabilities that a given piece of behaviour will result in a specific outcome (such as the expectation that elderly people who have sexual interactions will inevitably have heart attacks). Imaginative responses involve self-generated fantasies and those of others (such as erotic dreams and printed erotica). Physiological sexual responses include the various physiological changes that precede and accompany sexual excitement (such as increased vasocongestion in the genitals). It should be remembered that these responses often are initiated by the conditioned stimulus object, the potential sexual partner.

The behaviour towards which all of these internal and external factors are directed includes many possible preparatory acts (such as a smile, locking a bedroom door, or dispensing cash) and sexual interaction itself. Cognizant that it is the functioning couple that is of prime interest, we propose that two behaviour sequences are operating simultaneously, each individual serving as the stimulus for the other.

Finally, a major factor in changing a given behaviour sequence or making progress into a stronger relationship is the positive or negative outcome associated with each sexual interaction. Note that the two individuals may experience different outcomes related to the same sexual interaction. In such a situation, depending on the extent of the divergence in outcomes, the individuals may be propelled in directions incompatible with the maintenance of a relationship. The framework presented here allows comparisons among the central variables in terms of their importance or relative contribution to each partner's behaviour within the sexual relationship, over the course of its development. While each process is influenced by external events and by the other five processes, each is a partially independent determinant of behaviour exerting some influence on the sexual relationship. It is useful to consider each of the six internal processes shown in the figure.

Affective processes

Much of an individual's experience includes responses of feeling good or bad, finding things to be pleasant or unpleasant, making us happy or sad. With respect to sex, the basic innate response to sexual stimulation and to sexual activity is clearly a positive one. It is easy enough, however, to learn to associate negative affect with sexuality. Individuals can learn in a variety of ways that sex and people who engage in it are dirty, shameful, disgusting, and so forth. Most individuals eventually experience some mixture of positive and negative emotionality attached to each sexual cue and each piece of sexual behaviour (Byrne et al., 1974). Individuals differ in what they have learned, so they differ with respect to the degree to which a given sex-related activity evokes positive and/or negative feelings within them. Individuals also experience affective responses as a result of interpersonal encounters. While one person may respond positively to another on a level of non-genital exchange, negative affective responses to a partner's choice of specific sexual practices, or to some other aspect of the first interaction between the sexual partners would probably inhibit the development of a relationship.

Evaluative responses

Byrne (1971) and Clore and Byrne (1974) have established that the attitudes towards another individual are based on the proportion of positive feelings associated with the target (with each feeling weighted according to its strength). Each time one meets an individual or engages in a sexual act, his or her judgements can be summarized by noting that he or she feels a given way about the other person or about a particular sexual practice.

With respect to sexuality, there is a general tendency to respond to most sexual cues in a consistently positive or negative judgemental fashion. As with feelings, negative attitudes tend to interfere with the formation of a sexual relationship. For example, negative emotional–attitudinal responses to sex can be sufficiently strong that the individual avoids sexual intercourse completely (Fisher et al., 1979). In a less extreme sense, negative attitudes about another individual or his or her preferred behaviour might preclude future interaction. It is more likely that similar sexual preferences will be evaluated most positively, at least initially, and will contribute to the relationship.

Informational responses

A third internal process involves the array of factual information in addition to inaccurate beliefs that an individual acquires about sexual interaction and about a potential sexual partner.

General knowledge about sexual interaction is likely to be acquired in a haphazard and unsystematic manner. The result is that individuals differ in precisely how much they know about the details of interpersonal and sexual functioning and in the accuracy of the information they do possess. Particularly relevant to information and beliefs dealing with sexual interaction are the areas of morality, normality, and legality. The individual learns to place various sexual practices, sexual attitudes, and sexual preferences along continua indicating the degree to which each is moral or immoral, normal or deviant, lawful or criminal. Such knowledge and beliefs tend to be associated with corresponding emotions and attitudes.

Furthermore, within a potential sexual interaction, each individual acquires information about the other in terms of attitudes, preference, and goals of interpersonal functioning. Much of this information is processed and categorized into personal codes of morality or normality. These pieces of information influence the sexual interaction primarily through the expectancies that are associated with them, as will be discussed in the next section.

Expectative processes

One's information and beliefs about a given individual very often include elements that lead him or her to expect relatively specific positive or negative consequences to result from specific behaviour. The content of an individual's expectations, his or her judgement as to the value of obtaining a positive consequence or avoiding a negative one, and the person's subjective probability that a piece of behaviour is going to be followed by a consequence each act to determine whether a given behaviour will or will not occur.

If two individuals find themselves in a situation in which they might engage in intercourse for the first time, there are numerous ways in which their expectancies operate. For example, if an anonymous male in a homosexual encounter believes that the odds are against the disclosure of his identity, the encounter is more likely to be carried out. If both males believe that anal intromission strips away masculinity, it is not likely to occur. If two males believe that frequent one-time encounters are impersonal and degrading, a relationship is a likely alternative. The expectancies held may be true, false, or untestable. The important thing is what the individual thinks will happen. Further, the relative effect of each expectancy rests on the value the person places on sexual anonymity, sexual satisfaction, and the specific contexts of sexual expression.

Along with the other, less rational determinants of behaviour, a person weighs the various consequences, the pluses and minuses, until the balance favours one piece of behaviour or another.

Imaginative processes

Motives expressed in our fantasies are also expressed in overt behaviour. Sexual behaviour is much more dependent upon fantasy than most types of behaviour because it tends to be a private activity observed only by the individual and his or her sexual partner. Sexual fantasies seem to ensure excitement, to enhance sexual pleasure, and to facilitate an orgasmic response. Part of imaginative acitivity seems to involve the evocation of memories of one's own past sexual acts, interactions, and other fantasies, and arousal tends to be greatest in response to reminders of what the individual has personally experienced (Griffitt, 1975). Thus a potential sexual partner is likely to become the object of imaginative activity, particularly if he or she becomes associated with any of these past sexual partners, sexual interactions, or sexual fantasies.

Physiological processes

The final internal process in the model refers to the variety of bodily changes associated with various stages of the sexual act. Arousal is initiated by external stimulation such as touching sensitive body areas, and internal stimulation such as pressure on the seminal vesicles of the male and erotic daydreams. As sexual excitement increases (in the context of the present discussion, largely in response to the sexual partner) the probability of sexual behaviour increases. Arousal propels the individual towards engaging in sexual act without regard for emotions, attitudes, information, expectancies, or fantasies. In other words, the entire system can be at least partially "short-circuited" by intense arousal. In the light of the powerful influence of sexual excitement, the occurrence of one-time, impersonal sexual encounters is not surprising.

Application of the Behaviour Sequence

A sexual relationship may begin with physical infatuation and then grow and mature into a realistic and more mature sort of love. As individuals gather knowledge about each other, blind love or blind passion may be transformed into feelings of deep attachment, mutual caring, and positive evaluation of one another's intelligence and good judgement (Rubin, 1974; Walster and Walster, 1978). As in other phases of the acquaintance process, even the most loving relationship involves learning more and more about one another and, if all goes well, becoming better and better friends; even a predominantly physical sexual relationship, the goal of which is to attain unbridled mutual satisfaction, requires repeated interactions that are rewarded or punished and go on to contribute to the formation or dissolution of the relationship.

Research reported in the preceding pages has indicated that members of both sexes actively seek out sexual partners. That these partners are chosen from the masses based on some system of subjective preference indicates that each of us holds imaginative conceptions of potential sexual partners. The role of imaginative processes across the development of the relationship relative to the other central variables suggested here, is one potential area of investigation and will serve in a hypothetical application of the model.

It is reasonable to assume that initiating, responding to, or fulfilling an imaginative fantasy often serves to initiate a sexual interaction. And quite likely, these imaginative acitivites are more central than a breadth of information or a variety of evaluations concerning the potential partner in establishing an initial interaction.

If a relationship is to progress beyond a physical infatuation, however, fantasy responses may become less central to future sexual interactions. For example, individuals within the sexual dyad will come to evaluate one another's activities, attitudes, and so forth. Previous evaluations laden with positive affect initiated by the individual's imaginative activity may change, becoming more realistic or even negative when the novelty or initial thrill has passed. Information gathered by the individual relative to his or her partner's behaviour may serve to infringe upon his or her fantasy. While sexual partners in the imagination unerringly respond and fulfill, the physical presence of another individual introduces new preferences, new needs and new fantasies! Either partner has the option of changing or accommodating his or her behaviour or dissolving the interaction.

As a relationship becomes committed over time, it is conceivable that the individuals involved share an aura of positive regard. Irrespective of new information regarding social or genital behaviour within the dyad, this positive affect may be enough to maintain the relationship. Alternatively, we have seen that in ageing dyads, whether or not this positive regard is present, one or both partners may cease to become sexually attractive to the other. At such a point, it is likely that imaginative fantasy would become central in any initiation of sexual activity within the dyad.

While the framework in its present form falls short of claiming specificity in its predictive powers, it can be used to derive hypotheses to be tested. In addition, research has to be undertaken to verify the hypothesized associations among the processes in the model, specifically related to sexual interaction and the development of relationships.

Nevertheless, we feel that this framework suggests a meaningful organization of the processes leading to sexual interaction. Based on successful applications of a similar model to contraceptive behaviour (Byrne and Fisher, 1981), it is expected that appropriate operationalization of each process will contribute to our ability to predict and understand interpersonal sexual behaviour. Confronted with the many approaches to the study of different types of sexual relationships, this method offers continuity and facilitates comparison and generalization.

CHAPTER 7

Heterosexual Cohabitation Relationships

Michael D. Newcomb

This chapter will attempt to integrate the many studies that have been conducted during the past 15 years on cohabitation (i.e. living together without the sanction of marriage), and its main method of achieving such integration will be a focus on the psychological issues that have been investigated. However, since cohabitation is not a singular life style, various functions and types of cohabitation have been studied and theoretical integration of such studies necessitates a critique of the methodological and conceptual issues that researchers have faced. Some studies have focused on attitudes towards, and incidence of, cohabitation (e.g. Macklin, 1972), others on the factors that distinguish those people who cohabit from those who choose not to (e.g. Henze and Hudson, 1974; Yllo, 1978), whilst others attempt to understand the differences in the nature and quality of the relationships formed (e.g. commitment, Lewis *et al.*, 1977; division of labour, Stafford *et al.*, 1977; marital outcome, Newcomb and Bentler, 1980b). This chapter will argue that psychological dimensions such as commitment and satisfaction need to be placed in the broader context of relationship management, sex roles and sexual behaviour, as well as a range of individual differences (between cohabitors and non-cohabitors) in religiosity, personality, lifestyle or personal and family background. In such a way I hope to treat cohabitation not merely in terms of its incidence, or in terms of attitudes towards it, but through an examination of cohabiting as a personal relationsnip to place it in the broader context of other personal relationships, whilst yet retaining its particular flavour.

Though cohabitation is neither a modern invention nor an occurrence prevalent only in our society (Berger, 1971), it has not been widely practised by large numbers of middle class whites until recently (Macklin, 1972). From national samples it appears that between 2% and 5% of the entire population are currently cohabiting (e.g. Clayton and Voss, 1977), yet evidence from college campuses suggests that 24% of all students have at some time cohabited, not necessarily currently (Macklin, 1978a), whilst 44% of sampled students find cohabitation acceptable (Hobart, 1979). As will become clear, such complexities are occasioned in some cases, by the variety in sample types employed by different investigators (students, 20–30-year-old males nationwide in USA, all age groups. . .) and in others by methodological differences.

Issues in Cohabitation Research

By far the most significant variations among investigators of cohabiting occurs in the definition of cohabiting that they employ. Researchers have used several definitions that have ranged from the somewhat ambiguous, "Have you ever lived with someone of the opposite sex?" (Peterman *et al.*, 1974), to the strictly defined, "share a bedroom for at least four nights per week for at least three consecutive months with someone of the opposite sex" (Macklin, 1972). Cole (1976) and Clayton and Voss (1977) raised the required time together to six months, and Cole allowed no more than one separation longer than three weeks. Conceptually also there is debate about what exactly is cohabitation. Some workers feel that self-definition is an adequate criterion (although, behaviourally this would probably include a wide diversity of patterns); others contend that it is important that the couple consistently share a common residence and do not maintain separate living accommodations; and yet others feel that a common residence is not a critical factor, but rather that the couple spend the majority of their nights together. Although this is not a complete listing of all patterns that could conceivably be called cohabitation (see Cole, 1977), it does underscore the difficulties inherent in not having a standard definition that is adhered to by all researchers. For purposes of this review, cohabitation will be broadly defined as any unmarried, heterosexual couple who consistently share a common residence and regularly engage in sexual intercourse.

Typologies of cohabitation

It has long been accepted in the literature that cohabitation is not a singular entity, but rather consists of a heterogeneous collection of relationship types that have in common the structural fact of a couple living together in a sexual relationship without being married (Ridley *et al.*, 1978; Macklin, 1978a). Lumping all cohabitors together, without making important distinctions within the group about such things as expectations of the relationship, length of time together, position in the life cycle, and the function the relationship is serving, would only wash out critical differences. For example, it seems quite plausible that major differences exist between couples who cohabit as a temporary and casual lifestyle and those who cohabit as a permanent and stable substitute for marriage. These differences could include many qualities, such as characteristics of the relationship (e.g. commitment, adjustment), as well as outcome of the relationship.

Several typologies have been offered that may be helpful in conceptualizing the various forms, functions and motives of cohabitation but, unfortunately, few of these categorizations have been empirically investigated and most have been generated in the context of different sorts of samples — a fact that makes their comparability problematic. Lewis *et al.* (1977) proposed three types of cohabital relationships: temporary or casual; preparation for or trial marriage; and an alternative or substitute for marriage. They assume that each of these will have different qualities and characteristics. Alternatively, Macklin (1974) and other researchers suggest that cohabitation is an optional, new stage in the courtship sequence interposed between steady dating and marriage — an idea that seems aesthetically pleasing and has received some empirical support. For instance, Lewis *et al.* (1977) found that dyadic commitment levels, the amount of commitment for being and remaining in their relationships, were similar between cohabitors and individuals engaged to be married; and Newcomb and Bentler (1980a) found that almost one-half of their sample of married couples had cohabited before marriage. It is worth noting, however, that this structural placement of cohabitation actually meshes nicely with the Lewis *et al.* typology, if one assumes that the group that uses cohabitation as a substitute for marriage has simply truncated the typical courtship sequence by eliminating the usual end-point: marriage.

In student populations, Ridley *et al.* (1978) believe, the type of interpersonal relationship created by cohabital partners determines the quality and potential benefits of the union. Looking over their previous data (Peterman *et al.*, 1974), they propose four patterns of cohabital dynamics that appear common for students:

The first type they called *Linus Blanket*. In this relationship there is an overwhelming need for one of the partners to simply be in a relationship, no matter what or with whom — the primary goal is emotional security based upon a strong dependency need. A sound basis for the growth of interpersonal skills and competence seems minimally present in this type of relationship.

A second type they labelled *Emancipation*, which involves one or both partners being suddenly freed of parental constraints, typically by moving away to college. This pattern has been particularly noted in Catholic women who may be caught in a conflict between internalized pressures from their religious upbringing, their own needs and peer pressures (Peterman *et al.*, 1974).

A third type they termed *Convenience*. This pattern is characterized by a short duration and allows "a regularized sexual outlet and the luxuries of domestic living without the responsibilities of a committed relationship". They point our that this has the benefit of teaching important aspects of "surviving" within interpersonal relationships, even though this learning may be painful for one or both of them. Ridley *et al.* generally conclude that these three relationship types are not particularly conducive to creating a long term, highly adjusted relationship.

Their fourth type, *Testing*, has the highest potential for growth and personal development. Here, the partners are generally mature and possess a reasonably high level of interpersonal skills. One of the major conflicts will be to create a satisfying intimate relationship, while maintaining individuality and autonomy (Macklin, 1974).

These four distinctions are intriguing but are currently only speculative. It is clear that the relevant empirical testing of such a proposed typology would focus on the needs and dynamics that underlie and differentiate the formation and qualities of these cohabital types.

Cohabitation can thus no longer be considered a category unto itself but must be subdivided and analysed in terms of what distinguishes these subtypes and what function each serves in interpersonal relations. Categorizations and types are mostly speculative at this point and need greater clarification and empirical verification to be productive ways of structuring research. Once a typology has been more adequately defined and validated, detailed analyses of relationship qualities, effects and characteristics can be more readily studied.

Methodological issues

A common problem in many studies is the sample: with few exceptions only college students are used as subjects and they are frequently not selected using a probability sampling design. This situation has improved over the years so that fewer and fewer studies use convenience, *ad hoc* or pieced-together samples and this has allowed more confidence to develop in the description and understanding of cohabitation as a student phenomenon. But it is not confined to students, as several studies have shown (e.g. Clayton and Voss, 1977; Yllo, 1978) and previous studies have left possibly the majority of cohabitants largely untouched by researchers. Newcomb and Bentler (1980a) aptly point out that it would be a grave error to generalize results obtained from college samples to the general population in that students face rather unique life dilemmas that may very easily and indeterminably alter important features of cohabitation.

Although national surveys have been utilized in a couple of instances, the time and expense are usually prohibitive, and a less cumbersome way to obtain non-student samples is to use resources from a limited geographical area (e.g. Newcomb and Bentler, 1980a) but this, of course, raises the issue of introducing error by studying only a specific locale. Both methods have been used by researchers to obtain samples that will be representative of more than the student sector, and thus to broaden the data bases that have been criticized as inadequate and biased (Cole, 1977; Macklin, 1978a).

Another issue related to sample selection is the problems in using volunteers. The bias that this method introduces may be particularly prevalent when studying areas of sexuality and intimate relationships which cohabitation represents. A preliminary investigation of couples research has indicated that women are generally more interested in participating than men (Hill *et al.*, 1979). One implication of this might be that research on intimate relationships attracts a broad range of women (from traditional to liberal), but attracts a more narrow range of primarily liberal men.

A final comment on samples regards their actual size. All too frequently, samples are used with only ten or 20 couples or individuals in each criterion group. The problems with this are obvious and do not need to be dwelt upon.

Until recently, the most usual measures employed in this context were cross-sectional survey/interview type instruments to assess the quality and character of cohabitants. Whereas these techniques may be the most appropriate to evaluate areas such as attitudes towards and incidence of cohabitation, they lack the ability to delve into the more intricate personal and relational qualities that are also extremely important areas of study. To an extent, the vast array of psychological assessment devices has been ignored. Fortunately, this is changing as more sophisticated, reliable and valid instruments are being included in research designs allowing a finer and more detailed understanding of cohabitation. Even though more sophisticated tools are being used, there are still very few studies that have incorporated observational or behaviourally orientated instruments, and longitudinal data are rarely collected.

Features of Cohabitation

As noted above, much research on cohabitation is deficient conceptually because it has not treated cohabitation as a personal relationship but rather as something whose incidence should be charted and about which attitudes may be assessed. Such an emphasis overlooks the context and the dynamics which influence the formation of a cohabital relationship. However, such research cannot be entirely ignored and I shall now review such work with the intention of working towards a model of cohabitation that emphasises three stages in the development of cohabitation as a personal relationship.

Characteristics of cohabital relations

This section will address a group of studies that have looked at differences in the nature of the cohabital relationship itself, and the cohabitants' involvement in it. In most of these studies, couples who have experienced cohabitation either currently or premaritally are compared to couples who have never chosen to cohabit. Four areas that have received attention in this manner will be discussed in this section: commitment, satisfaction, sex roles and sexual behaviour.

Commitment

Perhaps the most widely investigated variable in the cohabitation literature is the concept of commitment. It is commonly assumed in other relationship research that a certain level of commitment is necessary to maintain the existence and quality of a personal relationship and it has been speculated that this critical level is not present in cohabitation since the partners have not made a legal and social declaration of their commitment, by marrying. Commitment has been looked at in three ways: (1) personal commitment or the extent to which one is invested in the pair-bond and its continuation, (2) behavioural commitment or the personal and/or peer forces that abet longevity in a relationship, e.g. negative consequences of termination, and (3) the level of desire to marry their current partner.

Budd (1976) and Johnson (1973) found that married couples reported a greater dedication to continuing their relationship, as well as more external constraints against terminating, than did cohabitors. Lewis *et al.* (1977) found that married couples reported significantly higher commitment to their relationship, and to marriage in general, than did cohabiting couples. They also compared cohabiting with engaged couples and found that the engaged group were significantly more committed to marrying their partners than the cohabiting group. (This is quite understandable in that, in a sense, this finding only reflects the definitions of the criterion groups. Engaged and cohabiting couples did *not* differ on their degree of pair-bond commitment.) Lewis *et al.* then subdivided their cohabiting sample into three groups: temporary involvement, preparation for marriage, and substitute for marriage. For both sexes, pair-bond commitment (desire to remain together) was least for those involved in a self-reported temporary involvement. Those cohabiting as a preparation for marriage had a significantly higher level of pair-bond commitment than the temporary group, and less than the substitute for marriage group.

Lewis *et al.* (1977) also looked at correlations of commitment within cohabiting, engaged and married couples. For cohabitants, four factors — happiness, homogamy, dyadic consensus and interaction — correlated with commitment and were all classified as qualitative factors. For engaged couples, length of acquaintance and mother's education correlated with commitment and were categorized as quantitative factors. Finally, commitment, in the married couples, correlated with couple happiness, length of acquaintance and father's occupation. Lewis *et al.* concluded that the stability of a relationship, as reflected in commitment levels, is primarily a function of the qualitative aspects for cohabitors, quantitative factors for engaged couples and a combination of both qualitative and quantitative components for married couples.

If we look at relative levels of commitment between partners in cohabital relationships, we find that contradictory results have been reported. Johnson (1968) and Lyness *et al.* (1972) report that males show less commitment to their relationship than do their female partners but Milardo and Murstein (1979), on the other hand, found no differences in male and female commitment levels. Milardo and Murstein suggest that researchers who have found such differences typically use a looser definition of cohabitation and as a result include couples who have spent little time together. Even if this definitional criticism was valid — which it probably is — it does not account for the sex difference early in a cohabital relationship. The explanation seems even less convincing when one considers the finding of Hill *et al.* (1976) that men tend to fall in love sooner than women. If falling in love can be loosely related to an amount of commitment, it would be expected that males would have a higher commitment level than females early in their relationship. A confounding issue in this problem is having virtually no information about how long or how far a relationship needs to have progressed before a couple decides to cohabit.

Satisfaction

The degree of intra-couple satisfaction has been examined in many ways by several researchers. When married couples are compared with cohabiting couples with regard to contentment and satisfaction, no differences have been found (Cole, 1976; Yllo, 1978). Similarly, levels of satisfaction and adjustment have been compared between married couples with and without premarital cohabitation, and again no reliable differences were found (e.g. Budd, 1976). Methods used in these studies to evaluate satisfaction have included self-report ratings (e.g. Yllo, 1978) and standard indices of marital adjustment (Newcomb and Bentler, 1980b), as well as behavioural and observational techniques (Cole, 1976).

It seems reasonable to conclude that the legal status of a relationship or whether partners have cohabited in the past has little to do with inhibiting or increasing the satisfaction of the partners. Rather, it is the quality of the relationship itself, reflected in the behaviour and defined roles of the participants, that determines the amount of happiness and adjustment each couple can achieve (Cole, 1976). Another way of stating the same idea is that the within-group differences are greater than the between-group differences and that similar processes probably create the variance in each group.

Sex roles

Since cohabitation is a new and innovative lifestyle for a large segment of the population (Macklin, 1978a), and one that attracts people with liberal attitudes (Newcomb and Bentler, 1980a), some workers hypothesize that it may be a fertile structure for androgynous and egalitarian behaviour to flourish (e.g. McCauley, 1975). This question has been addressed basically from two standpoints. The first way is to look at attitude differences between cohabitors and non-cohabitors. This has been studied by using measures of personality (e.g. Lewis and Guittar, 1974) and scales of egalitarianism (e.g. McCauley, 1975). The second method involves assessing actual behaviour either by self-report or by observation (e.g. Stafford *et al.*, 1977). With the exception of personality and attitude differences (that indicate more androgyny for cohabitors than non-cohabitors) the other methods of assessing sex role differences have revealed essentially no distinctions.

As will be presented later, Lewis and Guittar (1974) found personality differences indicating that cohabitors report counter-traditional sex role attitudes more frequently than non-cohabitors. The personality differences reported by Bower (1975) also support the notion that cohabitors exhibit more counter-traditional, androgynous attitudes than the average.

Using a bipolar scale of traditional masculinity and femininity, Newcomb and Bentler (1980a) found that women who cohabited premaritally described themselves as significantly more masculine than did women who had not

cohabited before marriage. The converse was true for men. When considering the length of cohabitation before marriage, they found that men who
cohabited longer described themselves as more feminine, while women who
cohabited longer described themselves as more masculine than those who
cohabited for a shorter length of time. All of these personality results lend a
fair amount of support to the notion that cohabitors perceive themselves as
more androgynous and counter-traditional than do non-cohabitors.

In a study that specifically assessed egalitarian attitudes, however, the
findings were inconclusive. McCauley (1975) found that while cohabitors of
both sexes subscribed to higher levels of egalitarianism than non-cohabitors,
the differences were not significant. She did find, however, that in both
groups women consistently had significantly higher levels of egalitarianism
than men. McCauley concludes that, even though cohabitation might presumably allow or foster egalitarian attitudes, this effect was not clearly found
and she fears that cohabitation may eventually be assimilated by society as
another double-standard institution.

Sex role differences have also been examined behaviourally in terms of
household activities and the division of labour. Even if more egalitarian
attitudes and androgynous personality qualities are expressed by cohabitors,
this is quite a different matter from living them in actual behaviour. Makepeace (1975), comparing cohabiting and married couples, found no significant differences in the performance of household tasks. She did find a difference based on the presence of children in the relationship. Both cohabiting
and married couples without children were more egalitarian than couples
with children. Segrest (1975) also compared cohabiting and married couples
on the basis of role expectations for doing household tasks and decision
making. She found that married couples, regardless of student status, were
more egalitarian than cohabiting couples and both groups were more
egalitarian than societal norms. Yllo (1978) found essentially no differences
on division of labour or decision-making power between cohabitors and
married couples.

Stafford et al. (1977), in a nicely designed and executed study, found that
although ". . . married couples are significantly more traditional in the
performance of household tasks than cohabiting couples, . . . they are not
different in the distribution of responsibility". In other words, both married
and cohabiting women perform the vast majority of household tasks to a
relatively equal degree. However, cohabitors more often perform cross-sex
traditional tasks (e.g. the woman mowing the lawn and the man helping with
the dishes) than is true in the married group. Overall, there were few major
distinctions between the groups. Stafford et al. proposed three hypotheses to
account for these findings: non-conscious sex-role ideology, authority, and
time available. From their data, Stafford and her colleagues concluded that

neither the time available nor the authority hypotheses account accurately for the patterns that they observed. The socialization-ideology hypothesis (Bem and Bem, 1970), which assumes that a non-conscious sex role typing maintains traditional patterns, seems to describe the results most effectively. The origins of this non-conscious ideology lie in the modelling of parents, as well as peer, school and mass media influences. Whitehurst (1974) supports this idea by contending that it is more difficult to put egalitarian attitudes into practice than simply to hold or philosophize about them. In order to maintain egalitarian roles within a relationship it is necessary constantly to reassess and examine the dyadic patterns that develop and are influenced by the non-conscious ideology and socialization. This is often a very tedious process, and frequently cohabitants find themselves slipping back into traditional sex role behaviour even though they endorse other attitudes.

Whereas the potential for deviating from traditional sex roles in both attitudes and behaviour does seem to be present, only attitudes are apparently different for cohabitors. Other factors — e.g. unconscious ideology — play an important role in maintaining traditional behavioural patterns in cohabital living. The longer a cohabital relationship endures, the more both sexes seem to move towards an androgynous role definition (Newcomb and Bentler, 1980a), but longitudinal confirmation of this trend is still required, and needs to incorporate behavioural indicators.

Sexual behaviour

Sexual behaviour has been looked at in two ways: exclusivity and specific activities. In general, cohabitors tend to have had their first intercourse experience at a younger age (Clayton and Voss, 1977; Markowski *et al.*, 1978), and to have had more sexual partners than non-cohabitors (Macklin, 1976; Markowski *et al.*, 1978).

Several studies, looking only at cohabitors, have found that between 8% and 31% have had sexual relations outside the dyad; this being more prevalent for males than females. However, it is unclear how many of the couples knew about and/or condoned this extra-couple sexual contact. Huang (1977), therefore, studied several cohabiting couples who chose to engage openly in outside sexual behaviour. These couples felt that possessiveness and jealousy are destructive forces in a relationship and that social and sexual non-exclusivity is one way to avoid these problems. On the whole, cohabitors seem to feel that sexual freedom should be available, although a large majority voluntarily choose monogamy as a reflection of their commitment to the relationship (Montgomery, 1972). Comparing married couples who had and had not cohabited premaritally, Clatworthy and Shied (1977) found that about 25% of each group had engaged in sex outside of their marriage — a figure that is about the same as for cohabiting, non-married couples.

Two studies examined specific sexual activities and reported contradictory results. Newcomb and Bentler (1980a) found a higher level of sexual experimentation and sophistication in premarital cohabitors, relative to non-cohabitors who married. The bulk of this difference was accounted for by cohabitors engaging in more oral sex behaviour, and female cohabitors being more active (e.g. initiating and performing more activities on their male partners) than couples who married without cohabiting before hand. Markowski *et al.* (1978), on the other hand, compared the sexual behaviour and attitudes of cohabiting and married couples, and found few differences. The married males were more satisfied with their first sexual intercourse experience than male cohabitors. In general, the married people were more satisfied with the majority of their intercourse experiences, had fewer group sex experiences, and were less inclined to seek an abortion than cohabiting individuals. Markowski *et al.* did not find differences between the groups regarding specific sexual activity (e.g. oral sex), which contradicts the Newcomb and Bentler (1980a) findings. However, in the Markowski *et al.* study subjects were selected so that it least one partner is or was a college student, they lived within five miles of a college campus, and they had no children nor had been previously divorced.

Characteristics of cohabitors

Currently, cohabitation is not the modal behaviour for any age group or ethnic segment of society. Since it has an aura of deviance, several investigators have tried to understand the phenomenon by studying personal and family qualities that distinguish individuals who cohabit from those who do not.

Religion

One of the most consistent findings is that cohabitors report dramatically lower religious commitment than do non-cohabitors. This finding holds whether the concept of religiosity is measured by frequency of church attendance (e.g. Clayton and Voss, 1977), scales designed to assess religious commitment, or affiliation with an organized religious system (Newcomb and Bentler, 1980a). Of particular interest is the finding that there is an over-representation of Catholics who cohabit (Henze and Hudson, 1974; Yllo, 1978). For college student samples (e.g. Henze and Hudson, 1974), this over-representation of Catholics may reflect a pattern of young college students who are experiencing their emancipation from parental and parochial control, which themselves may be more pronounced for Catholics. Supporting this idea, Lautenschlager (1972) found that cohabiting students more often perceived their parents as more strict and restrictive than those students who have not cohabited. Yllo (1978) contends that her finding a greater proportion of Catholics among cohabitors, in her non-student national sample, can be attributed to Catholic doctrines that allow only one marriage and no divorce. She suggests that this makes Catholics more wary about their one marriage, and thus they may test the relationship by cohabiting: further, since Catholics are less likely to remarry if separated, cohabitation or singlehood may be viewed as viable alternatives.

Newcomb and Bentler (1980a) found quite the opposite in their non-student sample of married couples with and without premarital cohabital experience: more non-cohabitors were Catholic or Protestant than cohabitors. This seems more intuitively consistent since religious affiliation or commitment typically has an inhibiting effect on non-marital intimate and sexual behaviour, which is an aspect of cohabitation. The couples in this sample were all married, which makes Yllo's theory that Catholics may choose to cohabit rather than remarry, not applicable in their population. On the other hand, Newcomb and Bentler noticed an over-representation of Jewish women who had cohabited, as did Yllo. They suggest that this could reflect a greater liberalism often associated with Judaism.

There seems no clear reconciliation to these apparent differences, except to conclude that each explanation may be valid in a particular context or situation. In other words pressures and motivations unique to specific populations may somehow alter the expected effects of religious affiliation when choosing to cohabit.

Personality

There is some evidence that personality differences exist between cohabitors and non-cohabitors. Lewis and Guittar (1974) found that female cohabitors described themselves as more competitive, aggressive, independent, and managerial than non-cohabiting females. Cohabiting males, on the other hand, described themselves as more emotionally dependent, less aggressive and less managerial than non-cohabiting males. Only one of these differences was statistically significant (male dependence), yet they tend to indicate that cohabitors have counter-traditional sex-role self-perceptions, relative to noncohabitors. Arafat and Yorburg (1973) found that cohabitors of both sexes described themselves as more out-going, independent and aggressive, than non-cohabitors. Bower (1975) found that male cohabitors reported more intraception and succorance than college males in general. Cohabiting women, on the other hand, had higher mean scores on autonomy, dominance and aggression than female student norms.

Using a variety of personality traits and behaviour, Newcomb and Bentler (1980a) were able to abstract two constellations of qualities that distinguished couples who had and had not cohabited premaritally. They found that cohabitors had fewer internalized constraints on their behaviour and self-perception, than non-cohabitors. This was evidenced by cohabitors being less religious and more androgynous, liberal, sexually experimental and accurately self-perceptive, than non-cohabitors. Secondly, they found that cohabitors were less inhibited in their outward transactions with society and less adherent to social norms, than non-cohabitors. This was apparent when cohabitors were found to be less style conscious, introverted and law abiding, while having more leadership qualities than non-cohabitors. These differences were found in both sexes, but were the most pronounced for the females. Unexpectedly, Newcomb and Bentler found that cohabitors of both sexes saw themselves as more attractive than non-cohabitors and that cohabiting females described themselves as more interested in art and more intelligent than did non-cohabiting females.

There seems little doubt, then, that major personality differences exist between cohabitors and non-cohabitors. Since all of these studies were cross-sectional, it is impossible to say whether these differences were caused by the cohabital experience or whether these underlying qualities were pre-existent and themselves influenced the choice to cohabit initially. Newcomb and Bentler (1980a) favour the latter possibility, in that they view the choice to cohabit as a behavioural indicator or correlate of these personality variations, and demonstrated that certain traits (e.g. androgyny) became correlationally more non-traditional the longer one cohabits.

Lifestyle

Lifestyle differences have been examined in terms of attraction to various innovative living arrangements and actual behaviour. Bower and Christopherson (1977) and Henze and Hudson (1974) found that cohabitors expressed a greater attraction to alternative lifestyles or quasi-marriage relationships (e.g. group marriage, communes) than non-cohabitors. In terms of behaviour, cohabitors report engaging in unconventional activities such as attending an outdoor rock festival, being vegetarian, studying astrology, ESP or the occult, bumming around the US or living in a commune, much more frequently than non-cohabitors (Clayton and Voss, 1977). Cohabitors also report greater use of illicit drugs, of all types, than non-cohabitors (Clayton and Voss, 1977; Henze and Hudson, 1974).

Personal and family background

Few consistent differences have been found between cohabitors and non-cohabitors in regard to family characteristics such as parental divorce, parent educational level, type of discipline and who administered it (Henze and Hudson, 1974; Newcomb and Bentler, 1980a; Yllo, 1980). Lewis and Guittar (1974) found one parent/child interactional factor to be significant: they compared engaged with cohabiting individuals on how close they felt to their parents during adolescence and found that engaged people were significantly closer to their same-sex parent, than were cohabitors. Lewis and Guittar interpret this to mean that a lack of closeness to same-sex parent may lead to less identification and effective modelling of parent behaviour by the child, and as a result s/he may choose to cohabit instead of immediately marrying.

Personal backgrounds have been studied by several researchers and have generally yielded few differences. The one exception to this is marital history. Using student samples, this important variable was logically omitted from studies since students have typically not been married and/or divorced. Yllo (1978) found that significantly more cohabitors of both sexes, had been previously divorced, compared with married couples in her national non-student sample. Newcomb and Bentler (1980a) found this to be significantly true for women in their sample, but not for men. Apparently, cohabitation is more attractive to those with a previous divorce, perhaps since it offers a testing ground before they risk another possible marital failure. Other background variables such as educational level, occupational level and previous children revealed no differences between cohabitors and non-cohabitors (Newcomb and Bentler, 1980a). Some distinctions have been found regarding age and will be discussed in the following section.

It seems clear that the choice to cohabit is probably not determined by demographic or background qualities to any large extent, except previous divorce. Many researchers have noted this lack of differences and stress the importance of studying other variables — e.g. personality and contextual factors — that may be more explanatory of cohabitation (Macklin, 1978a; Newcomb and Bentler, 1980a). However, most of these studies were conducted on college students and further substantiation is needed with more diverse populations.

Impact on marriage

Several possible effects of cohabitation upon marriage have been proposed and studied but much of this has been speculative.

A few studies have compared married couples on the basis of whether they had or had not cohabited premaritally but unfortunately, only one of these studies was longitudinal, and that one only followed the couples from the time they got married. This is clearly an area that needs more research.

Based on clinical, anecdotal or experiential information, opinions vary on how cohabitation influences a subsequent marriage. Some people feel the effects will be negative; Urie Bronfenbrenner suspects that cohabitation will undermine the basic family structure by allowing the avoidance of the commitment, responsibility and obligation that are necessary to make a relationship work. He fears that this pattern, developed as a consequence of cohabiting, will continue in marriage and the couple will suffer as a result (Schwartz, 1977). Harper (1975) contends that cohabitation has certain attractions (such as rebellion against parents and society, ease of termination, and avoidance of parenthood) that would disappear once married, and thus may cause disruption in the relationship if and when they do marry.

Others feel that cohabitation can have a positive and beneficial effect on a subsequent marriage. One of the most common beliefs is that cohabitation can be a screening device, to test the compatibility of the partners and quality of the relationship, before deciding to marry (Danziger, 1976). Some workers contend that cohabitation offers a unique opportunity to develop interpersonal skills and competence in an intimate relationship that is not provided in either traditional educational practices or courtship patterns in this society (Peterman, 1975; Peterman et al., 1974). To the extent that this individual maturation and development can occur during cohabitation, a subsequent marriage should be positively affected.

These speculations raise the question of what type of change a relationship undergoes when a couple moves from cohabitation to marriage. Unfortunately, this is an important area that research has barely touched. Berger (1974), using a retrospective analysis of 21 couples, concluded that the quality of a relationship remained largely unchanged in the transition from cohabitation to marriage but in contrast to this, Keaough (1975) found that couples felt a pressure to adopt traditional roles and as a result experienced a loss of identity. Although marriage may increase commitment and foster greater acceptance by relatives and society, it may also bring more role playing, possessiveness, and a reduced sense of independence and autonomy. Some might wonder if this is a fair exchange.

Even more basic is the totally unanswered question of what motivates a cohabiting couple to decide to marry: the reasons given for changing the status of their relationship may be an important factor in predicting how the marriage will eventually turn out. Some workers suspect that cohabitors decide to marry when they want to have children but this was not supported by the Newcomb and Bentler (1980b) study. They found that cohabitors who married produced significantly fewer children during their first four years of marriage than married couples who did not cohabit. However, this should be viewed in relation to the finding of Bower and Christopherson (1977) that cohabitors planned to have fewer children in their lifetime, than non-cohabitors.

Some researchers have observed the drastic reduction in marriage rates and the concomitant increase in non-marital cohabitation in Sweden (Trost, 1978), and fear that this may also be occurring elsewhere; but it seems that the vast majority — over 90% — of all cohabitors do plan to marry sometime in their life (Bower and Christopherson, 1977; Macklin, 1976; McCauley, 1977), so there is little basis for the fear that large portions of society will choose permanent cohabitation as a substitute for marriage. What has been found is that cohabitors plan to marry at a significantly older age than non-cohabitors (Bower and Christopherson, 1977), and this has been borne out in the findings of Newcomb and Bentler (1980a) and Olday (1977). Rather than reducing the overall rate of marriage or percentage of couples who are married, cohabitation may only delay marriage to a later point in life, as trends indicate younger people are doing in general (Glick, 1975).

To date, only one research project has longitudinally followed a sample of couples through their first several years of marriage, and then compared the outcomes of these marriages in terms of whether or not they had cohabited premaritally (Bentler and Newcomb, 1978). Overall, there was no significant difference between divorce rates of premarital cohabitors (36%) and married couples who did not cohabit (26%). Either the speculations discussed earlier have little validity, or else the positive and negative influences cancel out, since there is no apparent difference in divorce rates. Perhaps Whitehurst (1974) is correct when he contends that ''. . . the crucial factors making for long-term stability or instability are structural and essentially beyond the ability of persons to control . . .''

Upon closer examination of the Newcomb and Bentler (1980b) data, some interesting patterns emerge. Although there was no difference on marital satisfaction between the groups, cohabitors who divorced did so while reporting significantly greater marital adjustment, than non-cohabitors who divorced. This is consistent with the finding of Cole (1976) that cohabitors perceived fewer barriers to terminating their relationship, than non-cohabitors, and apparently, this quality is carried into marriage. Newcomb and Bentler interpret this to mean that the cohabitors had less commitment and motivation to continue their marriage in the face of difficulties and/or did not want to allow the relationship to deteriorate to great depths, by sticking it out. The cohabitors may have divorced more amicably and with less interpersonal devastation than non-cohabitors.

Newcomb and Bentler also examined the longitudinal predictability of marital success, for cohabitors and non-cohabitors, using a variety of personality and background variables assessed at the beginning of each marriage. Using the same set of six predictor variables in multiple regression analyses, they found that the cohabitor equation predicted marital success significantly more effectively than the non-cohabitor equation. Further, none of the six variables had a similar direction of influence in both groups. For example, age was positively related to marital success for the cohabitors but had virtually no predictive power for the non-cohabitors. Previous divorce, on the other hand, had a positive influence for cohabitors and a negative effect for non-cohabitors. Even though cohabitors are typically less traditional than non-cohabitors, the more traditional they were, relative to their own group, the better marriage they had in terms of several variables — and the converse was true for non-cohabitors. Apparently, cohabitation alters or is reflective of vast differences in the way certain variables predict marital success, and marital outcome is not as simple as the similar divorce rates would lead one to believe.

Several researchers have tried to determine whether married couples had greater or less difficulty with specific problem areas depending on whether or not they had cohabited premaritally. Olday (1977) examined conflict and emotional closeness and found no differences between her two married groups. Although noting many similarities, Budd (1976) found that cohabitors were more concerned with loss of love; they felt trapped and seemed to have poorer communication methods than non-cohabitors.

Clatworthy and Shied (1977) also found many similarities, in addition to some important differences. In regard to conflict, they found that cohabitors more frequently disagreed on responsibility for household tasks and choice of recreational pursuits, were less dependent on their mates and more tenacious in arguments than were non-cohabitors. In terms of their marriage, cohabitors had broken up more often, sought counselling more often, and considered marriage a less important part of their life than did non-cohabitors.

Newcomb and Bentler (1980b) examined 19 potential problem areas and found seven differences. Premarital cohabitors reported greater difficulty coping with adultery, attention being given to an outside person, alcohol, drug abuse and independence, compared to couples who had not cohabited premaritally. On the other hand, career conflicts and constant bickering were relatively greater problems for non-cohabitors. Macklin (1978a) points out that these differences may be due to pre-existent personality and attitude differences, rather than the actual experience of cohabitation. With the type of data available currently, it is impossible to determine for certain whether these differences were actually caused by cohabitation or were only reflected by it.

Cohabitation as a Personal Relationship

Cohabitation is a type of intimate relationship and as such has features that are important in the understanding of any relationship. For example, all relationships have a beginning, but the antecedents of initial attraction may differ in different types of relationship, and so may the manner in which different types of relationship emerge as realities for the partners. Importantly, the manner in which a relationship emerges probably determines to a large extent the nature and enduring qualities of that dyad. In addition, relationships are not accidentally chosen, but reflect the personality, expectations, and needs of the individuals involved. In this section, therefore, I shall present and discuss theory and data bearing upon the formation, nature and qualities of the cohabital dyad, and influences on its persistence.

The choice to cohabit

Why some people choose to live together without being married and others do not is an interesting and pivotal question that, surprisingly, cohabitors themselves frequently do not address. In one study, only 25% of cohabiting students discussed whether they would cohabit before actually doing so (Macklin, 1974). Although this lack of expressed forethought may be most prevalent among young college students, it is perhaps illustrative of a more general ambivalence or associated with engaging in a new, deviant and not totally accepted type of behaviour.

Macklin (1978a), presenting the general thinking of the Groves Conference cohabitation research group on the formation of a cohabital dyad, proposed two critical factors in the progression to cohabitation: perceived opportunity to cohabit and willingness to act on that opportunity. Within each of these factors are several important variables. The degree to which a person perceived the opportunity to cohabit is influenced by the availability of partners and living accommodations that allow cohabitors; social and peer norms and behaviour; removal from social control agents (e.g. parents); and interpersonal attractiveness. Assuming these conditions are favourable to cohabitation, an individual can then decide whether s/he will avail him/herself of the opportunity. This willingness factor is influenced by religious commitment, personality, previous sexual and dating experience, and affection and desire to be with their partner.

The two constellations of personality traits, presented by Newcomb and Bentler (1980a), fit interestingly into this framework. They found that cohabitors were less adherent to social values and less inhabited in their dealings with the world than were non-cohabitors. In other words, they would perceive the opportunity to cohabit more easily and readily, since they are less influenced by those factors that limit opportunity. Cohabitors were also found to have fewer internal constraints on their self-perception and behaviour, which would make them avail themselves of the opportunity to cohabit more frequently than non-cohabitors. Clatworthy's (1975) hypothesis also fits into this opportunity/willingness framework: she proposed that the degree of social disapproval (opportunity) and amount of guilt (willingness), affects whether a person will choose to cohabit or not.

Cole (1977) and Newcomb and Bentler (1980a) tried to explain why some choose to cohabit, and others do not, within social exchange theory (Scanzoni, 1972). Newcomb and Bentler found that cohabitors perceived themselves as having significantly more positive characteristics (e.g. attractive, intelligent, out-going, aesthetic appreciation), than do non-cohabitors. It is possible that these positively valued traits in cohabitors may make them more careful and choosy about committing themselves to a partner by marriage. Perhaps, cohabitation serves to delay marital commitment, allowing time to determine whether these positive qualities will be adequately compensated and reciprocated by their partner. On the other hand, non-cohabitors who see themselves as having fewer of these positive qualities may not want to risk the uncertainty of cohabiting, and may prefer to marry immediately. Milardo and Murstein (1979) studied 20 cohabiting couples and found that the degree of exchange orientation was inversely related to happiness and commitment within that relationship. In other words, the more a cohabiting couple defines their relationship in exchange principles the more difficulty they will experience in feeling content and satisfied in that relationship. So, as with other pairbonds, it is the mutual expectations for the relationship that largely determine the quality of the union, rather than the structural context (e.g. cohabitation versus marriage). However, the type of structure may attract people with similar personalities, expectations and values, as suggested by Newcomb and Bentler (1980a).

The nature of the dyad

The next area that theorists have begun to address is the dynamic characteristics that may make a cohabital relationship different from other dating, engaged or married couples. The theories and conclusions of Stafford *et al.* (1977) (finding no differences in the division of labour between cohabiting and married couples) have already been discussed, although they would appropriately fit in here, too.

Montgomery (1973) feels that cohabitors need more dyadic commitment or "internally generated cohesion" to remain intact than do marrieds. He bases this on the assumption that cohabitors have few external unifier and many external disrupters that act against the relationship, compared to married couples. He concludes that steady increases in commitment are needed for a cohabital relationship to survive, and further, each of these steps toward more commitment by one partner needs to be reciprocated by the other.

In a similar vein, Cole (1976) used a social learning framework to hypothesize that if partners are experiencing satisfaction in their relationship (a high ratio of pleasing to displeasing behaviour), continuance of the union would be attributed to internal attractions and factors in the relationship. Conversely, if dissatisfaction is felt, persistence of the relationship would be attributed to externally perceived termination barriers. They found that satisfaction was related to the number of perceived barriers to termination for both cohabitors and non-cohabitors. In addition, cohabitors reported significantly fewer termination barriers, than married couples. This would predict that cohabitors who experience distress, would separate more readily than married couples having the same level of dissatisfaction. Married couples have more external unifiers, than do cohabitors and these are likely to prevent divorce until a high level of discomfort and dissatisfaction are felt. Another way of looking at this would be that cohabitors would separate while experiencing higher levels of adjustment than marrieds who divorce. These were exactly the findings of Newcomb and Bentler (1980b), although their sample contained only married couples, with and without premarital cohabitation. This indicates that cohabitors, even when they marry, perceive fewer barriers to the termination of their relationship than do married couples who did not cohabit. One is also reminded of the finding of Clatworthy and Shied (1977) that cohabitors who married considered their marriage a less intrinsic part of their life than did married couples who did not cohabit.

Delora and Delora (1975) attempted to test a theory that related cohabitants' satisfaction to the structure of their relationship. They assumed that the cohabital relationship can be viewed as a two-person social system that falls on a structural continuum that ranges from *Gemeinschaft* to *Gesellschaft* (Tonnies, 1957). *Gemeinschaft*-like relationships are characterized by having diffuse and emotional objectives, and close, egalitarian contact, while *Gesellschaft*-like systems have more specific and rational objectives, are unequal in authority, and have little close contact. They suspect that a *Gesellschaft*-like system may be similar to contract cohabitation (Van Deusen, 1974). They found consistent support that *Gemeinschaft*-like cohabital relationships were the most satisfying for the partners. They also concluded that, in general, most cohabital relationships are *Gemeinschaft* in nature.

Persistence of the dyad

Factors that allow for the continuance or perpetuation, and those that lead to dissolution, of the cohabital relationship, have also been theorized about and examined. Hennon (1975) feels that conflict management plays a vital role in the maintenance of the cohabital dyad. All pair-bond relationships are systems in conflict, and the manner in which this conflict is handled will decide whether the dyad will dissolve or be enhanced. Hennon offers three, as yet uninvestigated, ways in which conflict could function as a consequence of cohabitation. Perhaps, since cohabitors cannot take their relationship for granted as much as married couples, they may be more sensitized to areas of disagreement and how these are dealt with. On the other hand, cohabitors may be less secure in their relationship, and feel that it is more fragile than if they were married, and thus may be less willing to disclose or confront areas of disagreement. The other possibility that Hennon entertains is that cohabitors may be in a romantic stage and thus tend to minimize and distort real conflict. The scant evidence bearing on these possibilities indicates that cohabitors who marry may have poorer communication tactics (e.g. walking out or refusing to talk) than marrieds who had not cohabited (Budd, 1976).

Ganson (1975) found that cohabitors who separated did so for reasons that involved infringement on personal freedom and incompatibility. He found, as did Hill *et al.* (1976) in regard to cohabiting and non-cohabiting couples, that women felt more dissatisfied, or saw a greater degree of difficulty in their relationship when separating than men. Ganson feels that women may be more emotionally involved, and typically give up more autonomy, than men, when in a relationship. If cohabital relationships are as traditional and sex-biased as some studies indicate, a liberated and independent woman would have difficulty adjusting to cohabitation or marriage, and might feel trapped or hemmed-in. Hill *et al.* contend that since a woman's social status is largely dependent on the man she chooses, rather than vice versa, she needs to be extremely evaluative of the man she is with and the relationship she is in.

A final theory regarding the continuance of a cohabital relationship is offered by Newcomb and Bentler (1980b). They suggest that while, generally, non-traditional couples cohabit, it is a degree of traditionality that keeps the couple together. If a cohabiting couple are too extreme in their non-traditionalism, they run the risk of moving into areas where there is no sociocultural precedent or support, and thus have no guideline about how to integrate their deviant qualities interpersonally. Within a particular context, for a cohabital relationship to endure and succeed in the traditional sense relatively traditional qualities and characteristics of the partners may very well be essential.

A Theoretical Perspective on Cohabitation

Theoretical development and hypothesis testing have lagged far behind the accumulation of interesting data and facts on cohabitation. When theories are offered (which has been extremely rare) they are for the most part explanations for pieces of data, focusing on a small segment of the cohabital phenomenon. Several of these incipient theoretical formulations were presented in the previous section. In an effort to provide a more broad and inclusive theoretical structure to understand the various facets of cohabitation, a new model will be offered in this section that can integrate several of the other mini-theories, as well as highlighting areas for future research. This model is not being advanced as a finished product, but rather as a beginning that will undoubtedly need confirmation and extensive modification to determine its usefulness, validity, and viability. The components of the model have been drawn from the research literature already presented in this chapter.

Figure 1 graphically illustrates the general structure of the model. Three stages or phases of the cohabitation process are identified as essential to understanding the phenomenon. Each of these stages will be briefly presented, including the broad factors affecting each phase. More detailed discussion of the influencing factors at each stage will follow.

The first stage is the *choice of relationship form*. Cohabitation is only one of several types of relationships that can be chosen by a person and a couple to meet their intimacy needs at a particular time. It is important to determine what factors influence the choice to cohabit as opposed to other options. Only three other relationship choices are considered aside from cohabitation. These three — singlehood, dating, and marriage — are offered as alternative examples and are certainly not exhaustive of the possibilities. The many influences affecting the decision to choose cohabitation as a relationship form can be subsumed under three factors: contextual, individual, and dyadic. Each of these factors helps to determine and understand why someone would choose to cohabit, rather than engaging in any of the other personal relationship types. Presumably each of the factors directly influences the choice to cohabit. However, it is also hypothesized that the contextual and individual levels are reciprocally influential (indicated by the two-headed arrow between them), while the individual factor directly affects the dyadic factor (single-headed arrow).

The second stage in the model, following the choice to cohabit, is the *nature or quality of the cohabital relationship*. In other words, this is a descriptive phase rather than a transition point which characterizes the choice to cohabit, and will lead to the outcome of the relationship stage. It is assumed that the factors affecting the choice to cohabit also influence and create the characteristics of the cohabital dyad; since, as pointed out earlier in this chapter, the beginning of a relationship has a major impact upon the subsequent nature of that relationship. However, there are several contextual and individual variables that have their most direct influence on the qualities and characteristics of the dyad, as indicated in the Figure.

The third and final segment of the model attempts to understand and explain the *possible outcomes of a cohabital relationship*. The relatively exhaustive and mutually exclusive set of outcomes are marriage, continue cohabitation, and termination of the relationship. Again, as in the choice of relationship form, there are three sets of factors that affect and determine the outcome of the relationship. These broad factors of variables are the contextual, individual, and dyadic influences.

This model attempts to account for and explain two decision points

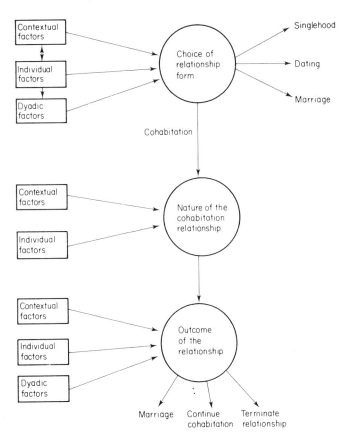

FIG. 1   Model of cohabitation process.

(choice to cohabit and outcome of cohabitation) in terms of three general influencing factors: the context, individual variables, and characteristics of the couple. The model also addresses the nature of the cohabital dyad by hypothesizing the influence of individual and contextual variables, as well as at least the individual and dyadic factors that determined the choice to cohabit. The following three sections will examine in greater detail each of the three segments of the model in the light of the factors impinging upon each segment. Many of the variables included and discussed in each factor are drawn from the information already presented in this chapter. Other variables are speculative and will need verification in future research.

Choice of relationship form

Table I delineates several of the possible variables under each of the three factors influencing the decision to choose cohabitation as a relationship form. The items are generally worded in a manner that reflects support for the choice of cohabitation. Contextual factors are hypothesized to have an influence on the individual factors, and vice versa. For example, individual attitude changes can be reflected in societal mores, while social attitudes can affect personal attitudes. The individual factors are hypothesized to affect the dyadic factor uni-directionally. For example, a certain amount of heterosexual competence is necessary to develop and maintain a close, intimate, and loving relationship. Although it is also true that being in a romantic relationship can have a profound affect upon increasing one's heterosexual competence, this would occur over a longer time-scale than represented in this segment of the model. However, this does illustrate the tentative nature of this model and emphasizes the need for more solid research to determine and verify specific pathways of influence.

Contextual factors

Contextual factors include all the influences that are external to the individuals and dyad, but still bear upon the decision to cohabit or not. Economic variables include Social Security payments to the elderly that encourage cohabitation rather than marriage, as well as a lack of dependence on parent financial support, since such support could be withdrawn as a sign of disapproval for cohabiting. The main legal concern is that cohabitation is still considered a crime in several US states, although these statutes are rarely, if ever, enforced (King, 1975). Opportunity to cohabit includes the availability and proximity of willing partners and, for students, the restrictiveness of dorm regulations and university policy. Peer and parent attitudes and

TABLE I   Model of cohabitation process: factors influencing choice of relationship form

Contextual factors	Individual factors	Dyadic factors
Economic	*Background*	*Sexual*
Social Security payments	Previous divorce	Satisfaction
Independence from	Parental divorce	Confidence
parental support	Generally younger	
	Lack of closeness	
	to same-sex parent	*Affective*
Legal		Support
Some laws	*Personality*	Expression
forbid cohabitation	Need for independence	
	Low religious	
	commitment	*General happiness with the*
		relationship
Opportunity	Comfort with ambiguity	
	and change	
Available partners	Low inhibition and	
Dorm regulations	adherence to external	
	constraints	*Companionate goals*
		Meeting emotional needs
	Attitudes	Companionship
Parental attitudes and	Willingness to engage in	
influences	alternative lifestyles	Love
	Liberal views	
Peer attitudes and		
influences		*Exchange orientation*
	Sexual experience	
Social Climate	Many partners	
High divorce rate	Early first sexual	
	intercourse experience	
Extended adolescence		
Need for advanced	*Heterosexual competence*	
education	*and attractiveness*	
Societal attitudes		
Feminist movement		
More premissive sexual		
mores		
Easier access to		
contraception		
Greater tolerance for		
alternative lifestyles		
Distance from control		
agents,		
e.g. parents		

influences are also major contextual determinants in the decision to cohabit or not. The greater the distance from social control agents, such as parents, the greater the likelihood of cohabitation. Finally, broad societal changes affect the choice to cohabit in terms of social climate (high divorce rate, extended adolescence, and need for advanced education) and societal attitudes (e.g. feminist movement, more permissive sexual mores). All of these factors, and probably others, create a relatively favourable context or environment regarding the choice to cohabit or not.

Individual factors

Reciprocally influenced by the context variables, the individual variables play a crucial role in the choice of relationship form. Background variables such as previous divorce, parental divorce, being generally younger, and a lack of closeness to one's same-sex parent help predispose a person to cohabit. In terms of personality, need for independence, low religious commitment and inhibitions, and comfort with ambiguity and change allow a person to be attracted to cohabitation as a relationship alternative. Liberal views and a willingness to engage in alternative lifestyles are attitudes that would lead one to cohabit. Early and more extensive sexual experience are also reflected in the choice to cohabit. Finally, an individual needs at least a minimal level of interpersonal competence and attractiveness to initiate and maintain a meaningful heterosexual relationship, which is a prerequisite for cohabiting.

Dyadic factors

Partly determined by the individual variables, the dyadic variables' contribution to the choice to cohabit lie in the establishment of a close, satisfying, and intimate relationship. In other words, a couple generally need to feel happy, and emotionally and sexually fulfilled in the relationship before considering cohabitation. However, the need for equity and exchange orientation are relatively more prevalent for cohabitors than other heterosexual couples (Milardo and Murstein, 1979), which has been suggested as an influence on the choice to cohabit (Cole, 1977; Newcomb and Bentler, 1980a).

Nature of the relationship

Once cohabitation has been chosen as a relationship form by a couple, various influences come into play in determining the characteristics of that relationship. Table II shows the contextual and individual variables influencing the dyadic qualities, as well as a description of the dyadic characteristics.

Clearly, the factors involved in choosing to cohabit also help to determine the nature of the relationship but need not be repeated here.

TABLE II   Model of cohabitation process: factors influencing the nature of the cohabital relationship

Contextual factors	Individual factors	Dyadic description
Traditional sex-role values	*Non-traditional sex-role attitudes and personality*	*Sexual* exclusive
Model of marriage	*Belief in social and sexual non-exclusivity as an ideal*	greater range of activities
Lack of total acceptance and place in society	*Needs and desires for validation and contact external to the relationship*	*Conflict negotiation*
Pressure to "legitimize" relationship by marriage		*Internally generated cohesion because of lack of external unifiers*
		Focus on qualitative aspects Happiness, homogamy, dyadic concensus, posiiive interaction
		Maintenance functions Sex-typed behaviours Non-conscious sex-role ideology Sharing of finances *Marital processes* Happiness Adjustment Problems

Contextual factors

Only a few other additional context variables are prominent in defining the character of the dyad, as opposed to the choice to cohabit. Society offers and reinforces traditional sex-roles and attitudes, as well as only offering traditional marital roles for a heterosexual couple living together. Although there is increasing acceptance by society of alternative lifestyles, this acceptance remains relative and cohabitation is not broadly considered as an ideal, and thus there are varying degrees of pressure to "legitimize" the relationship by marriage.

Individual factors

Persons who cohabit generally have egalitarian attitudes and relatively androgynous sex-role identities and personality traits. They often have a strong belief in social and sexual non-exclusivity as an ideal in their relationships. As a result, they allow and condone needs for validation, meaning, and fulfilment external to and independent of the relationship.

Dyadic description

All of the above-mentioned variables affect to differing, and as yet undetermined, degrees the character and qualities of the cohabital relationship. In terms of sexual behaviour, the majority of cohabiting couples are exclusive, even though they profess to the ideal of non-exclusivity. They typically choose monogamy as a behavioural sign of commitment to the relationship. On the other hand, their own sexual behaviours are more diverse than other heterosexual couples. Some researchers have speculated that conflict negotiation may be different in cohabiting, and in other, couples (Hennon, 1975), although the specific nature of these differences will need to be addressed by future research. For example, some data suggest that cohabitors avoid issues and do not solve difficulties as effectively as other couples. On the other hand, Hennon (1975) suggests that since the relationship cannot be taken for granted (at least not as much as a married couple), cohabitors may have a heightened awareness and sensitivity to their conflicts and the methods they employ to resolve them. Since cohabitors do not have many external unifiers to their relationship (e.g. a marriage contract), they need to generate internal cohesion to remain stable (Montgomery, 1973). One way to do this is to focus on the qualitative aspects of the relationship. Compared to engaged and married couples, the stability or cohesion of a cohabital relationship is determined by qualitative concerns such as happiness, homogamy, dyadic consensus (agreement on couple concerns), and positive and rewarding interactions (Lewis *et al.*, 1977). However, many of the processes observed in married couples also exist in cohabiting couples. For example, they face similar problems, share finances and recreational pursuits, have similar levels of happiness, and experience similar levels of distress if the couple separates. In addition, in spite of their egalitarian attitudes and androgynous personalities, cohabitors generally have sex-typed behaviour patterns in the performance of household duties. The context factors seem to have over-ridden the individual factors, through the strength of the non-conscious sex-role ideology imparted and modelled by the contextual influences.

Outcome of the relationship

Once a cohabitation relationship is formed, there are three outcomes that could come about: marriage, continued cohabitation, and termination of the relationship. Contextual, dyadic, and individual factors can affect these outcomes in different ways, depending upon the direction of their influence. These factors and how they affect the possible outcomes are presented in Table III.

Marriage

The contextual factors that would encourage a cohabiting couple to marry include a general pressure to marry from peers, parents, and society, a greater acceptance of marriage, and less prejudicial practices (e.g. some landlords will rent to married couples but not cohabiting couples). In addition, married couples have an accepted nomenclature and referents (i.e. husband, wife) that cohabitors do not have. Individual factors that could motivate cohabitors to decide to marry include the fact that most cohabitors do want to marry sometime in their lives, a need for security and to settle down, and a need to eliminate the tensions between lifestyle and religious upbringing and beliefs, even if these are weak. Dyadic factors conducive to marriage include a desire to have children, a need to increase behavioural commitment that is largely based on a greater certainty in the endurance of the relationship, and the couple's need for greater stability and reliance on the relationship. Each of these variables would help influence a cohabiting couple to decide to marry.

Continue cohabitation

Increased acceptance, or at least tolerance, for cohabitation by peers, parents and society could help allow the relationship to continue as is. The high divorce rate might make happy cohabiting couples fearful of marriage, while there may be some peer pressure to remain non-traditional and marriage might "sell out" their aura of deviance. These are some of the contextual factors that would lead to the continuation of a cohabital relationship. Among the individual variables that tend to lead to the continuance of the relationship as it is are a certain enjoyment of non-traditionalism, fear of commitment, resistance to change, and indecision regarding one's future. Some personality traits for males and females also motivate a couple toward

Table III   Model of cohabitation process: factors influencing the outcome
of the relationship

Outcome	Contextual factors	Individual factors	Dyadic factors
Marriage	Pressure to marry from peers, parents, society Greater acceptance if married Prejudice against cohabitors e.g. from potential landlords Lack of appropriate nomenclature	Eventual desire to marry Need to settle down Need for greater security Desire for congruity with religious beliefs and upbringing	Desire for children Need to increase behavioural commitment Increased certainty in the viability of the relationship Need for increased security and interdependency
Continue Cohabitation	Increased acceptance by peers, parents, society High divorce rate Pressure to remain non-traditional	Enjoy non-traditionalism Fear of commitment Resistant to change Undecided about future Males: secure, androgynous, low vulnerability, self-sufficient Females: intelligent, androgynous, sophisticated, liberal, self-sufficient	Satisfied with relationship Increasing reciprocal commitment No desire for children Mutual comfort as is
Termination	Parents vehemently against relationship Peers need for attention Alternative attractions Lack of support for non-traditionality	Infringement on freedoms Female: feels too dependent on partner Dissatisfaction Need for change	Unhappiness Fewer perceived barriers to ending relationship Incompatibility Stagnation Inability for traditionalism, interdependence, support Over-dependence

a lengthy cohabitation, as shown in Table III, and are generally qualities of self-sufficiency and androgyny. Dyadic factors encouraging the continuation of cohabitation include mutual satisfaction with the relationship as is, no immediate desire for children, and a process of increasing reciprocal commitment without the immediate need for marriage as a sign of that commitment. Each of these factors helps motivate a cohabiting couple to continue cohabiting and discourage any major changes in the relationship.

Termination

Contextual variables that would mediate the break-up of a cohabital relationship include parents vehemently against the relationship, friends' need for greater attention, alternative attractions (e.g. other sexual partners, a job in a different city), as well as a general lack of support for non-traditionalism and alternative lifestyles. Among the individual variables are infringement of freedom, dissatisfaction with partner, need for change, and, particularly for females, a sense of becoming too dependent on their partners. Cohabitors perceive fewer barriers to the termination of their relationship than married couples, which would allow them to end the relationship more readily if they felt unhappy, incompatible, or stagnated in the relationship. The couple may also feel over dependent on each other and terminate the relationship to find their own support and self-sufficiency. Finally, for a relationship to endure, a certain acceptance of traditional qualities is necessary (e.g. interdependency, mutual support), and if cohabitors are too non-traditional in such areas they may be incapable of responding to each other in these important ways and the stability of the relationship may weaken to the point of termination. All of these factors would encourage a cohabiting couple to break up rather than marry or continue their relationship.

Summary of the model

This model has been presented in a very broad and inclusive manner with no particular type of cohabital relationship implied (for example, only certain subsets of variables may be important to a specific type of cohabitation; or they may have differential importance) but it does indicate areas for future research and theoretical refinement. It may be necessary to include only certain variables or different weightings in the general structure of the model to account for variations in cohabital types. The model may be useful in conceptualizing the possible variables and influences that are specific to a particular cohabital type.

One of the main advantages of the model is that it attempts to account for many facets of the process of cohabitation, including decision points and description of the relationship, under one omnibus structure. Within this overall theoretical framework, it is possible to place other theories that address a smaller segment of the process, such as exchange orientation applied to the choice of cohabitation (Cole, 1977), and Levinger's (1979) social psychological perspective applied to the dissolution of the marital couple. Clearly, greater refinement and definition will make the model more viable, although as it stands it accounts reasonably well for many important features of cohabitation. As such, it may stimulate more directed and focused research, which in this area of study has been sorely lacking. It is no longer acceptable simply to collect interesting data and facts on cohabitation: it is now important to integrate and develop a broader and deeper understanding of the phenomenon. Future research needs to be precise and clear regarding its conceptualization of the questions and underlying hypotheses being investigated. A model such as that presented here should be a useful guide and heuristic tool in advancing this future work.

Cohabitation in the Context of Personal Relationships

Cohabitation is one type of intimate personal relationship, and as such has some qualities similar to other personal relationships, while possessing other unique qualities that differentiate it from other types of relationships. Macklin (1974) temporally or sequentially places cohabitation between steady dating and marriage, while Libby (1977) conceptualizes the characteristics of cohabitation falling between the needs of singlehood and marriage. The qualities of singlehood that make it an attractive alternative for some people include the fact that one can exercise relative autonomy and independence over a diversity of personal areas in one's life (Libby, 1977). For example, a single person has relative financial, sexual, and emotional independence, as well as having the major determination as to how s/he spends his/her time. Complementary with these autonomous qualities of singlehood, Kieffer (1977) suggests that a person's need for intimacy cannot be met by only one other person or one relationship. Rather, intimacy needs can be met most fully by a variety or "patchwork" of friendships and relationships (cf. La Gaipa's chapter, this Volume, p.67). Among the traditional lifestyle options, only singlehood allows for this divergent approach to meeting intimacy needs, since the relative independence of this lifestyle encourages, or at least makes acceptable, a person having a variety of intimate and/or personal relationships. On the other hand, marriage is traditionally defined as a closed, self-sufficient unit, where all of the social, emotional, and sexual needs of the partners are supposed to be met within the relationship (Whitehurst, 1977). Whether this is an actual possibility is debatable, but for many people it is conceptually and experientially distasteful, repugnant, or dissatisfying (McMurtry, 1977; Roy and Roy, 1977).

There appears to be a growing realization that not all of one's personal needs for intimacy, validation, and self-esteem can be met entirely as a member of one interdependent couple. Furthermore, there is a trend for people to deemphasize the crucial importance of a primary relationship in providing fulfilment and meaning in one's life. For example, the role of housewife has become too narrow and restrictive for many women to feel a sense of self-worth, self-esteem, and self-confidence. They are finding that they need to look beyond their primary relationship (marriage) in order to meet these needs. This does not indicate that primary or monogamous relationships have lost their meaning, only that people are realizing that they can receive or gain self-worth and personal validation from other sources as well.

For many individuals, and particularly young people or divorced persons, a compromise needs to be made. On the one hand, they want to retain the autonomous and independent qualities of singlehood, while on the other hand wanting the emotional and sexual closeness and companionship of marriage. Cohabitation seems to offer this unique combination of qualities to many individuals. Cohabitation is a type of personal relationship where there is intense intimacy, sexuality, and emotional closeness, in many ways similar to marriage, but also where individual independence and autonomy are strictly respected, as in singlehood. It is this quest for interdependence, and at the same time independence, that has made cohabitation viable for many people. One can maintain a sense of individualism, while enjoying the intimacy, sexuality, and emotional contact and support of a close, hetero-sexual relationship. But unlike Libby's (1977) conception of cohabitation, where he hypothesized a high degree of sexual non-exclusivity, most cohabital relationships are sexually monogamous. Their need for indepen-dence and intimacy respects non-exclusivity as an ideal, but rarely carries it through as a fact. In other words, cohabitors' need for autonomy and inde-pendence is not primarily an excuse for infidelity, as some opponents of cohabitation suggest.

This conceptualization or characterization of cohabitation is appropriate for only certain types of cohabital relationships. For example, it does not exemplify the elderly couple who cohabit because of economic inequities in the US Social Security system. Nor does it represent the major underlying determinants that create the Linus Blanket or Emancipation types of student cohabitation described by Ridley *et al.* (1978), although in many ways it serves a similar function and is descriptive of a similar pattern. For example, even though the Emancipation pattern of student cohabitation is motivated by a strong reaction to the removal of oppressive parental control, the relationship remains a compromise between the personal fulfilments of marriage and the autonomy aspects of singlehood, without the finality and long-term commitment implied by marriage. So, the conceptualization of cohabitation as a means of gaining the best of both worlds of the advantages of marriage and singlehood without the long-term commitment of matrimony, seems applicable to many types of cohabital relationships, at least at some levels of analysis.

When and if cohabitors do marry, their marriages often reflect the compromises involved in cohabitation. There is obviously an increment in commitment, but frequently the basic structure of the relationship remains the same. Apparently, non-traditional qualities are carried into marriage, as evidenced when these marriages are compared to marriages not preceded by cohabitation. For example, married couples who cohabited premaritally have greater difficulty with their negotiation of independence, see their marriage as a less central focus of their lives, and have greater difficulty integrating external interests, than married couples who did not cohabit premaritally. Obviously the balance of independence (singlehood) and interdependence (close relationship or marriage) is not an easy one to find and may involve a constant or intermittent struggle, negotiation, and re-evaluation of the relationship.

For most people, cohabitation is not a permanent or lifelong alternative to marriage. It allows a person to enjoy the rewards and satisfactions of a close and intimate relationship, while delaying the need to make a long-term commitment to another person. It also allows individual development to progress in areas other than the relationship, through respect for independence, autonomy, and external validation. As a response to the high divorce rate, it is possible that traditional marriage may adapt and expand to meet the changing needs of people, along the lines of cohabitation. However, this modification does not seem to be immediately imminent, and thus cohabitation will probably maintain its usefulness as an alternative personal relationship form offering its unique and attractive advantages. Cohabitation is clearly not for everyone, but for those who, as a function of age or circumstance, feel lonely at the thought of singlehood or trapped at the thought of traditional marriage, cohabitation offers a unique alternative.

Acknowledgement

The writing of this report was supported in part by USPHS grant DA01070.

CHAPTER 8

Intimate Relationships:
A Perspective from Equity Theory

Elaine Hatfield and Jane Traupmann

Equity theorists have explored men's and women's reactions in a variety of casual encounters and equity principles have been found to be important in such diverse contexts as industrial relations, exploiter/victim relationships, philanthropist/recipient relationships, and the like (see Walster *et al.*, 1978 for a review of this research). Equity theory has proved to be surprisingly successful in predicting people's reactions in such casual interactions, but, until recently, researchers never explored whether or not Equity theory was equally successful in predicting men's and women's reactions in the most profoundly important of human interactions: intimate relationships.

In the last few years, however, a revolution has occurred. Social psychologists have begun to theorize about intimacy (e.g. Hatfield, in press; Kelley, 1979; Cook and McHenry, 1979; Walster and Walster, 1978); feminists agree that intimacy is a profoundly important concern (Firestone, 1970); Marxists have discovered it (e.g. Foucault, 1978); and even gerontologists have begun to recognize its importance (e.g. Huyck, 1977).

In this chapter, we will explore the insights that formal Equity theory gives us into romantic and marital relationships. Having briefly reviewed Equity theory in the first section we will go on to examine theorists' sharp disagreements as to whether or not Equity considerations should operate in intimate relationships. Subsequently, we will review the current research which indicates that, indeed, considerations of fairness do seem to be critically important in intimate relationships, as in all other.

The Equity Formulation

Equity theory is a strikingly simple theory (more fully described in Walster *et al.*, 1978). It is comprised of four interlocking propositions:

(I) Individuals will try to maximize their outcomes (where outcomes equal rewards minus punishments).

(IIa) Groups can maximize collective reward by evolving accepted systems for equitably apportioning rewards and punishments among members. Thus, groups will evolve such systems of Equity and will attempt to induce members to accept and adhere to these systems.

(IIb) Groups will generally reward members who treat others equitably, and generally punish members who treat other inequitably.

(III) When individuals find themselves participating in inequitable relationships they will become distressed. The more inequitable the relationship, the more distress they will feel.

(IV) Individuals who discover they are in an inequitable relationship will attempt to eliminate their distress by restoring equity. The greater the inequity that exists, the more distress they will feel, and the harder they will try to restore equity.

The conceptual definition of equity

Equity theorists provide a precise conceptual definition of what is meant by an equitable relationship: an equitable relationship exists when the person evaluating the relationship — who could be Participant A, Participant B, or an outside observer — concludes that all participants are receiving equal *relative gains* from the relationship; i.e.

$$\frac{(O_A - I_A)}{(|I_A|)^{k_A}} = \frac{(O_B - I_B)}{(|I_B|)^{k_B}}$$

where I_A and I_B designate a scrutineer's perception of Person A and B's Inputs; $|I_A|$ and $|I_B|$ designate the *absolute value* of their Inputs (i.e. the perceived value of their Inputs, disregarding sign); O_A and O_B designate the scrutineer's perception of Person A and B's Outcomes. The exponents k_A and k_B take on the value $+1$ or -1, depending on the sign of A and B's Inputs and A and B's gains (Outcomes – Inputs). The value k_A or k_B is $+$ if A or B make a positive contribution $(+)$ and reap a gain $(+)$. . . . or make a negative contribution $(-)$ and incur a loss $(-)$, from the relationship. Otherwise k_A or k_B is $-$.

Operational definitions of equity

Several theorists have developed scales to assess how equitable men and women perceive their intimate relationships to be and for this purpose the two most popular Equity scales are *The Traupmann–Utne–Hatfield (1978) Scale* and *The Hatfield (1978) Global Measure*. With the former scale subjects are asked to estimate how well they do (how good a deal they get) in relation to their partner in each of 25 areas of concern found to be more important to marriages (for example, personal concerns, emotional concerns and opportunities gained and lost); while the latter yields a single global estimation of the relationship.

Typically researchers have used scales such as these to determine whether intimates feel Overbenefitted, Equitably treated, or Underbenefitted in their most intimate of relationships.

The psychological consequences of inequity

From time to time, men and women find themselves caught up in relationships where they feel they are getting either far more or far less than they deserve. For example, one new mother whom we interviewed classified herself as "over-benefitted" $(+3)$ on the *Hatfield (1978) Global Measure*. Soon after her child was born, she had had a nervous breakdown and had been "good for nothing" since then; she was deeply depressed, she had no energy, and her husband had been saddled with the care of their child while trying desperately to keep his faltering business afloat (-3). Another interviewee classified herself as "underbenefitted" (-2). She had tried to understand her husband, had worked hard to put him through school, but now felt really "ripped off" because the day he completed medical school he filed for divorce and her own plans to continue her education went down the drain.

According to Equity theory in such cases both the beneficiaries and the victims should feel uncomfortable about the iniquitous position, and, indeed in studies of casual encounters, and in a few studies of intimate affairs, researchers have found that equity and distress are typically related as depicted in Fig. 1. (For reviews of this research, see Walster *et al.*, 1978, and Hatfield *et al.*, in press.) In such cases, Equity theory proposes that the over-benefitted person will feel guilty, whilst the underbenefitted person will feel angry.

Techniques for reducing the distress caused by inequity

Proposition IV proposes that people who find themselves caught up in inequitable relations will try to reduce their distress — their guilt or anger — by restoring equity to their relationships. There are only two ways that people can set things right: they can re-establish *actual* equity or *psychological* equity. In the first case they can inaugurate real changes in their relation-ships, e.g. the underbenefitted may well ask for more out of their relation-ships, or their overbenefitted partners may offer to try to give more. In the latter case couples may find it harder to change their behaviour than to change their minds and so prefer to close their eyes and to reassure themselves that "really, everything is in perfect order".

At this point, Equity theorists confront a crucial question. Can they specify when people will try to restore actual equity to their relationships and when they will settle for restoring psychological equity instead? Equity theorists argue that people should follow a Cost/Benefit strategy in deciding how to respond. It has been found that decisions to respond to injustice by attempting to restore actual equity, by distorting reality, or by doing a little of both, depend on the costs and benefits that individuals expect will be associated with each strategy.

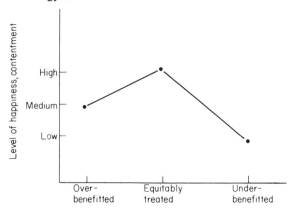

FIG. 1   The effect of equity on contentment / distress (after Austin 1974).

Of course, if couples find themselves enmeshed in inequitable relationships and cannot "set things right" — they have one last resort: they can abandon the relationship. Some couples "abandon" their relationship by withdrawing psychologically — they start spending less and less time with one another, and more and more time at work, with their children, or with friends; they have affairs. Sometimes couples make a more clear-cut break; they separate or divorce. Fuller details of these and other features are given in Walster *et al.*, 1978a.

Equity Theory and Intimate Relations

If one asks: "*Should* intimates be concerned about whether or not they are getting or giving their fair share in their love relationship?" most theorists find they have mixed feelings.

On the one hand, for most people, the family *is* "a haven in a heartless world" (Lasch, 1977). Zaretsky (1976), in his analysis of the place of the family in capitalist society, observes:

> In addition, the family is the institution in which one's personal uniqueness is central. It is the crucible in which our emotional life first takes shape and throughout life is the major institution in our society in which we expect to be recognized and cared for, for ourselves. . . . But even as adults, our "personal life" is confined to the family or to relationships — friendships, love affairs, communal life — that closely resemble it or are based upon it (p. 17).

Zaretsky points out that the family is the last refuge from the demands of capitalist society. So, in part, most of us feel that in a family, everyone is entitled to unconditional love; fairness should not "count" in love relations.

On the other hand, if intimates were *really* totally insensitive to issues of fairness, then intimate relationships could not survive, since real people are simply not willing to give and give with no thought of return. Hay and Horton (in press) go one step further: they argue that one should be suspicious of those who romanticize love relations. Paradoxically, they argue, such "romantics" may have a vested interest in mystifying love relations; as they wryly observe, one reason so many men can argue so eloquently that love should transcend concern with equity (transcend the minutiae of marriage contracts) is that they don't want clean the bathroom. So there may be a certain logic to the argument that a high-flown concern with altruistic love may cloak a desire to maintain an inequitable *status quo*.

Equity theorists have predicted that equity considerations should have a critical impact on intimate relations at six different points and this can be expressed in terms of a number of hypotheses (Walster *et al.*, 1978a):

Hypothesis 1: Men and women should be most likely to continue to date, to live together and to marry, if they feel their relationships are equitable. *Hypothesis 2:* Men and women in equitable relationships should be fairly content whilst men and women who feel they've received either far more, or far less, than they deserve, should be uncomfortable (the more inequitable their relationships, the more uncomfortable they should be).

Hypothesis 3: Intimate relationships which are perceived as equitable will be more satisfying overall than relationships in which men and women feel either overbenefitted or underbenefitted.

Hypothesis 4: Intimate relationships which are perceived as equitable will be more sexually fulfilling than relationships in which men and women feel either overbenefitted or underbenefitted.

Hypothesis 5: In all marriages there are certain crisis periods. For example: when a dating couple marries, moves in together, and begins to discover what marriage is really like; when their first child arrives; when the children leave home; when someone loses his or her job. . . . . or retires. At such times of precipitous change, a couple may find that their once equitable relationship is now woefully unbalanced.

Hypothesis 6: Equitable relationships will be especially stable relationships.

Let us consider the data which exist to support, or to rebut, these six Equity hypotheses.

Equity theorists have accumulated considerable support for *Hypothesis 1* (see Walster *et al.*, 1978a; and Hatfield, in press). To consider a typical study: Walster *et al.*, (1978b) interviewed 537 college men and women who were casual or steady daters. Their first step was to find out how equitable couples perceived their relationships to be, using a measure which asks:

> Considering what you put into your dating relationship, compared to what you get out of it. . . . . . and what your partner puts in compared to what (s)he gets out of it, how well does your dating relationship stack up?

Men and women are asked to estimate self Inputs, partner Inputs, self Outcomes, and partner Outcomes. From these estimates, men and women were classified as overbenefitted, equitably treated, or underbenefitted in their love affairs.

Walster *et al.* (1978b) attempted to assess whether or not the couples seemed to be moving towards more intimate relationships in two ways: (1) by asking couples how confident they were that their relationships would last, and (2) by asking couples how far they had progressed sexually. As predicted, the authors found that men and women in equitable relationships generally believed their relationships would last for quite some time. They were confident that they would still be together "one year from now" and "five years from now", and their confidence may well have been warranted. In a follow-up study (four months later) couples in equitable relationships *were* more likely to be still dating than were other couples. Both the overbenefitted (who would seem to have some reason to hope their relationships would last) and the underbenefitted (who would seem to have every reason to hope that something better would come along) were pessimistic about the future. If their relationships were not already in disarray, they expected they they soon would be.

Men's and women's perceptions of the equitability or inequitability of their relationships seemed to have a considerable impact on how willing they were to chance a sexual relationship. Walster *et al.* (1978b) found that couples in equitable relationships had the most sexual relationships, generally including sexual intercourse. Both the greatly underbenefitted and greatly overbenefitted however tended to stop before "going all the way".

The authors then asked respondents who *had* had intercourse, why they had gone so far. The participants in relatively equitable relations were most likely to say that they had intercourse because they *both* wanted to, (i.e. to say that "Mutual curiosity", the fact that "We are/were in love", "We like/liked each other", or "Mutual physical desire, enjoyment" were their reasons for having intercourse). Those who felt extremely overbenefitted or extremely underbenefitted were less likely to say that sex was a joint decision.

Thus research in this area seems to suggest that in the casual and steady dating period, it is couples in equitable relationships who expect their relationships to evolve into permanent ones.

The predicition of *Hypothesis 2* is an intriguing one. It is easy to see why men and women who feel they are being exploited by their partners would be furious, but the other side of the coin is less obvious. Men and women who feel they are getting far *more* than they deserve are involved in inequitable relationships, too, and if Equity theorists are right, the overbenefitted should have mixed feelings about their excessively good fortune. On the one hand they may well be delighted to be receiving such benefits, but they know that they don't deserve them and this should make them uncomfortable.

Several studies have explored these issues. Walster *et al.* (1978b) asked casually and steadily dating couples to estimate how equitable their relationships were on a global measure. They then assessed how contented the individuals were in their relationships via Austin's (1974) measure of Contentment/Distress and found that men and women who were involved in relatively equitable relationships were far more content and happy than were their greatly underbenefitted or greatly overbenefitted peers. As might be expected, the *greatly* overbenefitted felt extremely guilty about their favoured position, whilst the *greatly* underbenefitted felt extremely angry about the way they were being treated.

Traupmann (1978) and Utne (1978) interviewed a range of 118 newly wed couples from a variety of occupational backgrounds between three and six months after their marriage, the average age being around the mid-20s. They used an array of both global and detailed measures of perceived equitability, and Austin's (1974) Measure of Contentment/Distress. As predicted, the spouses who felt their relationships were equitable felt most content and happy and least angry and guilty in the relationship. Such data make it clear that even newly wed couples, who might be expected to be "honeymooning" for at least the first two months, are distressed by inequity. Together these two studies seem to suggest that from the dating years onwards, well into married life, couples are deeply concerned about the fairness or unfairness of their relationship.

To see whether this concern lasts throughout one's life or not, Traupmann and Hatfield (in press) interviewed 106 older women ranging in age from 50 to 82 years of age, using measures of equitability and contentment, but they found almost no differences between the women who felt overbenefitted, those who felt equitably treated, and those who felt underbenefitted. Virtually all of the women reported feeling very content and happy and not at all angry about their relationships. Although the overbenefitted were slightly distressed, and the underbenefitted even more distressed, by existing inequities, the predicted differences were not significant.

Because the studies have produced cross-sectional rather than longitudinal data we cannot be sure if this apparent lack of concern about equity reflects differences between young women's and older women's attitudes about how intimates *should* feel or if, after many years of marriage, intimates do become less concerned about issues of fairness. This question will remain unanswered until longitudinal studies on equity and marriage are completed.

Hypothesis 3: Intimate relationships which are perceived as equitable will be more satisfying than relationships in which men and women feel either overbenefitted or underbenefitted.

Do inequities in intimate relations have any effect on couple's *overall* satisfaction from them? Equity theory clearly predicts that marital inequity should detract from a couple's satisfaction with that relationship, but critics might argue that intimate relations are more complex than that. People may well be concerned about the equity/inequity of their relationship (as Hypothesis 2 suggests they are) but that will have little impact on their satisfaction/ dissatisfaction with the relationship *as a whole*.

Recent studies both using dating couples (Traupmann *et al.*, in preparation) and using married couples (Traupmann, 1978; Utne, 1978) have shown clearly that partners' evaluations of Equity and their satisfaction are related. People in equitable relationships report the highest levels of satisfaction, those who felt overbenefitted came next, and those who felt underbenefitted were least satisfied and least happy with the relationship.

There is evidence, then, that inequities in intimacy are distressing and can influence the overall level of satisfaction which dating couples and newly-weds may derive from their partnerships. It is the Equitable intimate relations, not relationships in which the man or the woman has the upper hand, which seem to be most fulfilling for both men and women. Men and women feel uncomfortable receiving either far more or far less than they deserve. It is only very late in life, if ever, that couples cease to be concerned with whether or not their relationships are "fair".

Hypothesis 4: Intimate relationships which are perceived as equitable will be more sexually fulfilling than relationships in which men and women feel either overbenefitted or underbenefitted.

According to Equity theory, men's and women's perceptions that they are fairly/unfairly treated should have a considerable impact on their sexual relations such that couples in equitable relationships should feel fairly comfortable about their sexual relations whilst couples in inequitable relationships should not. But how does this relationship to sexuality come about? Many sociologists have argued that marital satisfaction and sexual satisfaction are linked in the following ways:

(1) *Sexual satisfaction generates marital satisfaction.* It is argued here that sex is critically important to couples, that intensely passionate or companionate feelings contribute to marital happiness whilst routine, dismal, frustrating sex can threaten the best of relationships (see Kinsey *et al.*, 1948 and 1953; Bell, 1966; Hunt, 1974).
(2) *Marital satisfaction generates sexual satisfaction.* Sex is a delicate interaction. If couples like or love one another, if they feel equitably treated, if they feel comfortable with one another, sex may go well. If couples dislike or hate one another, feel trapped in inequitable relationships, feel uncomfortable in one another's presence, their deepseated resentment or guilt may corrode their sexual encounters (see Berne, 1964; Hunt, 1974; Kinsey *et al.*, 1948 and 1953; Masters and Johnson, 1976).

Traupmann *et al.* (in preparation) interviewed 189 dating couples about their sexual relationships and measured the equity of the couple's relationship, their level of overall sexual satisfaction and their feelings immediately after a sexual encounter. The results, however, were not totally consistent. Looking at men and women's estimates of their *overall* sexual satisfaction, there is no evidence that equity considerations are important in determining how satisfied couples are with their sexual relationships. It is only when we begin to ask about the specifics of sexuality — ask how psychologically satisfied they are by a given sexual encounter (how close and loving they feel immediately after a sexual encounter) and how physically satisfied they are with sex — that we secure any evidence that men and women care about equity. The results, then, provide only partial support for the contention that equity considerations do have some impact on men and women's sexual satisfaction in a marriage.

These latter results are however, buttressed by earlier research. Walster *et al.* (1978a) found that couples in equitable relationships had the most intensely sexual relations, and that most couples in equitable relationships were having sexual intercourse whilst couples in inequitable relationships were not. Taken together, then, these results provide a certain amount of support for the contention that equity considerations *might* be an important determinant of whether or not people engage in sexual behaviour at all and if they do, how satisfied they will be with their sexual encounters, though the data are not conclusive. In addition, there seems to be a consistent though statistically non-significant difference between men's and women's reactions to equity and sexuality (Hatfield *et al.*, in press). On the whole, results in this area are intriguing but at the moment inconclusive, and a great deal more research is required to provide a clear picture.

Hypothesis 5: In all marriages there are certain crisis periods. For example, when a dating couple marry, live together, and begin to discover what marriage is really like; when the first child arrives; when the children leave home; when someone loses his or her job. . . . . or retires.

At such times of precipitous change, a couple may find that their once equitable relationship is now woefully unbalanced. Equity theorists would predict that if we contacted couples just before such crises, in the midst of such crises, and then again, after couples had a chance to deal with the crisis, we would find that the couples would have found the crisis period very unsettling, and worked hard to reestablish the equitableness of their relationship. . . . . or that their relationships would be floundering.

Couples may *start off* in fairly well matched relationships (see Hypothesis 1), but sooner or later dramatic upheavals in the marital balance inevitably occur. One question that Equity theorists have asked is: what effects do such wrenching changes in the equity of a relationship have on the dynamic equilibrium of a marriage? Equity theorists have maintained that such changes in a marriage's balance should send reverberations throughout the entire system. When couples are confronted with the fact that there is a gross imbalance in their relationship, they should try to set things right. They should: (1) try to make their relationship actually more equitable, (2) try to convince themselves (and their partners) that things are fairer than they seem, — or — if all else fails, (3) withdraw from their relationship.

Unfortunately when we turn to the effects of shifts in marital balance most of the evidence in support of the contention that couples *do* try to readjust their relationships is anecdotal. There are some data which suggest that when people's physical appearance changes drastically — through accident, plastic surgery, or dieting — their expectations may change too. For example, Jones (reported in Palmer, 1974) warned *Weight Watchers* magazine readers that:

Marriage, like all relationships, is a balance. When one partner is overweight, the fact has been considered, perhaps unconsciously, in setting up the balance. Obviously, when you remove the obesity, you upset the balance. The relationship shifts and takes on a different complexion.

In the same article, Palmer adds:

Gone are. . . . . the attempts to buy love through acquiescence and the overweight's traditional don't-make-waves-they-may-throw-you-out policy. In their place comes a new pride, an awareness of rights and a tendency to speak up for those rights (pp. 23–50).

There is also a limited amount of survey data which support the contention that any change in the equity of a relationship affects the entire system. For example, the Depression afforded Komarovsky (1971) a tragic opportunity to study the impact of a dramatic change in the marital balance. Komarovsky reasoned that:

In the traditional patriarchal view of the family, the husband is expected to support and protect his wife. . . . . she , in turn, is expected to take care of his household, to honor and obey him (p.2).

What happens, then, Komarovsky asked, when a man loses his job? Does he begin to lose authority?

During the Winter of 1935–36, Komarovsky contacted 58 families who were receiving public assistance. In all the families, before the Depression the husband had been the family's sole provider but when the Depression hit, all this changed: the men lost their jobs and were forced to go on relief. Komarovsky interviewed family members to find out what impact, if any, this change had on the husband's and wife's relationship, and he found that, in 13 of the 58 families, when the husband lost his ability to support his family, he began to lose his authority.

Two major types of changes occurred in families. (1) in some families, the couple's relationship began to evolve into a more egalitarian one. For example, in one family, the man began, for the first time, to take on part of the household duties. In another family, a Protestant father who had forbidden his children to go to a Catholic school relented. (2) In a very few cases, the husbands' and wives' status was reversed and the dominant husband became totally subordinate. For example, in one family, so long as the husband was employed his wife had treated him with careful respect, but, once the economic depression hit, she no longer bothered to be so polite and began to blame her husband for his unemployment, to ignore his wishes, to complain about his behaviour, to argue with him, to nag him constantly, and to criticize him sharply even in front of the children.

There is further survery evidence that men's and women's economic contribution to a family determines their relative power . . . . and that profound changes in the economic *status quo* produced equally profound changes in the relative power in a couple. For example, Cavan (1973), studying the effects of unemployment, found that men who become unemployed soon lost power in the family. Gillespie (1971) found that wives who work and thus have an independent source of income have more power than those who stay at home and have no independent income. Finally, after his studies of divorce, Goode (1956, p. 63) commented that "wilful failure in the role of breadwinner is often met by wilful destruction of the sexual and social unity of the marriage".

There is, then considerable *anecdotal* evidence that marital crises do send reverberations throughout the system and do provoke couples to try to set things right.

Hypothesis 6: Equitable relationships will be especially stable relationships.

According to Equity theory, if a couple's relationship becomes grossly inequitable, and the partners can envisage no way to set things right, then they should be tempted to abandon that relationship. Of course there are many ways of "withdrawing" from a relationship: for example, if casually dating couples are unhappy with a casual date, it's easy enough for them to put a swift end to things and, as we saw in discussing Hypothesis 1, most inequitable dating relationships do simply end. Once couples marry, however, things change. Marriages are supposed to be for "better or worse" and divorce is still costly in both emotional and financial terms (see Bohannan,

1971). Thus, many married men and women, upset by the marital give-and-take, withdraw *psychologically* from the situation — they bury themselves in their work, or give their all to their children, to their friends, or to backgammon. Yet, if a marital relationship is unbalanced enough, for long enough, couples do sometimes opt for separation or a divorce. (In 1973, for instance, in the United States, 913 000 couples opted for an annulment or a divorce and Udry, 1974, has estimated that 20-25% of first marriages end in annulment, desertion, or divorce.)

In the previously cited studies by Utne (1978) and Traupmann (1978) attempts were made to examine whether equitable marriages were more stable, and this was done by interviewing newlyweds and following them up a year later. It was found that immediately after their marriage, overbenefitted and equitably treated men and women were confident that their marriage would last, and only the underbenefitted were willing to entertain any doubts. One year later, however, both the overbenefitted *and* the underbenefitted had begun to worry that their relationship might not be a stable one. As one might expect, the underbenefitted were especially sceptical that things would last.

One source of instability, then, comes from within. Another may come from without. Hatfield *et al.* (1979) speculated that inequitable relationships may be fragile relationships for yet a second reason: Men and women who feel they are not getting their just deserts from one affair, may be especially likely to risk exploring a fleeting, or even a more permanent, love affair. To test this notion, they re-analysed some data collected by Berscheid *et al.* (1973) from a large sample of *Psychology Today* readers and formed support for the idea that equitable relations are more stable because couples in such relationships are extremely reluctant to rush into extramarital affairs. Both overbenefitted and equitably treated men and women were very reluctant to experiment with extramarital sex (on the average, they waited 12-15 years before chancing an extramarital involvement with someone else), while deprived men and women began exploring extramarital sex far earlier — only 9-11 years after marriage. Overbenefitted and equitably treated men and women had the fewest extramarital encounters (0-1); the deprived had the most extramarital liaisons (1-3). Again it would seem, then, that equitable relations are likely to be more stable than inequitable ones — since *both* partners are motivated to be faithful.

Future Directions

In general, it would seem that Equity theory does provide a convenient paradigm for examining romantic and marital relationships. The sparse data which do exist provide at least suggestive evidence that Equity principles do operate in determining the choice of a mate and how partners get along, day-to-day and thereafter.

Clearly more, and more careful, research is needed in the whole area to resolve important outstanding issues; and when this is done it may well be found that both Equity theorists and their critics have been at least partially right — love relationships have both unique characteristics and important similarities to other kinds of relationship. Instead of merely continuing the debate, however, it may be more fruitful to change the focus of investigations and examine questions such as the following.

1. What sorts of *people* are especially concerned with equity? What kinds of people keep a careful, methodical count of who does what for whom, when? What kinds of people just drift along assuming that things will balance out somehow? Who is intensely upset by overbenefit — racked by guilt and shame? Who really only cares if they themselves are underbenefitted? Who becomes upset when they detect even a short-term inequity? Who takes a far longer perspective?

2. Under what *conditions* are people especially concerned with equity? Foucault (1978), for example, argues that in different eras there are different reigning paradigms: e.g. in one era, morality is seen as the proper guide to behaviour; whilst in other, more rationalistic eras, logic is critical. Was morality the reigning paradigm of the nineteenth century, and are rational-istic, economic principles seen as the proper guide for behaviour now?

We are hopeful that intimacy researchers will soon be on the way to finding out answers to these questions.

Acknowledgement

Research reported here was supported in part by National Institutes of Health Biomedical Research Grant and in part by HEW-AoA Grant #90-A-1230 for multidisciplinary research on Aging Women, awarded to the Faye McBeath Institute on Aging and Adult Life, University of Wisconsin-Madison, 1977-1979.

CHAPTER 9
Relationships in Marriage and the Family

Robert L. Burgess

My charge in this chapter was to concentrate on the sorts of relationships that occur in the domestic context, including the relationships which transpire between marital partners as well as their relationships with their own children. This is obviously a considerable undertaking for one chapter. Consequently, I have decided to limit my discussion to those aspects of marriage and the family that are especially suitable to this book on personal relationships such as marital interaction, satisfaction, conflict, parent-child interaction and divorce. Clearly, certain important topics are missing such as mate selection, relationships between parents and their adult offspring, and sexual interaction. The first is covered by two chapters in the companion volume "Developing Personal Relationships" (Chapters by Cunningham and Antill, and Huston *et al.*), the second by Reisman in that volume and the third by Przybyla and Byrne in Chapter 6 of the present volume. Coverage of other relevant topics is given by Orford and O'Reilly and Newcomb and Bentler in "Personal Relationships in Disorder". Even so, the topics I am covering could make up an entire book; thus, the reader is forewarned that this chapter is designed simply to be an introduction to the study of relationships in marriage and the family.

The oldest tradition in the systematic analysis of marriage and the family is sociological. As early as 1924, G. V. Hamilton (reported in Hamilton, 1948) began secretly investigating the sexual behaviour of couples. Through interviews with 100 couples, he discovered that men were apparently more satisfied with their marriages than were women and that, as a group, women tended to be more seriously disappointed in their unions than were their husbands. He also pioneered the exploration of such variables as income, female employment and extramarital affairs and their influence on the degree of marital satisfaction.

At about the same period of time, Terman *et al.* (1938) were exploring the correlates of marital happiness, examining such factors as personality traits and the frequency of sexual intercourse. While they did not find a significant relationship between personality and happiness, they did find a strong correlation between (a) the discrepancy between desired and actual frequency of intercourse and (b) marital happiness. This finding led them to conclude that the most important variables influencing marital happiness were likely to be these and other relationship variables. For example, in their investigation of "domestic grievances" they were led to conclude that "the greatest single danger to marital happiness is for one spouse to like and the other to dislike to argue" (Terman *et al.*, 1938, p. 29). Research by Burgess and Cottrell (1938) produced results largely consistent with Terman's: they reported that "the outstanding features in marital adjustment seem to be those of affection, temperamental compatibility, and social adaptability" (Burgess and Cottrell, 1938, p. 349).

For decades, these researchers profoundly influenced the course of family studies. During this period, attempts were made to classify families and marriages according to various indices such as the complementarity of partners' needs (Winch, 1958), the congruence of values (Tharp, 1963), the totality of the relationships (Cuber and Haroff, 1965), the degree of marital adjustment (Locke, 1951), and marital satisfaction (Terman and Wallin, 1949). This pattern continues today as exemplified by the study of dyadic adjustment in marriage (Spanier, 1979). Interestingly, the questionnaires that were constructed to assess each of these apparently different concepts or dimensions correlated very highly. This led Burgess and Wallin (1953) to conclude that these measures were all tapping the same underlying dimension which they called "marital success".

Subsequent research supports their assertion as well as the argument that the variables most predictive of marital and family stability and satisfaction are relationship variables. Thus, Murstein's (1970) study of the development of intimate relationships indicates that the future stability of the dyad from engagement into marriage depends to a considerable extent on discussions that the partners have had about their respective values and their perceptions of appropriate role behaviour. In the same vein, Gottman (1979) has argued that marital satisfaction is ultimately related to a couple's ability to resolve differences. Similarly, Burgess (1979) in his study of parent–child conflict has written that coercive patterns of parent-child interaction are immediately traceable to contingency histories located within the family itself.

Social Relationships: Definitions and Dimensions

So far I have suggested that relationship variables and processes are important in studying marriage and the family: yet, I have not made clear exactly what I mean by the term "relationship". Even though the first part of this book deals extensively with the nature of personal relationships, I feel that I should make explicit my own approach and illustrate the particular meaning of such relationships in the context of the family. As I see it, there are at least three major levels of social involvement or social contact. One individual may simply be orientating his or her behaviour towards another as when one person visually attends to the behaviour of another. In this case, the behaviour of one person is being influenced by the behaviour of another but that influence is unidirectional: the person observed may be totally unaware that s/he is being observed and is influencing the actions of another (e.g. when a child imitates the behaviour of an esteemed uncle). I will refer to this kind of event as *social behaviour*. It is social because at least one person's behaviour is being controlled by the behavioural or physical characteristics of another.

Secondly, two individuals may each be attending to and influencing each other's behaviour. This bi-directional influence may be either simultaneous or alternating and, moreover, the degree of influence may range in intensity. For example, two conversants may simply be affecting each other's listening and speaking behaviour; but on the other hand, two people may exert substantial control over the course of each other's lives. Illustrations would include a marriage proposal or the negotiation of marital roles, respectively. When two or more persons mutually affect each other's behaviour in such ways, we have what I shall call *social interaction*.

Should the individual interactants know each other (interacting frequently over time), and should the nature of those interactions be influenced by the individuals' previous history of interacting with one another, we would have our third level of social involvement, namely a *social relationship* (Hinde, 1976b; 1979; this volume). Examples would include a love affair, a close friendship, and a business partnership.

There are several features to each of these three levels of social contact which should be noted. To begin with, each level is capable of affecting and being affected by the others. Thus, the way in which we interact with someone may be determined by our relationship with that person. If a friendship or a marriage has come to involve increasing mutual distrust, the nature of any particular interaction episode may be quite different from what it was when there was trust between the two individuals. Similarly, a relationship may change as a result of a recent interaction: these changes may be as transitory as a simple change in mood or as long lasting as growing disaffection and disengagement.

Social contacts may also vary along several dimensions (Hinde, 1976b). For instance, contacts can vary in terms of the *content* of the interaction. Hence, a given relationship may involve mutual assistance in problem solving, competition for scarce resources, aggression or sexual intercourse. Relationships may also be differentiated according to the *diversity* of interactions that occur. One relationship might be based almost exclusively upon mutual sexual interests. Another might cut across intellectual, recreational, occupational, as well as sexual spheres.

Family and marital relationships — as well as other sorts — may vary in terms of the *quality* of the interaction. One of the more useful ways to examine the quality of interaction in this context is in terms of the relative frequency of certain kinds of behaviour such as the proportion of positive to negative contacts (Burgess and Conger, 1978). For example, one relationship may be characterized largely by the exchange of positively reinforcing, affectionate or other similarly supportive behaviour, whilst another relationship may be characterized by coercive exchanges (Patterson, 1977). Still another relationship may be highly charged emotionally with accelerated frequencies of both positive and negative behaviour.

A related way to assess the quality of a relationship is in terms of clusters of specific behaviour. Thus, a close or intimate relationship might be described as one with all or some of the following characteristics (Hinde, 1976b, this volume; Levinger and Snoek, 1972).

(i)   frequent interaction;
(ii)   face-to-face interaction;
(iii)   diverse interactions across several behavioural and situational domains;
(iv)   substantial influence on each other's lives;
(v)   repeated attempts to restore proximity during absence;
(vi)   alleviation of anxiety upon return of the partner;
(vii)   unique communication systems;
(viii) synchronized goals and behaviour;
(ix)   mutual self-disclosure;
(x)   seeing separate interests as being inextricably tied to the well-being of the relationship.

Part of the notion of the quality of a relationship, then, obviously includes the *amount of involvement* between two individuals. One relationship might be superficial and be characterized by periodic interaction. Another could involve considerable intensity, emotional affect, commitment and a high degree of mutual self-disclosure.

One final dimension of relationships that I shall mention here is the *degree of reciprocity* in interaction. This is a dimension of social relationships whose presumed importance is matched only by the controversy which surrounds its measurement and its role in family relationships. Gottman (1979), for example, equates the term reciprocity with "the contingent nature of the interaction between two conspecifics" (p.63). Consequently, "reciprocity involves one person's behaviour's changing the probability of subsequent behaviour by the other. Reciprocity is, thus, a *probability change* concept" (p.64). On the other hand, as Patterson and Reid (1970) commented: "Reciprocity describes dyadic interaction in which persons A and B reinforce each other at an equitable rate" (p.133). There are obvious problems with each definition. Gottman's seems to confuse contingent behaviour change, which is what I have termed social interaction, with the contingent exchange of functionally equivalent behaviour, which is the more customary notion of reciprocity. By confusing the two concepts, interaction and reciprocity, Gottman falls into the trap of assuming that "reciprocity" can occur only from moment-to-moment or episode-to-episode, and the possibility of delayed reciprocity is overlooked. Yet, there is reason to suspect that the intensity or quality of a relationship may be assessed in terms of the deferred nature of reciprocal interchanges: indeed, "contiguous", as opposed to "delayed" reciprocity may best characterize either the opening stages of a relationship, or a relationship in distress (Levinger, 1979). There are also problems with the Patterson and Reid definition which seems to confuse the concepts of reciprocity and equality or equity; terms which are conceptually and empirically distinct (Burgess and Nielsen, 1974).

Despite these terminological problems, there is general agreement among family researchers that the nature and degree of reciprocity is an important dimension in family relationships. Moreover, attention to, awareness of, and concern for reciprocity may vary across relationships in much the same way that the importance of contiguous or immediate reciprocity does. That is, each of these may be especially salient in the initial stages of relationships and in distressed relationships. We obviously still have much to learn about the role of reciprocity in marriages and families just as we need to know more about how the distribution of rewards varies across relationships. One possibility deserving of investigation is that the incidence of both equal and equitable reward distributions is high at all stages of intimate relationships involving age-peers except for those relationships in distress. Similarly, I would expect departures in equality and equity in parent–child and certain other cross-generational relationships.

While there are undoubtedly other dimensions along which social contacts in general, and social relationships in particular, may vary, these represent the major ones identified so far in studies of marital and family interaction. I shall be referring back to these dimensions as the following discussion proceeds.

Marital Relationships

Functions, roles and satisfaction in marriage

The word "marriage" conjures up certain images for most of us. These include a loving husband and wife and their children who live together in a single dwelling. The family is an economically independent unit with the husband being at least the major provider, while the wife's chief responsibilities include care of the household and the children. The image also includes the family engaged in mutual support and problem solving and the spouses meeting each other's sexual needs. Finally, it is expected that this relationship will continue until death do them part.

However, this image portrays marriage and the family as people believe they should be, not as they actually are. Indeed, at best, it may only describe a middle-class model of the family. In any case, family sociologists have been documenting a number of changes in both family structure and function. For example, some of the functions that the family has historically performed such as economic production, education and protection are presently being performed, at least in part, by other social institutions (Burgess and Locke, 1953). Admittedly, other functions such as reproduction, socialization, the provision of affection and emotional support and recreation still are performed largely within the family and even though children may be born to a woman who is not married, this is not the usual arrangement. Also, while much socialization takes place outside the house, the family is still the primary influence especially during the early years of life.

Nonetheless, changes have been taking place, which are perhaps most noticeable when we examine the economic function of the family. With industrialization, the family as a unit of production is found less and less often, and the family's economic role has become largely that of a spending unit. Associated with this change, is increased emphasis upon the companionship and emotional support function of both marriage and the family; but, this restriction in functions, as Slater (1968) has noted, has also placed new demands on the marital relationship.

Spouses are now asked to be lovers, friends, and mutual therapists in a society which is forcing the marriage bond to become the closest, deepest, most important and most enduring relationship of one's life. Paradoxically, then, it is increasingly likely to fall short of the emotional demands placed upon it and be dissolved (p.99).

One of the basic reasons for, or concomitants of, changes in marriage and family relationships today is the redefinition of sex role expectations that is taking place. Husbands are no longer seen as being solely responsible for economic support nor are wives solely responsible for housework and child rearing. Yet, while changes in sex role expectations are occurring, there remain patterned differences in role performance for males and females in marriages and families. Looking first at the male role in marriages, it would appear that to be a man in a largely male-dominated culture would be both desirable and beneficial. Certainly, men still dominate most professions, run most corporations, and occupy positions of power and prestige in political, cultural and educational institutions. Similarly, men usually get paid more for the same jobs when women also do them and they typically have greater freedom of movement within marriage.

Yet, there are costs as well. Men are more vulnerable to stress, they have more heart attacks and more ulcers, and they die at younger ages than women. Likewise, they commit more serious crimes, abuse drugs and alcohol more and they are more likely to commit suicide. Interestingly, most of these problems tend to be alleviated somewhat by marriage: thus, compared to single men, married men have superior mental health, lower suicide rates, greater career prospects and longer lives (Bernard, 1973).

When we examine the female role in marriage we find just the opposite pattern. Married women, when compared to unmarried women, have more neurotic symptoms, they are more depressed, more fearful and anxious, have lower self-esteem, and they are less happy (Bernard, 1973). They are also less satisfied with their marriages than are their husbands.

There is a very considerable research literature reaching back over a generation which shows that: more wives than husbands report marital frustration and dissatisfaction; more report negative feelings; more wives than husbands consider their marriages unhappy, have considered separation or divorce, have regretted their marriages; and fewer report positive companionship (Bernard, 1973, p.28).

Several reasons have been offered for these different responses to marriage and the family be men and women. First, it has been suggested that marriage changes a woman's life more than it does a man's. The transition from being a single woman to being a full-time wife and mother may be particularly abrupt. A young woman must move from a single world with little sexual segregation such as school or work to one where there are quite different experiences for men and women. She may move from a highly diverse and stimulating environment to one which is much more predictable, has clearly defined boundaries and which requires her to be someone who is charged with taking care of others. Secondly, she is often required to do tasks which she finds aversive: for instance, house-cleaning and child-rearing can become dull, monotonous and highly repetitive; and many of these duties are not intrinsically rewarding yet they require considerable effort. Thirdly, she must often perform these tasks in relative isolation without the support and assistance that could be provided by others since the main potential sources of support are a husband (who is absent for most of the day) and children (who can hardly be expected to perform that function adequately). Fourthly, a married woman often experiences a loss of control over her own life. Her husband's success determines their life style, their social status and where and how well they shall live. Their mobility is also determined by her husband's job. Meanwhile, wives are left to sell their houses, pack and move the family.

Thus, women often feel helpless and victimized (Melville, 1972). Little wonder, then, that after marriage women tend to become more submissive and conservative. While education may have taught the young woman to be creative and to think and act independently, marriage may teach another lesson. Thus, we find that a wife is more likely to adjust her behaviour, attitudes, and values to her husband's than is a husband to his wife's. Given both the pattern of hypergamy discussed above and the fact that marriage seems to be more important to a woman's overall happiness with her life, she has more to lose; and, given the principle of least interest, the balance of power weighs in favour of her husband and we witness what Jessie Bernard (1973) calls "the Pygmalion Effect" (p.43). In short, women make more adjustments in marriage than men do because they see themselves as having more at stake.

One factor which can significantly increase a woman's psychological well-being, including her satisfaction with her marriage, is work. Not only will a married woman's entry into the labour force relieve some of the family's financial strains, it will also often increase her self-esteem and equalize the balance of power in the family (Hoffman and Nye, 1974). Women in lower-income families, however, may gain more power by working than women from higher-income families because their wages have a proportionately larger impact on total family earnings. It should not be surprising, then, to learn that men in blue-collar families are more likely to resist their wives going to work and when their wives do enter the labour force, it is more likely to be a source of marital conflict and dissatisfaction (Hoffman and Nye, 1974).

Of special interest is the dual-career pattern where both spouses are committed, though perhaps not equally, to the world of work. In these cases, it is usually assumed that neither household tasks nor child-bearing and -rearing take precedence over the woman's career. This pattern seems not to be too difficult for childless couples but it can clearly complicate matters where children are involved. Rhona and Robert Rappoport (1971) in their study of dual-career couples found that these marriages are high in both strains and satisfactions. The most common strain for these couples is resource overload, with time an especially scarce resource. Another common problem in such marital relationships is the tension which develops over whether the woman is really being a "good wife and mother" while pursuing her career. As Safilios-Rothschild (1970) has noted, marital equality is still more of an ideal than an accomplished fact. Significantly, in a survey of college men, Komarovsky (1973) found that only seven percent said they would change their own marital roles in substantial ways in order to facilitate their wife's career (p.873).

Apart from the issue of marital equality and male-female differences in marriage, a number of studies have shown that marital satisfaction begins to decline soon after the newlywed period (Burgess and Wallin, 1953; Campbell, 1975; Cuber and Haroff, 1968). For example, Campbell (1975), using a national probability sample of 2000 couples, found that marital happiness was highest among newly married couples without children, that satisfaction dropped with the birth of children, and that it rose again once children left the home. However, a recent study by Spanier *et al.* (1975) using non-linear regression analyses, concluded that the presumed curvilinearity in marital satisfaction reported in earlier studies may have been premature.

> Whereas it is seemingly appropriate to conclude that couples report lower marital adjustment scores following the birth of their first child, and continuing through the early childhood years, current evidence does not yet warrant concluding that there is a leveling off followed by an increase in adjustment or satisfaction into the later years (p.271).

In any event, this decline in marital satisfaction with the birth of children is most true for the wife and is undoubtedly due to a host of factors including the fact that the couple may simply find it more difficult to be alone. Not only may sexual interaction be inhibited by the presence of children, but the time the couple does have together is likely to be task-orientated time. In addition, there may be child-induced family conflict resulting from sibling rivalry, school problems and disagreements between parents and children concerning matters of discipline. For example, in an analysis of family interaction in the homes of non-problem middle-class mothers and their pre-school children, Fawl (1963) reported an average of 3.4 disturbances per hour. Moreover, there were age-correlated differences. Thus, the average number of disturbances from two- to three-year-old children was more than twice that for four- to five-year-old children.

Marital conflict

As I noted earlier, we tend to have an idealized conception of marriage and the family. It is often portrayed as a romantic and intimate oasis. In reality, it is also often an intimate battleground. Goode (1971), for instance, has maintained that violence and physical force are among the major resources used to achieve desired ends in families as well as elsewhere. Stark and McEvoy (1970) found that approximately 25% of men and 18% of women felt that it was acceptable to slap one's spouse under certain conditions. Similarly, Levinger (1966) found that 23% of middle class couples and 40% of working class couples gave "physical abuse" as a reason for divorce. In their recent national probability sample, Straus *et al.* (1979) note that approximately 50% of their families reported at least one incident of husband–wife physical violence and 28% reported a minimum of one violent act during the survey year.

Several intrinsic characteristics of family life have been implicated in the persistent occurrence of marital and family conflict (Burgess, 1979; Gelles and Straus, 1979). Among these characteristics is the great amount of time family members spend in close contact: one consequence of spending a lot of time in face-to-face interaction with someone is that small annoyances can become exaggerated in importance. Another is that the more time individuals spend together, the greater the overlap of interests and activities so that these, in turn, may become events around which disputes and disagreements might arise. Moreover, given the fact that most family resources are finite in nature, the stage is set for recurring conflicts of interest. Thus, a husband and wife may fight over what they should do on Friday night, whether her mother may visit for a week, where they should take their vacation or which bills should be paid. As I have written elsewhere (Burgess, 1979), "These conflicts of interest are infinite in number and are the grist for escalating disengagement, disaffection, and domestic guerilla warfare" (p.144).

Other characteristics that set the stage for conflict include the high levels of emotional involvement that typify marriages and families. Indeed, the level of emotional affect is usually higher in the family than in any other social relationship. But, such mutual investment in one another generates its own risks and pains, as when one spouse deceives the other. Another related characteristic of family life that is important here is the assumption that membership in a family usually implies the right to influence and control each other's behaviour. Given the fact that in most societies the kinship and household structure insulates the family from the social constraints of other individuals, dissatisfaction with the conduct of another family member may be exacerbated by aggressive attempts to change that person's behaviour.

Resolution of such conflict remains a major task. As noted earlier, marital satisfaction may be influenced largely by a couple's ability to resolve their differences (Gottman, 1979). Several studies support this argument. For example, Dean (1966), while comparing happily married with unhappily married couples, found only low to moderate correlations between happiness and personality indices. In contrast, Navran (1967) found that marital satisfaction was related to the ways in which a couple communicated their differences of opinion and resolved those differences. Navran concluded that happily married couples

(a) talk more to each other, (b) convey the feeling that they understand what is being said to them, (c) have a wider range of subjects available to them, (d) preserve communication channels and keep them open, (e) show more sensitivity to each other's feelings, (f) personalize their language symbols, and (g) make more use of supplementary non-verbal techniques of communication (1967, p.182).

There is reason to suspect that there are styles of interaction unique to marital relationships. Ryder (1968), using a decision-making task, compared the interaction patterns found between husbands paired with their wives or with female married strangers. He found that husbands are more likely to be task oriented and directive with their wives. Wives are more likely to use disapproval with their spouses and they laugh less frequently with spouses than with strangers. In brief, he found that spouses generally treat strangers more gently and politely than they do each other.

Much of what we know about those patterns of interaction associated with marital success and failure we have learned from studies that compare "normal", non-distressed families with "disturbed" or distressed families. The nature of the disturbance has ranged from families where at least one member of the family has been diagnosed as schizophrenic to families where the parents sought marriage or family therapy. The results from these studies are quite consistent.

First, distressed families tend to display more ritualized patterns of interaction. Haley (1964) found that three-person disturbed families are more rigid and employ fewer response alternatives, whilst Ferreira and Winter (1968) found that in problem families there frequently occurred a "monologue-silence-monologue-silence" sequence with less information being exchanged and less spontaneous agreement than in normal families.

The major overarching construct is the amount of information that any act in a family adds to a sequence of acts, and the amount of information is less in distressed families. The amount of information added by an act is, thus, inversely related to the tightness of the interaction structure. The tighter the structure the less information each new event provides . . . (Gottman, 1979, p.49).

Secondly, distressed families exhibit lower frequencies of positive (for example, affectionate and supportive) behaviour. Hence, there is more humour, laughter, and emotional support in normal than in distressed families (e.g. Riskin and Faunce, 1970). In one interesting study, Weiss *et al.* (1973) had couples monitor daily the frequency of pleasing and displeasing events and they found that their marital therapy programme significantly increased the pleases-to-displeases ratio. Wills *et al.* (1974) found that the pleases-to-displeases ratio accounted for substantial portions of the variance in daily ratings of marital satisfaction by a group of non-distressed married couples.

Thirdly, distressed families have higher rates of negative interaction. Birchler *et al.* (1975) were able to discriminate distressed from non-distressed couples on the mean ratio of negative responses per minute on problem-solving and discussion tasks. Similarly, the ratio of agreements to disagreements is generally higher in non-distressed families (e.g. Riskin and Faunce, 1970).

Fourthly, there is some evidence that distressed families are less likely than normal families to reciprocate one another's positive acts, and more likely to reciprocate negative or coercive behaviours. For example, Birchler (1972) described a husband-wife correlation of 0.97 for positive behaviour in non-distressed marriages and 0.74 in distressed marriages, whilst the correlations for negative behaviours were 0.26 and 0.54, respectively. In another study of distressed couples (Wills *et al.*, 1974), there was evidence for the reciprocation of displeasurable but not pleasurable behaviour. They concluded that "in day-to-day affectional interaction, a displeasurable behaviour is more likely to be reciprocated than a pleasurable behaviour" (p.809). In sum, these studies, as well as a recent series carried out by Gottman (1979), indicate that distressed couples are more predictable, interact less often, are less positive, more negative and are more likely to reciprocate negative-affect pieces of behaviour. As we shall see, similar patterns have been found in parent-child relationships.

Family Relationships: Parent-child Interaction

The traditional approach to the study of parent-child relationships has been to focus on the impact of specific child-rearing practices on the child's subsequent behavioural and social development. Hartup (1978) has referred to this as the "social mould" conception of child-parent relationships. Recent efforts, however, have emphasized the bi-directionality of parent-child relations (e.g., Lerner and Spanier, 1980). Thus, this more recent view assumes that children and parents influence each other, and so engage in a relationship at more than one of the levels of involvement outlined at the beginning of the chapter.

In one prominent series of reports, Baumrind (1967; 1968 attempted to integrate the literature on parenting practices. In she identified three major clusters of parental behaviour. The labelled the *authoritarian parent*. This type of parent appare ___ to control and evaluate the behaviour of a child according to some absolute standard of behaviour. This parent stresses the value of obedience and often uses punishment to exact compliance. The second type of parent, Baumrind labelled the *permissive parent*. This parent attempts to relate to the child's behaviour in a non-punishing and accepting manner. The parent is more likely than the authoritarian parent to consult with the child about behaviour standards and offers the child rationales for those standards. Reason, rather than overt power, is used by this parent in child-rearing. The third type of parent is labelled the *authoritative parent*. This parent uses direction through reasoning to control the child. Thus, such a parent exercises firm control over the child but presumably does so through verbal give-and-take with the child.

According to Baumrind (1972), extremely authoritarian or permissive parenting has equally bad consequences for a child's development. Authoritative parents are seemingly more successful in producing children who are achievement orientated, independent, cooperative with adults and friendly with peers. Several other studies have presented data consistent with Baumrind's analyses. For example, Coopersmith (1967) found that mothers who were supportive, caring, accepting and who enforced rules consistently had children who were higher in self-esteem than did mothers who gave little guidance, enforced rules inconsistently or were punitive. Sears (1970) reported that when at least one parent was warm and accepting, children were likely to have high self-esteem.

A study by Santrock (1975) provides support for the view that different disciplinary techniques are related to moral development. It was found that boys who were exposed to power-assertive discipline were capable of making more advanced moral judgements than were boys who were accustomed to love-withdrawal discipline. Likewise Hoffman (1970) had noted earlier that love-withdrawal as a parenting tactic may contribute negatively to moral development.

Most of the research on the effects of children on their parents has been with infants and there is evidence that infant behaviour can, in some circumstances, decrease the probability of parental care. Thus, Robson and Moss (1970) found that mothers experienced decreasing attachment towards their three-month-old infants when crying and other demands for care-giving did not diminish over time and Bell and Ainsworth (1972) found that the more an infant cried in any one quarter of an infant's first year, the more the mother ignored crying in the next quarter. These studies suggest that infant-parent relationships are truly interactional and that the infant is capable of initiating and maintaining a relationship insofar as the infant does not exceed parental limits (Lerner and Spanier, 1980).

Just as we are learning more about marital interaction from comparing distressed and non-distressed couples, so are we learning more about the dynamics of parent-child relationships by comparing deviant and normal families. The deviant families receiving the most attention so far are those where there are either aggressive or delinquent children in the home or where the parents have seriously abused or neglected their children. This body of research indicates that breakdowns in parent-child relationships are largely due to deficient child management skills (e.g. Alexander, 1973; Burgess, 1979; Patterson and Reid, 1970). Moreover, these studies should be of particular interest to students of social relationships because they have all emphasized the interactional character of the parent-child bond in that these parenting deficits have been found to produce spiralling increases in coercive interactions among children and parents (Burgess and Conger, 1978; Patterson, 1976).

Dysfunctional patterns of parent-child interaction take five principal forms and, interestingly, are quite similar to those characteristics responsible for distressed marital relationships. First, these families have a tendency to accent the negative, i.e. to be critical and punitive in their interactions with each other (Burgess and Conger, 1978; Patterson, 1976). Parents in these problem families have also been found to issue significantly more commands than other parents and these commands function to elicit increased frequencies of familial conflict (Terdahl et al., 1976).

A second dysfunctional pattern is that the parents often are poor observers of their child's behaviour. Consequently, the parents do not track a child's deviant behaviour until it reaches an amplitude or frequency where child management becomes exceedingly difficult (Patterson and Reid, 1970). Since both the child and the parent are capable of influencing each other's behaviour, the outcome of this state of affairs is a heightened level of aversive exchange.

Given the parent's poor observing skills, these families are noted for a third characteristic, i.e. they use punishment in an inconsistent manner (Patterson, 1979). In other words, in these families, not only is punishment a frequent control tactic, but the parents are also found to punish a high proportion of prosocial child behaviour as well as deviant child behaviour (Patterson, 1979). Another feature of the inconsistent use of punishment is that many of these parents do a poor job of backing up their scolds and threats with the actual administration of punishing events. Consequently, their verbal threats become increasingly ineffective and simply serve to accelerate the level of coercive interchanges between themselves and their children.

The fourth characteristic of problem families is that the parents typically display significantly lower levels of positive contacts in general (Burgess and Conger, 1978), and positive reinforcement for appropriate child behaviour, in particular (Patterson, 1976). Fifthly, as with punishment, such parents when they do use positive consequences for child behaviour, are as likely to use them following deviant or disruptive behaviour as they are following pro-social child behaviour (McCord et al., 1961). What results, of course, is an essentially unpredictable and contingent schedule of positive reinforcement. There is other research evidence which indicates that such inconsistent schedules are ineffective in encouraging and sustaining appropriate behaviour (e.g. Barnhart, 1968). There are also several studies which suggest that out-of-control children are less effectively controlled by adult social reinforcement (Walker and Buckley, 1973). The outcome of all this is that as parents find their use of rewards ineffective in their attempts to control their children's behaviour, they come to use positive behaviour less and less often. As the frequency of positive contacts and positive reinforcement declines, the rise of coercive behaviour is inevitable.

In addition, there are data which show that the use of rewards in such problem families comes increasingly under the control of the coercive behaviour of other family members (Patterson and Reid, 1970). For example, an adolescent may be positively reinforced for attacks on her siblings by their acceding to her demands. Aggressive behaviour works; it produces compliance — and this is especially the case if there is a large difference in physical size or power. In this manner, the conflicts of interest which I described earlier are often resolved to the benefit of the aggressor and a cycle of aggression is begun. Once that occurs, subsequent coercive behaviour functions as a coping strategy for dealing with another family member's aggressive behaviour: the reinforcer for this behaviour soon becomes the termination of the other person's attack. As these patterns of coercion spread throughout the entire family, it becomes less and less possible to resolve conflicts of interest in a reasonable manner and attempts to do so often contain mixed negative as well as positive messages, as even attempts to be supportive are accompanied by qualifications or criticisms. Even if attempts at positive problem-solving are undiluted by negative connotations, they, nonetheless, are often rebuffed by attacks rather than cooperation. With this heightened level of aversive exchange, all parties come to take a general adversarial stance vis-à-vis each other and patterns of dominance and submission eventually emerge (Patterson, 1979).

A particularly promising outcome of our increasing ability to specify the interactional dynamics of distressed and non-distressed marital and family relationships is that we are becoming more able to assist those relationships in trouble. Thus, Gottman (1979) has reported success with an empirically derived marital therapy programme that concentrates on teaching such interpersonal skills as listening to and validating a spouse's position, pinpointing problem behaviour rather than attributing feelings and motives to the marital partner, following certain rules of politeness rather than continually engaging in bickering, and negotiating agreements. Data are provided which indicate significant changes in marital satisfaction following the intervention programme (Gottman, 1979).

Similarly, improvements in parent-child relationships have followed the application of intervention programmes based on the coercive system described above. These programmes usually involve such components as training a parent to give frequent amounts of love and praise throughout the day whenever the child is behaving appropriately or teaching the parents how to establish reasonable rules and to apply them consistently. Parents are also encouraged to spend time teaching and having their children practise new prosocial behaviour and to avoid hugging, picking up or physically loving the child when s/he misbehaves, all the while remaining as pleasant and calm as possible. Finally, they are taught to substitute "time-out" for physical punishment when the child behaves inappropriately (e.g., Reid and Taplin, 1978).

Divorce

Despite these promising attempts at modifying dysfunctional marital and family relationships, the fact remains that many marriages and families fail. Indeed, one of the most significant demographic changes in the United States since World War II has been the recent rise in the divorce rate to unprecedented levels. Using cohort analysis, Weed (1980) notes that for each of the annual marriage cohorts from 1963 to 1966, approximately 30% of the original marriages had already ended in divorce by 1977. Assuming that the divorce and death rates of American couples in 1976-77 would remain at the same level, Weed estimated that 41% of the marriages in the 1963 cohort will end in divorce and almost one-half of all marriages in the 1973 cohort will eventually end in divorce. In another recent study (Spanier and Glick, 1980) it was shown, further, that the divorce rate is significantly related to age at marriage. In brief, teenage marriages are twice as likely to end in divorce as are marriages involving persons in their twenties.

Attempts to explain rising divorce rates have a long history. Willcox (1891) proposed that the economic emancipation of women was a major factor, whilst Groves (1928) attributed the rise of divorce rates to an increased emphasis on individual pleasure-seeking at the expense of a code of behaviour based on social obligation and self-denial. Ogburn and Nimkoff (1955) suggested that the family was experiencing a loss of cohesion due to its losing some of its major functions to other institutions. In a recent study (Preston and McDonald, 1979) several other factors were found to account for especially high deviations from the general rising trend. These accelerators included "armed service mobilization and high unemployment rates in the year of marriage, and slow national economic growth between pre- and post-marital periods" (p.1).

Hidden behind all these hard facts, however, is a considerable amount of pain and trauma. As Donald Bogue (1949) noted:

"Few events in the life cycle require more extensive changes in activities, responsibilities, and living habits (or cause greater alterations in attitudes, re-ranking of values, and alterations of outlook on life) than does a change from one marital status to another" (p.212).

In fact, divorce turns out to be a major crisis for most people (Goode, 1963; Weiss, 1975). Gurin *et al.* (1960) discovered that approximately 25% of divorced men and 40% of divorced women seek some form of professional help for personal problems. And, while the experience of divorce may be troubling to us all, it is especially a difficult experience for women:

"Divorce hits women hardest. Most of them have to work (71%) and care for children (84%) without moral, economic, or psychological support from a husband or partner. They earn less than single women their age, certainly less than divorced men . . . And they lack the opportunities that divorced men have to date and remarry. For all these reasons, divorced women feel the greatest pressure and stress of any group, report the greatest dissatisfaction with their lives, and describe the emotional quality of their lives in gloomy terms" (Campbell, 1975, p.41).

Young people may have an easier time in adjusting to divorce since they can more easily mix with groups of young, never-married, persons. An important alternative source of support, especially perhaps for older persons, are kin groups, which often help out by providing companionship, lending money, offering child-care services and making their homes available (Weiss, 1975). Whether from kith or kin, adjustment to divorce can best be accomplished by active involvement in social interaction (Goode, 1963).

One of the more troublesome issues surrounding divorce is who will obtain custody of the children. Even though there has been an increase in the number of children living with their father, the proportion still is below two percent of all broken homes (Spanier and Glick, 1980). Hetherington (1979) has found, not surprisingly, that children find the transition from a two-parent to a single-parent household painful. Common responses are anger, fear, depression, and guilt. Moreover, the aftermath of divorce results in an increase of social discord in family relationships though this decreases in the year following divorce.

On the other side of the ledger, a high percentage of divorced people remarry; indeed, the remarriage rate and the divorce rate produce similar curves (Glick and Norton, 1973). Data from the US Bureau of the Census indicate that approximately 80% of the people whose first marriages end in divorce remarry, with the modal interval between first marriage and divorce being only two to three years (Spanier and Glick, 1980). However, it seems all is not a bed of roses, and people do not always learn from previous mistakes, since it has been reported that remarriages actually have a slightly higher probability of ending in divorce than do first marriages, though this difference declines very rapidly for marriages and remarriages of 15 years' duration or more (Weed, 1980).

Conclusion

In this chapter, I have attempted to introduce the reader to the study of relationships in marriages and families. In doing so, I have tried to cover topics that, to some extent at least, cut across the family life cycle. Given such a broad subject matter, I could not possibly have covered all the topics necessary for a complete description and explanation of family affairs. However, it is hoped that this contribution together with those of the other authors in this and the other volumes will at least serve to motivate readers to join in the task of charting and understanding the nature of personal relationships.

CHAPTER 10

Relationships at Work: A Matter of Tension and Tolerance

I. L. Mangam

It is customary to begin chapters such as this with a summary of the argument to be developed throughout the next several pages presumably either to serve as a guide or as the equivalent of a fly-leaf (the reading of which absolves many of us from reading the actual text). This chapter will not be an exception to that rule, but is unusual in that the essence of what I am addressing is contained in a quote from another writer; not another social psychologist nor yet a sociologist or psychologist. A jazz and blues singer, George Melly (1977) provides the introduction which is taken from the second volume of his autobiography and concerns his arrival on board the good ship *Dido*:

> To begin with it was total confusion, but after a day or two it began to make a little sense. I came to realize that everybody in the ship's company held a different if partial view. For the stokers and engineers, it was the engine-room and propellers which signified; for the gunnery officers and ratings, their neatly stacked shells and turrets — for the electricians, the ship was a nervous system of cables and power-points; for the writers, a list of names, each entitled to different rates of pay; for the cooks, the galleys and store rooms; for the Master at Arms, rebellious stirrings and acts prejudicial to naval discipline; for the Captain and senior officers, a view of the whole, detailed or vague, according to their competence; for the ship's cat, areas of warmth and comfort, and a jungle where the prey squeaked and scurried behind the bulkheads and sacks of provisions. Yet there were also intricate private

relationships, both official and unofficial. Every mess had its friends, enemies, and neutrals. Shared duty led to liaisons or enmities. Between ranks, commissioned or otherwise, there were tensions, tolerance, fierce vendettas fought out with the aid of King's Regulations or the sympathetic bending of the rules.

For me, Melly says it all, or nearly all. In what follows I will pick up and elaborate upon a number of themes expressed or implied in what he has to say; in particular I will be concerned with the division of labour, with the nature and consequences of hierarchy, with "partial views" and their effects and, throughout, with the tensions and tolerances which constitute the essence of relations at work. First, however, I wish to make some general comments about the nature of organization to set what follows in context (see also Mangham, 1978, 1979).

Melly's initial experience of the good ship *Dido* was one of confusion replaced within a very short time by an apprehension of the structure which surrounded him on all sides. Social life in any institution is patterned; the daily round is not one of constant interpretation and constant improvization since much of what passes for everyday interaction is in actuality taken for granted and well rehearsed. Much of what is deemed to be "normal" interaction at work, as elsewhere, is non-problematic. Social actors do not interact in a void and construct their social world *ab initio* on each and every occasion, but rather they approach interaction already influenced by past social experience and, to a marked extent, their choices (insofar as they are aware of choice at all) are limited, if not determined, by the patterns of behaviour most frequently used by other social actors past and present in what are taken to be similar circumstances. Such patterns of mutual accommodation arise as individuals seek to make the world more predictable by structuring their associations. For each person, theoretically at least, an encounter with another constitutes an opportunity to reduce equivocality and to achieve some personal goal. When a relatively stable working agreement is arrived at — the delicate balance where each anticipates some benefit by maintaining the association — it will be in the interests of both parties to preserve it. In such circumstances we have the elements of what may be termed a joint act. (Allport, 1955).

One form of joint action is created when a cycle of repetitive pieces of behaviour comes into being; a circumstance in which an individual regularly conducts himself in a manner which is compatible with another's expectations (and vice versa). The pattern of reciprocating behaviour thus created may lead directly to patterns of mutual expectation which gradually take on the character of a norm or a set of rules which both individuals (and others when faced with what they take to be a similar situation) accept as binding upon themselves and as defining their relationship. Thus, interactions may be characterized anywhere along a continuum at one end of which all behaviour is negotiated and at the other end of which are those interactions or relationships which are relatively stable, relatively structured and almost wholly taken for granted.

I am not claiming that an organization is nothing more than the joint action of its members, but I am saying that such behaviours and such relationships do constitute the basic elements of organizing. As Weick (1969) puts it:

> Interlocked behaviours are the basic elements that constitute any organization. They consist of repetitive, reciprocal, contingent behaviours that develop and are maintained between two or more actors. Each actor uses and is used by the other person for the accomplishment of activities which neither alone could accomplish.

Thus *organizing* may be conceived of as a process of creating, maintaining and, occasionally, dissolving relationships and *the organization*, at any one time, may be seen as a network of such joint actions.

Regularity and Innovation

A great deal of behaviour is likely to be orderly and routine: the various ranks and trades know what is expected of them and perform, with minor variations, in line with the expectations. Our performances in our own organizations, in management meetings, in union assemblies, parent-teacher associations, and so on are adequate testimony that in many, many circumstances we know how to conduct ourselves. At the other end of the continuum are the circumstances in which expectations and parts to be played are much less clear and much more subject to improvization and negotiation. The more novel or problematic the situation, the more consciously must the participants create and test out particular courses of action.

The distinction between the routine and the novel is, however, much less absolute than is implied above. In a number of routine circumstances there is room for improvization and innovation and even in the most novel there may be an element of the stable and predictable. However, both the routine and standard responses to circumstances as well as the improvised ones depend, *in the final analysis*, upon the process of interpretation, as Blumer (1969) observes:

> The meanings that underlie established and recurrent joint action are themselves subject to pressure as well as to reinforcement, to incipient dissatisfaction as well as to indifference; they may be challenged as well as affirmed, allowed to slip along

without concern as well as subjected to infusions of new vigor. . . . It is the social process in group life that creates and upholds the rules, not the rules that create and uphold group life. . . .

Negotiated order

The last quotation contains the nub of the argument that I am advancing: personal relationships acting in the social process create and uphold the rules, the rules do not create the process. Put another way, organization may be seen as a process — a continuous exchange of definitions and affirmation or otherwise of working agreements that depends on the relationships at work: it is not simply a structure of rules, regulations and procedures within which all is order. All shared understandings lack permanence and must be continually reaffirmed or renegotiated through personal means; rules, procedures, structure and order itself are not automatic occurrences (however taken for granted they may appear) but rather must be worked at and sustained by the repeated acts of participants in the relationships that they create and maintain. The working agreements which characterize organizational life initially arise from and are ultimately dependent upon the relationship processes of give and take, diplomacy, imposition and bargaining. Order and change within organizations may thus be seen to be the products of negotiations, the result of the pulling and hauling that constitutes the bargaining process which occurs between individuals and groups as they struggle to achieve their goals and objectives in association with, or at the expense of, others. The "tensions" and the "tolerances" which Melly mentions are, from this perspective, a necessary correlative of organizing, and arise from or depend on *personal* relationships.

Organizations are not the rational, orderly entities that some would have us believe. The various individuals and sub-units of the organization are heterogeneous, have some degree of discretion and autonomy (even in the most regimented of institutions) and may differ in terms of their goals. How, then, is some semblance of order maintained? In essence there is no discontinuity between processes which occur between individuals outside the workplace and those which occur within. Just as friends arrive at working agreements, as lovers do, as families do, so also do members of organizations. In this sense Melly is correct in referring to *Dido* as "a real community, a steel village". Relationships at work are marked by a continuous process of negotiation, one in which working agreements are created, consolidated or overturned. Strauss and his colleagues (from whose work the term "negotiated order" is taken) found, for example, that in one psychiatric hospital "hardly anyone knows the extant rules, much less exactly what situations they apply to, for whom and with what sanctions". Members had to agree on interpretations, had to invent temporary rules to guide their actions. Doctors and nurses "negotiated" understandings about who was entitled to do what and came to temporary working agreements: "temporary" because almost any day some new circumstance or some pressure upon existing arrangements arose such that, as Strauss and his colleagues note (Strauss, 1971), the outsider is never able to know "what the hospital is. . . . unless he has. . . . a comprehensive grasp of what combination of rules and policies along with agreements, understandings, parts, contracts and other working arrangements currently obtain".

The social order of a hospital, of a factory, of an office and even of the good ship *Dido* is sustained or created anew with each affirmation or renegotiation of particular working agreements. Joint action may be seen as a complex process of bargaining and negotiating and the model of organization that derives from such a perspective is one characterized by a complex and shifting network of competing *and* collaborating individuals or groups acting so as to control their own behaviour and that of others in what may be defined as their own self-interests.

The division of labour

This picture of negotiated order is immensely complicated by the application of the principles of the division of labour and of the practice of scientific management within the workplace. Of central importance to the reaching of mutual accommodation is the balance of power; work is designed in accordance with certain principles and priorities which tend to concentrate power within the organization and create circumstances in which the negotiation of order is conducted between groups rather than individuals (with qualifications to which I will return later). In order to develop this point I must first make some comments concerning the nature of the division of labour.

The organization of the good ship *Dido* reflects these principles and neatly establishes the point that work, at least for the most part in the Western world, is differentiated. The ship does not carry a complement of men of the same rank all carrying out the same tasks — the labour is divided. Such differentiation is obvious in every organization, in industrial organizations there are various departments and, as in the ship, various levels of management. In another sense, however, the *Dido* is not representative in that the differentiation of tasks aboard is not as extreme as that as experienced by many factory workers. Many jobs within organizations consist of frequently repeated operations, lasting half a minute or less. Garson (1972) captures this aspect well in his investigations of assembly line operations:

"Hanging around the parking lot between shifts, I learned immediately that to these workers, 'It's not the money'."

"It pays good," said one, "but it's driving me crazy."
"I don't want more money," said another. "None of us do."
"I do," said his friend. "So I can quit quicker."
"It's the job," everyone said. But they found it hard to describe the job itself.
"My father worked in auto for 35 years," said a clean-cut lad, "and he never talked about the job. What's there to say? A car comes, I weld it. A car comes, I weld it. One hundred and one times an hour."

No doubt life aboard the *Dido* varies not only in its degree of differentiation but also in its complexity or simplicity. The job of the navigation officer is likely to be more complex than that of a writer or a signalman, that of an electrician more complex than that of a cook and so on. Welding cars is both a highly differentiated task and a relatively simple one (now automated in some plants, thus eliminating the need for an operative at all). Most, but not all, shop-floor work is simple; indeed the logic of the division of labour dictates that it should be so.

The division of labour (and the philosophy of management that accompanies it) creates conditions in which the amount of "freedom" permitted to the employee varies: that which Schrank (1978) refers to as "schmoozing" time.

But compared to the repetitive work of the furniture factory, I preferred the machine shop, though many men I worked with did not. A day in the machine shop would go fast, and at least some work was a challenge. . . . However I found that one of the best things about being a machinist or a tool-maker was the freedom to move around, to schmooze. Often when a machine tool has been set up for an operation, there can be considerable time to schmooze with the guys around you — go get coffee, a Coke, or a smoke. And a considerable amount of time may get taken up in figuring out how to make the task easier.

The relative differences in freedom from control and specification, and the freedom to schmooze, to figure out your own task, or to just take time out are significant distinctions between and within organizations.

A question of discretion

Fox and others have argued that this schmooze factor is, indeed, the most significant distinction to be found within the workplace. He distinguishes three levels of discretion — high, medium and low — and devotes a considerable amount of space to them. Low-discretion jobs are those such as experienced by the car assembly workers at Lordstown referred to earlier in this chapter, and the kinds of task which are the lot of many workers both in factories and offices. The type of job which requires, in the words of F.W. Taylor (1911) — of whom more later — that the workers "do what they are told promptly and without asking questions or making suggestions. . . . it is absolutely necessary for every man in an organization to become one of a train of gear wheels''. Low-discretion jobs leave minimal room for schmoozing and are so prescribed, controlled and supervised that the amount of negotiation, in the sense outlined earlier, appears to be virtually non-existent. Again the Lordstown assembly line studies reflect this aspect of work experience graphically:

> I asked about diversions: "What do you do to keep from going crazy?"
> "Well, certain jobs like the pit you can light up a cigarette without them seeing."
> "I go to the wastepaper basket. I wait a certain number of cars, then find a piece of paper to throw away. . . ." (Quoted in Garson, 1972).

In factories and offices, for the mass of workers there is little or no discretion and for the few, the precious few, there is some room for judgement and initiative. F.W. Taylor (1911) has dignified this practice with the title of "scientific management", a philosophy which he advocated in the early years of this century and which has had a runaway success. He held that the worker should execute the work, but that the manager should design it and plan it. By this division of labour, however, not only would the management specify what was to be done but "how it is to be done and the exact time for doing it". Here is Taylor talking to Schmidt, a labourer, in a passage which Taylor wrote to illustrate his work-study method — he is persuading the immigrant worker to move 47 tons of pig iron per day:

> Well, if you are a high-priced man, you will do exactly as this man tells you tomorrow, from morning till night. When he tells you to pick up a pig and walk, you pick it up and you walk, and when he tells you to sit down and rest, you sit down. You do that right straight through the day. And what's more, no back talk. Now a high-priced man does just what he's told to do, and no back talk. Do you understand that? When this man tells you to walk, you walk; when he tells you to sit down you sit down and you don't talk back at him. Now you come on to work here tomorrow morning and I'll know before night whether you are really a high-priced man or not.

And the Consequences Were. . . .

It has not turned out to be quite like Taylor's dream. The very principles of simplification and differentiation taken in conjunction with the imposition of low-discretion tasks upon the mass of workers has resulted in no small measure of tension and antagonism between management and men. As Fox (1974) notes, the person subjected to heavy prescription of his work and tight supervision is likely to react: "The role occupant perceives superordinates as behaving as if they believe he cannot be trusted, of his own volition, to deliver a work performance which fully accords to the goals they wish to see pursued, or the values they wish to see observed''. In turn he is likely to respond with low trust of his employer.

Trust is an important, if little understood, variable in human relationships at work as well as elsewhere. It is arguable that in pre-industrial society (and, indeed, in some present-day small workshops), when the division of labour was minimal, the small scale of the operations made possible a personalized set of relations between the master and his servants. Although, as Dickens and others have shown, such personal relationships may not be to the benefit of the employee, at its best such a system approaches the condition of joint negotiation I have described earlier — the spirit of give and take. Such relationships are not characterized by *narrow* self-interest (though to be sure they are informed by self-interest) and specific contractual obligations. Throughout their existence there is a degree of accommodation to each other's needs, a mutual reciprocity, a fuzziness about rights and duties, that betokens that neither party will exploit the other. Thus an employee may agree to work late for no payment in order to finish an urgent job, knowing and *trusting* that his employer will respond should he have occasion to ask something in turn.

The effect of the division of labour and its associated features has been to weaken the relationship of trust which existed between master and servant. In substantial sectors of economic life there has emerged the characteristic pattern of relations between management and men — a pattern marked by impersonal and contractual attitudes and behaviour. As industrialization proceeded the employer *enforced* upon the employee what the latter experienced as a low-trust pattern of work. Put in terms of the points made earlier about negotiation of order, the employer chose less and less to have a vague mutually adjusting accommodation between himself and his employee, but sought to fulfil his own needs at the expense of the other by scheduling output and controlling every aspect of performance. Indeed the needs and aspirations of the workforce are cultivated by the management only insofar as they contribute to, or are at least compatible with, its own priority purposes. Significantly, perhaps, with the advent of the industrial revolution, persons (or even ''servants'') with all that the term implies for aspirations, needs and obligations became ''hands'' — a dramatic expression of the change in function and in relationship implied by large-scale, low-discretion operations.

The notion of a specific contract between the employer and his factory ''hands'' released the former from any other obligations to the latter. Beyond observing the letter of the law, the employer has no duties in respect of his employees. For the employee, however, the contract has frequently been imposed and enforced but often — as with Taylor — with the expectation that its imposition would not change the diffuse obligations of the employee towards the employer. In other words Schmidt is not only to shift 47 tons of pig iron, he is to be "glad of it"; that is, he is to continue to respond in a high-trust fashion with willing compliance, absolute loyalty, and complete confidence in Taylor (Fox, 1974).

In a number of circumstances employees have so behaved; it must be appreciated that although employees may perceive themselves as being used by management it is not inevitable that they will express this awareness or even consider it anything other than "natural":

> I mean what I say. People should stick to their own class. Life's a railway journey, and mankind a passenger, first class, second class, third class. Any person found riding in a superior class to that for which he has been given a ticket will be removed at the first station stopped at, according to the bye-law of the company. (Quoted in Robertson, 1956).

To the extent that Schmidt accepts that "life's a railway journey" he may be content to go along with others travelling in a higher class. For many, however, the response desired by Taylor and his kind was not forthcoming. As study after study attests, the imposition of low-discretion jobs results in employees working indifferently or to rule, with little or no personal commitment, practising restrictionism and generally behaving in a "bloody-minded" fashion. Others discovered the power of the informal group and, later, the formal unionized group. Study after study attests to the influence of the former, sufficient to fill this chapter, without straying too far into the broader field of industrial relations. Membership of the group serves to redress the power imbalance created by extreme differentiation and simplification. Relationships at work are frequently characterized by a strong desire to be part of a gang or team. Not necessarily or even primarily for the friendship it affords — in one study fewer than 10% of the respondents claimed particular friends at work (Crawford, 1976) — but as a reaction to the contracts imposed upon lower-level operatives by the management.

In the Bank Wiring room, for example, part of the famous Hawthorne studies, 14 men were studied over a period of six months in 1931 and 1932. Their behaviour was observed and monitored, but no attempt was made by the investigators to change anything. It was revealed that, contrary to management expectation, individuals did not attempt to maximize their earnings by working harder. Instead the group informally established its own norm of outputs and punished those who contravened it. If a man did turn out more than was thought proper by his peers, or if in their estimation he worked too fast, he was exposed to merciless ridicule. He was abused as a "rate buster" or a "speed king" and was treated with contempt. Similarly those who produced too little were abused as "chiselers" since they were seen as cutting down the earnings of the group as a whole. Abuse and ridicule were not the only penalties nonconformists had to suffer; those who transgressed the group norm on productivity were likely to be "binged". A man who was thought to be working either too fast or too slow and who proved unresponsive to ridicule might be approached and struck hard on the upper arm — "binged" as the operatives put it. "Binging" originated as a game, a test of strength to see who could hit the harder, but was clearly employed as a mode of social control. Roethlisberger and Dickson, authors of this part of the studies, note that the workers explained this behaviour in terms of insecurity — "if output were too high, something might happen — the 'bogey' might be raised, the 'rate' might be lowered, someone be laid off, hours might be reduced, or supervisors might reprimand the slower workers". (Quoted in Homans, 1951).

Such statements imply a conflict of interests between employer and employee which Roethlisberger and Dickson are quick to dismiss, but other studies — empirical and impressionistic — tend to reinforce the interpretation that informal relations arise at least as much as a response to attempts to control as for reasons of sociability. Schrank (1978) neatly captures the essence of this in the following extract from his autobiographical account of work in a carpentry factory:

> "My third or fourth week at the factory found me earnestly launched in my quest for holding the job but doing less work — or working less hard. This was immediately recognized and hailed by the men with 'Now you're gettin' smart, kid. Stop bustin' your ass and only do what you have to do. You don't get any more money for bustin' your hump and you might put some other poor bastard outa' a job.' "

Schrank was to learn an even more important lesson. He began to "find" pieces of completed work amongst the sawdust or behind the woodpiles and on one occasion, on drawing the attention of an operator to his "find", he was told in no uncertain terms to mind his own business. Dejected, he considered his future: "What the hell should I do? This job is terrible, the men are pissed off at me. . . ." He is put straight by Sam:

> " 'Let me tell you what it's all about. The guys around, that is the machine operators, agree on how much we are gonna turn out, and that's what the boss gets, no more, no less. . . .' *The more he talked, the more I really began to feel like the enemy.* . . . 'Look, kid, the boss always wants more and he doesn't give a shit if we die giving it to him, so we' (*it was that 'we' that seemed to retrieve my soul back into the community.* . . .) 'agree on how much we're going to give him. . . .' (*Sam put his arm on my shoulder. My God! I was one of them! I love Sam and the place. I am in!*) 'So look' he says, 'your job is to figure out how to move and work no faster than we turn the stuff out. Get it? OK?' " (Schrank, 1978, italics added).

Roy, another writer in this idiom, confirms much of what Schrank has to say about the nature and purpose of peer relationships in his much more thorough and extended study. He was employed for nearly a year as a radial-drill operator in one of the machine shops of a steel processing plant and he kept a daily record of his observations and experiences relating to work activity and social interaction. His major interest lay in the phenomenon which Taylor had much earlier disparagingly termed "soldiering", the deliberate restriction of output by workers. In a fascinating study Roy (1955) notes that "not only did workers on the 'drill-line' cooperate with each other as fellow members of a combat team at war with management; they also received considerable aid and abetment from other groups of the shop. . . ." He notes that machine operatives not only held back effort, but sometimes they cooperated to work hard. Always, however, as workers "we devoted ourselves to crossing the expectations of formal organization with persever-ance, artistry and organizing ability of our own."

His discussion of relationships between management and men around work-study illustrates the battle lines clearly. He notes that one belief, univer-sally accepted in the work group, may be characterized as: "You can't 'make out' if you do things the way management wants them done." He explains that job timing was a "battle all the way" between operators and time-study, a battle which united men against management:

> During the eleven-month study, machine operators, including the drill-line men, were enjoying the cooperation of several other shop groups in an illegal facilitation of the "make-out" process. This intergroup network effectively modified certain formally established shop routines, a too close attachment to which would hand-icap the operators. The "syndicate" also proved adequate in circumventing each of a series of "new rules" and "new systems" introduced by management to expur-gate all modifications and improvizations and force a strict adherence to the rules. (Roy, 1955).

Roy comments that a more complete picture of intergroup and inter-personal relations would include conflict as well as cooperation between operators and service groups, but he clearly demonstrates that changes in relationships accompany "in cyclical fashion, changes in basic conditions of work".

A Degree of Tolerance . . . . An Element of Collusion

The tension that exists between workers and management in many organi-zations is manifest; every newspaper, every broadcast attests it. But, as Melly perceptively remarks, relations on the good ship *Dido* were also marked by tolerances; he draws our attention to the fact that within organiza-tions people do reach some form of accommodation. However widespread, incipient, muted, overt, or covert, the conflicts that exist between individuals, groups and levels, in most cases they manage to negotiate some working agreement. The division of labour and the practice of scientific management may, as Fox and others have argued, produce at work relationships of continuing and constant conflict; may have indeed changed the nature of the contract between employer and employee, but the process of negotiation of order may still be observed. All is not tension and hostility, strife and dissension. The negotiation may now be between groups or representatives of groups, but it is negotiation for all that.

A much neglected study by Melville Dalton reveals that in the organizations he studied there was great heterogeneity and clashing of individual and group purpose, with people frequently working at cross-purposes — but it also documents in great detail the accommodations that they reached with each other. Relations at the plant level, Dalton notes, between management and labour necessitates relatively covert and *continual* negotiation. Relations are a blur of conflict, cooperation and compromise initiated and guided by cross-cliques; negotiation of order in the factories and stores that Dalton studied was pervasive, secretive and complex. I will quote liberally from this source to illustrate the reality of tension and tolerance to which Melly alludes.

Dalton (1959) points out, for example, that the men do not always unite against the employer nor do the management necessarily hold together. As a union official told him: "A man can have a good, legitimate grievance, but the union may pass him and his grievance up to keep on good terms with the company." Both unions and representatives of management collude to avoid "trouble". For example, he reports that when a foreman sent home a workman who was persistently late, the workman filed a grievance and was allowed to return to work by the foreman's superior. Naturally the foreman was incensed and asked why he had been let down on this occasion. As Dalton (1959) reports it, the superior said it "was a small item after all" and went on to declare that he (the superior) "might want a big favour from the union sometime in the future. . . . We have to trade back and forth. Sometimes we give in, sometimes they give in. That's why we never have any big trouble". The achievement of such an accommodation with the man and his union, however, has its costs. In this case the tension between the foreman and his boss clearly was increased, assuming vendetta proportions:

"If O'Brien (his superior) wants to make me look like a fool every time I make a decision, why, by God, he can make all the decisions. You know, two can play that game. I can give the boys every damn thing he can give them. Then when they come up with a big one that I know damn well he can't give 'em, I'll tell 'em to take it to him — that I don't want anything to do with it."

Much of the accommodation is covert and delicate and must remain so or the consequences may be dire, as Dalton clearly documents. A middle manager and a union official had agreed on additional bonus hours in order to raise the pay levels of three jobs but were thwarted in their attempts so to do by the activities of the time-study engineers who refused to change the rates since "unnecessary operations were being carried out". The manager talked to the head of engineering but at first was unsuccessful. There was open conflict and the manager was able to win a slight increase in rates by having the jobs restudied but not without subsequent cost to his career. "His attempts to have 'smooth relations' with the union trapped him into the unforgivable sin of openly bargaining for the union with a group of his colleagues. This was not forgotten when he was under consideration for the divisional post." He did not get it.

Failure to observe delicate and covert informal arrangements can be an embarrassment to all concerned. Dalton reports the case of a "straight" or "incorruptible" lady who ran one of the soda fountains who aroused much resentment by not giving the usual favours. Her superior was forced to examine her records, to imply that she was making errors, and to withhold the praise she obviously craved. Higher chain officials also asked her to explain her unique performance. They hinted that she could not be so superior in her performance as other fountain managers and, effectively, forced her to resign.

> The store manager regarded her as a failure because she did not understand what he could not tell her — that her margin of profits was too high and that some social use of materials, not theft, was expected. In his mind, she was too little concerned with the system's internal harmony and too devoted to formalities (Dalton, 1959).

One final example of a covert working agreement again illustrates a tolerance which allows the work to be done and protects the interests of a number of people. Dalton (1959) reports the case where head office wanted periodic surprise inspections and parts counts made in the departments. This was soon negotiated covertly into a situation where only "nominal surprise" visits would occur, all agreements having been made before as to the "walking route". Furthermore, not only were arrangements made with the workers to get certain parts out of the way, but also arrangements were made between the department heads to move parts around, using each other's storage areas. Thus what Dalton terms a "working adjustment" was reached. Head office was apparently satisfied that all was in order, the departmental chiefs "escaped nervous breakdown" and the local plant chiefs preserved "their conception of local rights and at the same time raised morale".

As Dalton indicated there is tension as well as tolerance in such a system of accommodation: the implied threat of reprisal lurks behind a great many of the covert working agreements. As he reports, staff officers permitted minor rule-breaking by the line "in exchange for aid" from the line during crises. They also agreed to transfer some funds of line accounts "in order to get more, or continued, cooperation. This last may never be expressed in such terms but it is understood." All of these agreements are "essential to prevent the line from revealing staff errors to the top". Another potential line of reprisal, Dalton noted, was for the workers to "stand pat" on the rules "at a time when the staff wants evasion". Such a trade-off "becomes simple and so unofficially acceptable that it seems natural". In any event the higher the stakes, "the more 'illegal' the past, the closer they were drawn to each other and the greater the fear of exposure".

Foremen are the men in the middle in this process of informal negotiation — the broker's men of the pantomime of work. In the Bank Wiring study we learn that the supervisor was in a difficult position since, as a representative of management, his duty was to enforce the rules and to do all that he could to maximize output. He was clearly aware that there were a good many things going on of which higher management would not have approved, but he was equally aware that there was little that could be done about it. As Roethlisberger and Dickson conclude: "To enforce the rules would have required his standing over the men all day, and by doing so he would have sacrificed all hope of establishing good relations with them. He would have lost even that minimum of influence that he needed if he was to do any kind of job at all." (Quoted in Homans, 1951).

There are clear indications of the kind of tolerance and collusion documented by Dalton in Roy's (1955) study also:

> Art (a foreman) was at the time cage when I punched off the day work of rereaming and on to the piecework of drilling. He came around to my machine shortly after. "Say" he said, "when you punch off day work on to piecework, you ought to have your piecework already started. Run a few, then punch off the day work, and you'll have a good start. You've got to chisel a little around here to make money". Apparently the rule for the broker's men is "to break the rules, but not too much, just within reason to keep the boys on production".

Detailed studies such as those undertaken by Dalton — and there are too few of them — reveal the complexity of relationships at work. Some relationships clearly contribute to the company's goals, some to the union's. Others, however, equally durable, equally strong, reflect the accommodations that are made covertly by those who work together in order to maintain some level of internal harmony. As Dalton puts it, a "web of commitments grows up, continuously reaffirmed or renegotiated as events and circumstances change".

Taylor Versus the Rest

Rising aspirations, or simple "bloody-mindedness" among occupants of low-discretion roles, may dispose them to be more resistant towards coercive policies and practices. As individuals they may, other things being equal (which they rarely are), go sick, work slowly or secure work elsewhere. As a group, particularly as a unionized group, they may challenge the contract which management seeks to impose upon them. In any event, as I have indicated, they will indulge in informal, covert as well as formal negotiations of order.

For Taylor and other senior managers the situation is somewhat different. Those occupying high-discretion roles are much less likely to be subject to coercion than other members of the organization: one cannot force a man to exercise judgement, initiative or real commitment to the organization, force at such a level runs the risk that not only will the member work "without enthusiasm", he may actively exercise his initiative in opposition to the desires of those at the very top. In terms of the model of negotiated order outlined earlier, he *as an individual,* unlike Schmidt as an individual, has the power to act against the interests of others, thus in the bargain that ultimately constitutes the order of the organization, every working agreement to which he is party will perforce provide him with a greater measure of satisfaction than obtains for the more lowly "hands" in the organization. Relations between Taylor the manager and his employer, therefore, are much less likely to be antagonistic than relations between Schmidt and Taylor. Relations between Taylor and his peers, however, may be much less warm and cooperative than those which obtain between Schmidt and *his* peers. For not only do the principles of scientific management and the practice of the division of labour divide men from management, they also promote intra-organizational conflict within the hierarchy. The consequences of the "partial views" which are such a feature of modern organizations can be as devastating as the consequences of hierarchy itself.

The "Taylors" engaged in different organizational tasks develop and maintain distinctive cultures and interests. A great deal of organizational conflict occurs between specialists and the groups they represent as they attempt to advance their interests and "build their empires". Within industry, conflict frequently occurs between sales and production, between personnel and production, between technical development, production and mechanical engineering, between finance and corporate planning and so on *ad infinitum:*

"What we need around here is some better control of the marketing people. Indeed what we need are some better marketing people, they are not up to the job. The

trouble is they can't say 'No'; they will promise the customer stuff we just cannot make. Anything for a quiet life. . . ."
"The people in the overseas sales division, I've got to say it, they must be fools, bloody fools. Even a child could understand the impact of taking an order on these terms, but not them, in particular not Eric Smith, he's a prize idiot and he's in charge of the rest of them." (Quoted from Mangham, 1980).

Such conflicts (and they are well documented and readily recognizable) are not confined to industrial organizations. Within universities, for example, it is no secret that schools, departments, and faculties compete for resources; members of such bodies fight often bitterly and frequently with considerable skill to have their views prevail. Schools and departments rarely cooperate over personnel or equipment and can usually only display concerted action in opposition to some other faculty or to the central administration. Individual academics jealously protect their freedom of action and manfully resist other academics who seek to control them through committees, unions, budgets or whatever. Relations within research teams are often experienced as highly competitive and are rarely seen to be free of conflict and mutual antagonism (Bailey, 1978). Similarly within hospitals, in the armed forces and within revered institutions such as the British Broadcasting Corporation, intra-organizational conflict and mutually antagonistic relations are frequently reported:

Cooperation between different departments of the BBC — strikingly lacking — as between, let's say, Current Affairs departments. An absence of any interplay at all. In fact positive rivalry, and a tendency to play down the contribution of others. . . . (Burns, 1977).

I could go on citing examples from virtually every kind of organization but I will conclude this section with the results of a couple of studies. When asked to describe the biggest problem over the previous few weeks, the majority of managers in one study did not list a technical or financial one but one involving relations with others. In another study, Handy (1976) reported:

(a) 87% of middle managers felt that conflicts were very seldom coped with, and that, when they were, the attempts tended to be inadequate.
(b) 65% thought that the most important unsolved problem of the organization was that the top management was unable to help them overcome the inter-group rivalries, lack of cooperation and poor communications.
(c) 53% said that if they could alter one aspect of their superior's behaviour it would be to help him see the dog-eat-dog communication problems that existed in middle-management.

Relations between managers, however, are not completely characterized by tension and conflict any more than those between management and men may be so characterized. They, too, show the characteristics of a negotiated order; occasionally, for example, they cooperate to defeat some third party situated elsewhere in the organization. As with all negotiations, individuals seek to establish with other individuals where they each stand with respect to particular issues, events or situations and, in so doing, seek to discover whether or not they have or can make common cause. Relations between managers, therefore, may often be very similar to those which obtain between professional politicians; indeed the senior levels of organizations are noted for their alliances, coalitions and caucuses. Roelofs' (1967) description of a political caucus may be constructively quoted:

> . . . . a meeting having a definable character, usually private, certainly informal, and often marked by the somewhat disguised bonhomie typical of relations between men who, even if not friends, know that they need each other and must respect each other as independently situated. A caucus is . . . . a personal meeting but one between men who come together to discover if among their several needs there may be personal advantages. . . .

In every nook and cranny, in every executive toilet, dining room, office and car park, gossip and talk provide the raw material of relationships between the managers and professionals. By hints and indirections, deals are done and temporary alliances are forged only to be overturned as events unfold and circumstances are seen to change.

Finally, as with the shopfloor, covert negotiations supplement or transgress formal relations. Burns (1977) in his splendid study of the BBC notes that a number of executives considered it smart or wise to "out-manoeuvre" the codes of practice laid down by the Board of Management:

> . . . . on my own programme, very often I have to do things which I know if I asked my boss, he'd say no. It would be right for my boss to say "No, you mustn't do that".

No doubt some accommodation has been reached whereby this particular executive does not ask and his particular boss does not watch his programmes.

Summary

Throughout this chapter I have attempted to present some of the "tensions" and the "tolerances" that constitute the experience of relationships at work. My argument has been that although the division of labour and the practice of scientific management may greatly exacerbate the tension which exists in any dependency relationship (such as much of work is), it does not preclude

Page

the element of negotiation which underpins all of social life. Indeed with its emphasis upon contractual obligations it may in fact enhance this aspect of relationships. Throughout I have adopted a pluralistic perspective on organizations, seeing them as coalitions of interest groups presided over by a senior management group — in a detailed or vague fashion according to competence — serving the needs of the entity by paying attention to all the interests affected. Such a perspective clearly implies no correct or proper objective or set of objectives, but rather the need for a balance to be established between the sometimes divergent claims of the participating parties. Put another way, organizations may be seen as arenas within which actors play out their own agendas; organizations — as I have maintained — may be seen as being enacted in process. Thus relationships at work may be subject to conflict and cooperation, indifference, friendship, war and peace, tension and tolerance; and this applies equally elsewhere — which gives the study of relationships at work more than local interest and importance.

References

ABBOTT, S. and LOVE, B. (1972). "Sappho was a Right-on Woman: A Liberated View of Lesbianism," Stein and Day, New York.

AJZEN, I. (1977). Information processing approaches to interpersonal attraction. *In* "Theory and Practice in Interpersonal Attraction," (Ed. S.W. Duck), Academic Press, London and New York.

ALBERT, S. and KESSLER, S. (1978). Ending social encounters. *J. Exp. Soc. Psychol.* **14**, 541-553.

ALEXANDER, J.F. (1973). Defensive and supportive communication in family systems. *J. Marriage Family* **35**, 613-617.

ALLAN, G. (1977). Sibling solidarity. *J. Marriage Family* **39**, 177-184.

ALLPORT, F.H. (1955). "Theories of Perception and the Concept of Structure", Wiley, New York.

ALTMAN, I. (1975). "The Environment and Social Behavior: Privacy, Personal Space, Territory, Crowding", Brooks/Cole, Monterey, CA.

ALTMAN, I. and TAYLOR, D. (1973). "Social Penetration: the Development of Interpersonal Relationships", Holt, New York.

ANDERSON, N.H. (1971). Integration theory and attitude change. *Psycholog. Rev.* **78**, 171-206.

ANDREYEVA, G.M. (1974). Towards the construction of a theoretical model of social perception. *Questions of Psychology* (Russian Journal).

ARAFAT, I. and YORBURG, B. (1973). On living together without marriage. *J. Sex Res.* **9**, 97-106.

ARAJI, S.K. (1977). Husbands' and wives' attitude-behaviour congruence on family roles. *J. Marriage Family* **39**, 309-320.

ARGYLE, M. (1975). "Bodily Communication", Methuen, London.

ARMISTEAD, N. (1974). Experience in everyday life. *In* "Reconstructing Social Psychology", (Ed. N. Armistead) Penguin, Harmondsworth, Middlesex, UK.

ARONSON, E. (1972). "The Social Animal", Freeman, New York.

ARONSON, E. and CARLSMITH, J.M. (1968). Experimentation in social psychology. *In* "The Handbook of Social Psychology", (2nd edn) Vol. 2. (Eds G. Lindzey and E. Aronson), Addison-Wesley, Reading, MA.

215

ASKHAM, J. (1976). Identity and stability within the marriage relationship. *J. Marriage Family* **38**, 535-546.

AUSTIN, J.L. (1962). "How To Do Things With Words", Oxford University Press, Oxford.

AUSTIN, W.G. (1974). Studies in "Equity with the World": A new application of Equity Theory. Unpublished doctoral dissertation. University of Wisconsin.

BABCHUK, N. (1965). Primary friends and kin: A study of the associations of middle-class couples. *Social Forces* **43**, 483-493.

BACK, K.W. and BOGDONOFF, M.D. (1964). Plasma lipid responses to leadership, conformity and deviation. *In* "Psychobiological Approaches to Social Behaviour", (Eds P.H. Leiderman and D. Shapiro), Stanford University Press, Stanford, CA.

BACKMAN, C. (1980). Promises unfulfilled: on the premature abandonment of promising research. *In* "The Development of Social Psychology", (Eds R. Gilmour and S.W. Duck), Academic Press, London and New York.

BACKMAN, C.W. and SECORD, P.F. (1959). The effect of perceived liking on interpersonal attraction. *Human Relations* **12**, 379-384.

BAILEY, F.G. (1978). "Morality and Expediency", Oxford University Press, London.

BAILEY, R.C., FINNEY, P. and HELM, B. (1975). Self-concept support and friendship duration. *J. Soc. Psychol.* **96**, 237-243.

BANFIELD, E.C. (1958). "The Moral Basis of a Backward Society", The Free Press, Glencoe, Ill.

BARNHART, J. (1968). The acquisition of cue properties by social and non-social events. *Child Dev.* **39**, 1237-1245.

BARTRAM, M., ROLLETT, B. and FRITZ, W. (1978). Zur Diagnose informeller Gruppierungen aufgrund taxometrischer Konzepte, *In* "Evaluation von Gruppenarbeit", (Ed. A. Knapp), 66-79. Akademische Verlagsgesellschaft, Wiesbaden.

BATESON, G., JACKSON, D.D., HALEY, J. and WEAKLAND, J. (1956). Toward a theory of schizophrenia. *Behavioural Sci.* **1**, 251-264.

BATESON, G. (1958). "Naven", Stanford University Press, Stanford, CA.

BAUMRIND, D. (1967). Child care practices anteceding three patterns of preschool behaviour. *Genetic Psychol. Monographs* **75**, 43-88.

BAUMRIND, D. (1968). Authoritarian vs authoritative parental control. *Adolescence* **3**, 255-272.

BAUMRIND, D. (1971). Current patterns of parental authority. *Develop. Psychol. Monographs* **4**.

BAUMRIND, D. (1972). Socialization and instrumental competence in young children. *In* "The Young Child: Reviews of Research", Vol. 2. (Ed. W.W. Hartup), National Association for the Education of Young Children, Washington, D.C.

BECKER, W.C. (1964). Consequences of different kinds of parental discipline. *In* "Review of Child Development Research", Vol. 1. (Eds M.L. Hoffman and L.W. Hoffman) Russel Sage Foundation, New York.

BEFU, H. (1977). Social exchange. *Am. Rev. Anthropol.* **6**, 255-281.

BELL, A.P. (1978). "Homosexualities: a Study of Human Diversity among Men and Women", Simon and Schuster, New York.

BELL, R.Q. (1974). Contributions of human infants to caregiving and social interaction. *In* "The Effect of the Infant on its Caregiver", (Eds M. Lewis and L.A. Rosenblum), Wiley, New York.

BELL, R.R. (1966). "Premarital Sex in Changing Society", Prentice-Hall, Englewood Cliffs, NJ.
BELL, S.W. and AINSWORTH, M.D. (1972). Infant crying and maternal responsiveness. *Child Development* **43**, 1171-1190.
BEM, D and BEM, S. (1970). We're all unconscious sexists. *Psychology Today* (Jan.), 4-22.
BENNIS, W.G., SCHEIN, E.H., BERLEW, D.E. and STEELE, F.I. (1964). "Interpersonal Dynamics", The Dorsey Press, Homewood, Ill.
BENTLER, P.M. and NEWCOMB, M.D. (1978). Longitudinal study of marital success and failure. *J. Consulting Clin. Psychol.* **46**, 1053-1070.
BENTLER, P.M. and NEWCOMB, M.D. (1979). Longitudinal study of marital success and failure. *In* "Love and Attraction", (Eds M. Cook and G. Wilson), Pergamon, Oxford.
BERGER, M.E. (1971). Trial marriage: harnessing the trend constructively. *The Family Coordinator* **20**, 35-43.
BERGER, M.E. (1974). Trial marriage follow-up study. Unpublished manuscript.
BERGER, P. and KELLNER, H. (1972). Marriage and the construction of reality. *In* "Woman in a Man-made World", (Eds N. Glazer-Malbin and H.Y. Maehrer), Rand McNally, Chicago.
BERNARD, J. (1972). "The Future of Marriage", World, New York.
BERNE, E. (1964). "Games People Play: the Psychology of Human Relationships", Grove Press, New York.
BERSCHEID, E. and WALSTER, E.H. (1974). A little bit about love. *In* "Foundations of Interpersonal Attraction", (Ed. T.L. Huston), Academic Press, New York and London.
BERSCHEID E. and WALSTER, E.H. (1978). "Interpersonal Attraction", (2nd edn), Addison-Wesley, Reading, MA.
BERSCHEID, E., WALSTER, E. and BOHRNSTEDT, G. (1973). The Body Image Report. *Psychology Today* **7**, 119-131.
BIRCHLER, G.R. (1972). Differential patterns of instrumental affiliative behavior as a function of degree of marital distress and level of intimacy. Doctoral Thesis, University of Oregon.
BIRCHLER, G., WEISS, R. and VINCENT, J. (1975). Multimethod analysis of social reinforcement exchange between maritally distressed and nondistressed spouse and stranger dyads. *J. Personality Social Psychol.* **31**, 349-360.
BLAU, P.M. (1964). "Exchange and Power in Social Life", Wiley, New York.
BLAU, Z.S. (1973). "Old Age in a Changing Society", Franklin Watts, New York.
BLOCK, D. (1969). Unwed couples: do they live happily ever after? *Redbook* (Apr.), 90-91.
BLOCK, J. (1977). Advancing the psychology of personality. *In* "Personality at the Crossroads", (Eds D. Magnusson and N.S. Endler), Erlbaum, Hillsdale, N.J.
BLUMER, H. (1969). "Symbolic Interactionism", Prentice-Hall, Englewood Cliffs, NJ.
BODALEV, A.A. (1970). The formation of the concept of another human being as a person. (Russian MS).
BOGUE, D. (1949). "The Population of the United States", Free Press, Glencoe, Illinois.
BOHANNAN, P. (Ed.), (1971). "Divorce and After", Doubleday Anchor, Garden City, NY.
BOISSEVAIN, J. (1974). "Friends of Friends: Networks, Manipulators and Coalitions." Blackwell, Oxford.

BOOTH, A. (1972). Sex and social participation. *Am. Sociolog. Rev.* 183-193.
BOTT, E. (1957). "Family and Social Network: Roles, Norms and External Relationships in Ordinary Urban Families", Tavistock Publications, London.
BOTWINICK, J. (1978). "Aging and Behavior", Springer, New York.
BOWER, D.W. (1975). A description and analysis of cohabiting samples in America. Unpublished Master's thesis, University of Arizona.
BOWER, D.W. and CHRISTOPHERSON, V.A. (1977). University student cohabitation: a regional comparison of selected attitudes and behavior. *J. Marriage Family* 39, 447-453.
BOWLBY, J. (1969). "Attachment and Loss, Vol. 1: Attachment", Hogarth Press, London.
BOWLBY, J. (1973). "Attachment and Loss, Vol. 2: Separation", Hogarth Press, London.
BOWLBY, J. (1980). "Attachment and Loss, Vol. 3: Loss", Hogarth Press, London.
BRAIKER, H.B. and KELLEY, H.H. (1979). Conflict in the development of close relationships. *In* "Social Exchange in Developing Relationships", (Eds R.L. Burgess and T.L. Huston), Academic Press, New York and London.
BRIAN, R. (1977). "Friends and Lovers", Granada, St. Albans, Hertfordshire, UK.
BRINGLE, R.G. and EVENBECK, S. (1979). The study of jealousy as a dispositional characteristic. *In* "Love and Attraction", (Eds M. Cook and G. Wilson), ·Pergamon, Oxford.
BROWN, J.S. and WOODRIDGE, P.J. (1973). Interpersonal attraction among psychiatric patients. *J. Health Social Behaviour* 14, 299-311.
BRUNER, J.S. and TAGIURI, R. (1954). The perception of people. *In* "Handbook of Social Psychology", (Ed. G. Lindzey), Addison-Wesley, Cambridge, MA.
BUCKLEY, W. (1967). "Sociology and Modern Systems Theory", Prentice-Hall, Englewood Cliffs, NJ.
BUDD, L.S. (1976). Problems, disclosure and commitment of cohabiting and married couples. Unpublished doctoral dissertation, University of Minnesota.
BURGESS, E.W. and COTTRELL, L.S. (1939). "Predicting Success or Failure in Marriage", Prentice-Hall, New York.
BURGESS, E.W. and LOCKE, H.J. (1945/1960) "The Family from Institution to Companionship", American Book Company, New York.
BURGESS, E.W. and WALLIN, P. (1953). "Engagement and Marriage", J.B. Lippincott, Chicago.
BURGESS, R.L. (1979). Child abuse: A social interactional analysis. *In* "Advances in Clinical Child Psychology", Vol. 2. (Eds B.B. Lahey, B.B. and A.G. Kazdin), Plenum Publishing, New York.
BURGESS, R.L. and CONGER, R.D. (1978). Family interaction in abusive, neglectful and normal families. *Child Development* 49, 1163-1173.
BURGESS, R.L. and HUSTON, T.L. (Eds) (1979). "Social Exchange in Developing Relationships", Academic Press, New York and London.
BURGESS, R.L. and NIELSEN, J. (1974). An experimental analysis of some structural determinants of equitable and inequitable exchange relations. *Am. Sociolog. Rev.* 39, 427-443.
BURNS, T. (1977). "The BBC: Public Institution and Private World", Macmillan, London.

BYRNE, D. (1971). "The Attraction Paradigm", Academic Press, New York and London.
BYRNE, D. (1977). Social psychology and the study of sexual behaviour. *Personality Soc. Psychol. Bull.* **3**, 3-30.
BYRNE, D. and BYRNE, L. (1977). "Exploring Human Sexuality", Crowell, New York.
BYRNE, D., ERVIN, C.R. and LAMBERTH, J. (1970). Continuity between the experimental study of attraction and real-life computer dating. *J. Personality Soc. Psychol.* **16**, 157-165.
BYRNE, D., FISHER, J.D., LAMBERTH, J. and MITCHELL, H.E. (1974). Evaluation of erotica: facts or feelings? *J. Personality Soc. Psychol.* **29**, 111-116.
BYRNE, D and FISHER, W.A. (1981). "Adolescents, Sex and Contraception", McGraw-Hill, New York.
BYRNE, D. and GRIFFITT, W. (1973). Interpersonal attraction. *A. Rev. Psychol.* **24**, 317-336.
BYRNE, D. and KELLEY, K. (1981). "An Introduction to Personality", Prentice-Hall, Englewood Cliffs, NJ.
CAMPBELL, A. (1975). The American way of mating: marriage *si*; children, only maybe. *Psychology Today* May, 39-42.
CASLER, L. (1973). "Toward a reevaluation of love" *In* "Symposium on Love", (Ed. M. Curtin), Behavioral Publications.
CASSELL, J. (1977). "A Group Called Women: Sisterhood and Symbolism in the Feminist Movement", David McKay, New York.
CATTELL, R.B. and NESSELROADE, J.R. (1967). Likeness and completeness theories examined by 16PF measures on stably and unstably married couples. *J. Personality Soc. Psychol.* **7**, 351-361.
CAVAN, R.S. (1973). Speculations on innovations to conventional marriage in Old Age. *The Gerontologist* **13**, 409-411.
CHADWICK-JONES, J.K. (1976). "Social Exchange Theory", Academic Press, London and New York.
CHAPMAN, A.J., SMITH, J.R., FOOT, H.C. and PRITCHARD, E. (1979). Behavioural and sociometric indices of friendship in children. *In* "Love and Attraction", (Eds M. Cook and G. Wilson), Pergamon, Oxford.
CLARK, A.A. and LA GAIPA, J.J. (1979). Sibling rivalry: the friendly answer. Unpublished manuscript, University of Windsor, Candada.
CLARK, A.L. and WALLIN, P. (1964). The accuracy of husbands' and wives' reports of the frequency of marital coitus. *Population Studies* **18**, 165-173.
CLATWORTHY, N.M. (1975). Couples in quasi-marriage. *In* "Old Family/New Family: Interpersonal Relationships", (Ed. N. Glazer-Malbin), Van Nostrand, Princeton, NJ.
CLATWORTHY, N.M. and SHEID, L. (1977). A comparison of married couples: premarital cohabitants with non-premarital cohabitants. Unpublished manuscript, Ohio State University.
CLAYTON, R.R. and VOSS, H.L. (1977). Shacking up: cohabitation in the 1970s. *J. Marriage Family* **39**, 273-283.
CLORE, G.L. (1975). "Interpersonal Attraction: an overview", General Learning Press, Springtown, NJ.
CLORE, G.L., and BYRNE, D. (1974). A Reinforcement–Affect Model of Attraction. *In* "Foundations of Interpersonal Attraction", (Ed. T.L. Huston), Academic Press, New York and London.

COHEN, Y.A. (1961). Patterns of friendship. *In* "Social Structure and Personality", (Ed. Y.A. Cohen), Holt, Rinehart and Winston, New York.

COLE, C.L. (1977). Cohabitation in social context. *In* "Marriage and Alternatives: Exploring Intimate Relationships", (Eds R.W. Libby and R.N. Whitehurst) Scott, Foresman, Glenview, Ill.

COLE, C.M. (1976). A behavioural analysis of married and living together couples. Unpublished doctoral dissertation, University of Houston.

COLLINS, J., KREITMAN, N., NELSON, B. and TROOP, J. (1971). Neurosis and marital interaction. III. Family roles and functions. *Br. J. Psychiatr.* **119**, 233-242.

COOK, M and McHENRY, R. (1979). "Sexual Attraction", Pergamon, New York.

COOLEY, C.H. (1956). "Human Nature and the Social Order", The Free Press, Glencoe, Illinois.

COOMBS, C.H. (1964). "A Theory of Data", Wiley, New York.

COOPER, J. (1976). Deception and role playing: on telling the good guys from the bad guys. *Am. Psychol.* **31**, 605-610.

CORY, D.W. and LeROY, J.P. (1963). "The Homosexual and His Society", Citadel, New York.

COTTON, W.L. (1975). Social and sexual relationships of Lesbians. *J. Sex Res.* **11**, 139-148.

COWAN, C.P., COWAN, P.A., COIE, L. and COIE, J.D. (1978). Becoming a family: The impact of a first child's birth on the couple's relationships. *In* "The First Child and Family Formation", (Eds W.B. Miller and L.F. Newman), Carolina Population Center, Chapel Hill.

COX, F.D. (1978). "Human Intimacy: Marriage, the Family and its Meaning", West Publishing Company, St. Paul, MI.

CRAWFORD, M.P. (1976). Retirement and disengagement. *Human Relations* **24**, 255-278.

CUBER, J.F. and HAROFF, P.B. (1965). "The Significant Americans", Appleton-Century-Crofts, New York.

CURRY, T.J. and EMERSON, R.M. (1970). Balance theory: a theory of interpersonal attraction? *Sociometry* **33**, 216-238.

DAILEY, D.M. (1979). Adjustment of heterosexual and homosexual couples in pairing relationships: an exploratory study. *J. Sex Res.* **15**, 143-157.

DALTON, M. (1959). "Men who manage", Wiley, New York.

DANZIGER, C. (1976). Unmarried heterosexual cohabitation. Unpublished doctoral dissertation. Rutgers University.

D'AUGELLI, J.F. and D'AUGELLI, A.R. (1977). Moral reasoning and premarital sexual behavior: toward reasoning about relationships. *J. Soc. Issues* **33**, 46-67.

DAVIS, A., GARDNER, B. and GARDNER, M.R. (1941). "Deep South" University of Chicago Press, Chicago.

DAVIS, J.D. (1978). When boy meets girl: sex roles and the negotiation of intimacy in an acquaintance exercise. *J. Personality Soc. Psychol.* **36**, 684-692.

DEAN, D. (1961). Romanticism and emotional maturity: a preliminary study. *Marriage Family Living*, **23**, 44-45.

DEAN, D.G. (1966). Emotional maturity and marital adjustment. *J. Marriage Family* **28**, 454-457.

DELORA, J.R. and DELORA, J.S. (1975). Social structure and satisfaction of heterosexual cohabiting dyads. Paper presented at the Groves Conference, Dubrovnik, Yugoslavia, 1975.

DERLEGA, V.J. and CHAIKIN, A.L. (1977). Privacy and self-disclosure in social relationships. *J. Soc. Issues* **3**, 102-115.

DERLEGA, V.J., HARRIS, M. and CHAIKIN, A.L. (1973). Self-disclosure reciprocity, liking and the deviant. *J. Exp. Soc. Psychol.* **9**, 277-284.

DERLEGA, V.J., WILSON, M. and CHAIKIN, A.L. (1976). Friendship and disclosure reciprocity. *J. Personality Soc. Psychol.* **34**, 578-582.

DION, K.K. and DION, K.L. (1975). Self-esteem and romantic love. *J. Personality* **43**, 39-57.

DION, K.L. and DION, K.K. (1976). The Honi phenomenon revisited: factors underlying the resistance to perceptual distortion of one's partner. *J. Personality Soc. Psychol.* **33**, 170-177.

DOHERTY, E.G. and SECORD, P.F. (1971). Change of room-mate and interpersonal congruency. *Representative Res. Soc. Psychol.* **2**, 70-75.

DOUVAN, E. and ADELSON, L. (1966). "The Adolescent Experience", John Wiley, New York.

DREWERY, J. and RAE, J.B. (1969). A group comparison of alcoholic and non-psychiatric marriages using the interpersonal perception technique. *Br. J. Psychiatr.* **115**, 287-300.

DRISCOLL, R., DAVIS, K.E. and LIPETZ, M.E. (1972). Parental interference and romantic love: the Romeo and Juliet effect. *J. Personality Soc. Psychol.* **24**, 1-10.

DUCK, S.W. (1973). "Personal Relationships and Personal Constructs: A Study of Friendship Formation", Wiley, London.

DUCK, S.W. (1976). Interpersonal communication in developing acquaintance. *In* "Explorations in Interpersonal Communication", (Ed. G. Miller), 127-147. Sage Annual Reviews, New York.

DUCK, S.W. (1977a). Inquiry, hypothesis and the quest for validation: personal construct systems in the development of acquaintance. *In* "Theory and Practice in Interpersonal Attraction", (Ed. S.W. Duck), Academic Press, London and New York.

DUCK, S.W. (1977b). "The Study of Acquaintance", Teakfield (Saxon House), London.

DUCK, S.W. (Ed.), (1977c). "Theory and Practice in Interpersonal Attraction", Academic Press, London and New York.

DUCK, S.W. (1980a) Personal relationship research in the 1980s: towards an understanding of complex human sociality. *Western J. Speech Commun.* **44**, 114-119

DUCK, S.W. (1980b) Taking the past to heart: one of the futures of social psychology. *In* Gilmour, R. and Duck, S.W. (eds) "The Development of Social Psychology", Academic Press, London and New York.

DUCK, S.W. and ALLISON, D. (1978). I liked you but I can't live with you: a study of lapsed friendships. *Soc. Behaviour Personality* **6**, 43-47.

DUCK, S.W. and CRAIG, G. (1978). Personality similarity and the development of friendship. *Br. J. Soc. Clin. Psychol.* **17**, 237-242.

DUCK, S.W. and SPENCER, C.P. (1972). Personal constructs and friendship formation. *J. Personality Soc. Psychol.* **23**, 40-45.

EHRMANN, W. (1959). "Premarital Dating Behavior", Holt, New York.

EKMAN, P. and FRIESEN, W.V. (1969). The repertoire of non-verbal behaviour. *Semiotica* **1**. 49-98.

EKMAN, P. and FRIESEN, W.V. (1975). "Unmasking the Face", Prentice Hall, Englewood Cliffs, NJ.

ELMS, A.C. (1975). The crisis of confidence in social psychology. *Am. Psychol.* **30**, 967-976.

FAWL, C. (1963). Disturbances experienced by children in their natural habitat. *In* "The Stream of Behavior", (Ed. R. Barker), Appleton-Century-Crofts, New York.

FEGER, H. (1978). The social structure of small groups: The role of asymmetric relations. Paper presented at the meeting of the European Association of Experimental Social Psychology, Weimar 1978.

FELLING, A.J.A. (1974). "Sociaal-Netwerkanalyse", Samson, Alphen aan den Rijn, Netherlands.

FERREIRA, A.J. and WINTER, W.D. (1968). Information exchange and silence in normal and abnormal families. *Family Process* **7**, 251-276.

FIRESTONE, S. (1970). "The Dialectic of Sex", Morrow Paperbacks, New York.

FIRTH, R., HUBERT, J. and FORGE, A. (1971). "Families and their Relatives: Kinship in a Middle-Class Sector of London", Routledge and Kegan Paul, London.

FISHER, W.A., BYRNE, D., EDMUNDS, M., MILLER, C.T., KELLEY, K. and WHITE, L.A. (1979). Psychological and situation-specific correlates of contraceptive behavior among university women. *J. Sex Res.* **15**, 38-55.

FOA, U.G. (1971). Interpersonal and economic resources. *Science (N.Y.)* **171**, 345-351.

FOA, U.G. and FOA, E.B. (1974). "Societal Structures of the Mind", Thomas, Springfield, Illinois.

FOOT, H.C., CHAPMAN, A.J. and SMITH, J.R. (Eds), (1980). "Friendship and Social Relations in Children", Wiley, London.

FOOT, H.C., SMITH, J.R. and CHAPMAN, A.J. (1979). Non-verbal expressions of intimacy in children. *In* "Love and Attraction", (Eds M. Cook and G. Wilson), Pergamon, Oxford.

FOSTER, G.M. (1961). The dyadic contract: a model for the social structure of a Mexican peasant village. *Am. Anthropol.* **63**, 1173-1193.

FOSTER, H.H. and FREED, D.G. (1978). Non-marital partners: sex and serendipity. *J. Divorce* **1**, 195-211.

FOUCAULT, M. (1978). "The History of Sexuality, Vol. 1: An Introduction", Pantheon Books, New York.

FOX, A. (1974). "Beyond Contract: Work, Power and Trust Relations", Faber and Faber, London.

FRANCHER, J.S. and HENKIN, J. (1973). The menopausal queen: adjustment to aging and the male homosexual. *Am. J. Orthopsychiatr.* **43**, 670-674.

FRANSELLA, F. and BANNISTER, D. (1977). "A Manual for Repertory Grid Technique." Academic Press, London and New York.

FREEDMAN, J.L. (1969). Role playing: psychology by consensus. *J. Personality Soc. Psychol.* **13**, 107-114.

FREUD, S. (1938). "An Outline of Psychoanalysis", Hogarth, London.

GADLIN, H. (1977). Private lives and public order: a critical view of the history of intimate relations in the United States. *In* "Close Relationships: Perspectives on the Meaning of Intimacy", (Eds G. Levinger and H.L. Raush), University of Massachusetts Press, Amherst, MA.

GANSON, H.C. (1975). Cohabitation: The antecedents of dissolution of formerly cohabiting individuals. Unpublished Master's thesis, Ohio State University.

GARSON, B. (1972). Luddities in Lordstown. *Harper's Magazine* June, 1972.

GELLER, D.M. (1978). Involvement in role-playing simulations: a demonstration with studies on obedience. *J. Personality Soc. Psychol.* **36**, 219-235.

GELLES, R.J. and STRAUS, M.A. (1979). Determinants of violence in the family: Toward a theoretical integration. *In* "Theories about the Family: Research-based Theories", Vol. 1, (Burt, Hill, Nye and Reiss, Eds), The Free Press, New York.

GERGEN, K.J. (1969). "The Psychology of Behaviour Exchange", Addison-Wesley, Reading, MA.

GERGEN, K.J. (1973). Social psychology as history. *J. Personality Soc. Psychol.* **26**, 309-320.

GERGEN, K.J. (1978). Experimentation in social psychology: a reappraisal. *Eur. J. Soc. Psychol.* **8**, 507-527.

GILLESPIE, D. (1971). Who has the power? The marital struggle. *J. Marriage Family* **33**, 445-458.

GILMORE, D. (1975). Friendship in Fuenmayor: patterns of integration in an atomistic society. *Ethnology* **14**, 311-324.

GILMOUR, R. and DUCK, S.W. (Eds). (1980). "The Development of Social Psychology", Academic Press, London and New York.

GLASSER, P.H. and GLASSER, L.N. (1962). Reversal and conflict between aged parents and their children. *Marriage Family Living* **24**, 46-50.

GLAZER-MALBIN, N. (1975). Man and woman: interpersonal relationships in the marital pair. *In* "Old Family/New Family", (Ed. N. Glazer-Malbin), Van Nostrand, London.

GLICK, P.C. (1975). A demographer looks at American families. *J. Marriage Family* **37**, 15-26.

GLICK, P. and NORTON, A.J. (1973). Perspectives on the recent upturn in divorce and remarriage. *Demography* **10**, 301-314.

GOFFMAN, E. (1959). "The Presentation of Self in Everyday Life", Doubleday Anchor, New York.

GOODE, W.J. (1956). "After Divorce", Free Press, Glencoe, Ill.

GOODE, W.J. (1963). "World Revolution and Family Patterns", Free Press, New York.

GOODE, W.J. (1971). Force and violence in the family *J. Marriage Family* **33**, 624-636.

GOTTMAN, J.M. (1979). "Marital Interaction: Experimental Investigations", Academic Press, New York and London.

GOTTMAN, J.M., MARKMAN, H. and NOTARIUS, C. (1978). The typography of marital conflict. *J. Marriage Family* **39**, 461-477.

GOZMAN, L.J. (1974). The relationship between friendship behaviour and personality characteristics. *Problems of interaction and upbringing (Russian).*

GREENFIELD, S. (1973). Love: Some reflections by a social anthropologist. *In* "Symposium on Love", (Ed. M. Curfin), Behavioural Publications.

GRIFFITT, W. (1975). Sexual stimulation and sexual responsiveness: sex differences. *Archives Sex. Behavior* **4**, 529-540.

GROVES, E.R. (1928). "The Marriage Crisis." Longmans, Green, New York.

GRUSH, J.E. and YEHI, J.G. (1979). Marital roles, sex differences, and interpersonal attraction. *J. Personality Soc. Psychol.* **37**, 116-123.

GUBENNESCH, H. and HUNT, L. (1971). The relative accuracy of interpersonal perception of high and low authoritarians. *J. Exp. Res. Personality* **5**.

GURIN, G., KEROFF, J. and FELD, S. (1960). "America Looks at its Mental Health", Basic Books, New York.

HALEY, J. (1964). Research on family patterns: an instrument measurement. *Family Process* **3**, 41-65.

HAMILTON, G.V. (1948). "A Research in Marriage", Lear Publications, New York.

HANDY, C.B. (1976). "Understanding Organizations", Penguin, Harmondsworth, Middlesex, UK.

HARARY, F. (1969). "Graph Theory", Addison-Wesley, Reading MA.

HARPER, D.M. (1975). Does living together before marriage make for a better marriage? *Med. Aspects Human Sexuality* **9**, 34-39.

HARRY, J. and DeVALL, W.B. (1978). "The Social Organization of Gay Males", Praeger Publishers, New York.

HARTUP, W.W. (1978). Perspectives on child and family interaction: Past, present, and future. *In* "Child Influences on Marital and Family Interaction: A Life-span Perspective", (Eds R.M. Lerner and G.B. Spanier), Academic Press, New York and London.

HARVEY, J.H., WELLS, G.L. and ALVAREZ, M.D. (1978). Attributions in the context of conflict and separation in close relationships. *In* "New Directions in Attribution Research", Vol. 2. (Eds J.H. Harvey, W.J. Ickes and R.F. Kidd), Lawrence Erlbaum Associates, Hillsdale, New Jersey.

HATFIELD, E. (in press). "Love, Sex and the Marketplace", Academic Press, New York and London.

HATFIELD, E., GREENBERGER, D., TRAUPMANN, J. and LAMBERT, P. (in press). Equity and sexual satisfaction in recently married couples. *Archives Sex. Behavior*

HATFIELD, E., TRAUPMANN, J. and WALSTER, G.W. (1979). Equity and extramarital sex. *In* "Love and Attraction: an International Conference", (Eds M. Cook and G. Wilson), 323-334. Pergamon, Oxford.

HAY, J. and HORTON, T. (in press). "A reply to Bernard I. Murstein: a feminist perspective". *In* "Love, Sex and the Marketplace", (Ed. E. Hatfield), Academic Press, New York and London.

HEIDER, F. (1958). "The Psychology of Interpersonal Relations", Wiley, New York.

HENDRICK, C. and BROWN, S. (1971). Introversion, extraversion and interpersonal attraction. *J. Personality Soc. Psychol.* **20**, 31-36.

HENDRIX, D. (1975). Kinship ties: movers and stayers in the Ozarks. *In* "Old Family/New Family", (Ed. N. Geazer-Malbin), Van Nostrand, London.

HENNON, C.B. (1975). Conflict management within pairing relationships: The case of non-marital cohabitation. Unpublished manuscript, University of Utah.

HENZE, L.F. and HUDSON, J.W. (1974). Personal and family characteristics of noncohabiting college students. *J. Marriage Family* **36**, 722-726.

HETHERINGTON, E.M. (1979). Divorce: A child's perspective. *Am Psychol.* **34**, 851-858.

HILL, C.T., RUBIN, Z. and PEPLAU, L.A. (1976). Breakups before marriage: the end of 103 affairs. *J. Soc. Issues,* **32**, 147-168.

HILL, C., RUBIN, Z., PEPLAU, L. and WILLARD, S. (1979). The volunteer couple: commitment and participation in research on interpersonal relationships. *Soc. Psychol. Q.* (   ).

HINDE, R.A. (1976a). Interactions, relationships and social structure. *Men* **11**, 1-17.

HINDE, R.A. (1976b). On describing relationships. *J. Child Psychol. Psychiatr.* **17**, 1-19.

HINDE, R.A. (1978a). Dominance and Role - Two concepts with dual meanings *J. Soc. Biol. Struct.* **1**, 27-38.
HINDE, R.A. (1978b). Interpersonal relationships — in quest of a science. *Psychol. Med.* **8**, 373-386.
HINDE, R.A. (1979). "Towards Understanding Relationships", Academic Press, London.
HINDE, R.A. (1980). The bases of a science of interpersonal relationships. *In* "Personal Relationships 1: Studying Personal Relationships", (Eds S.W. Duck and R. Gilmour), Academic Press, London and New York.
HINDE, R.A. and HERRMANN, J. (1977). Frequencies, durations, derived measures and their correlations in studying dyadic and triadic relationships. *In* "Studies in Mother–Infant Interaction", (Ed. U.R. Schaffer), Academic Press, London and New York.
HINDE, R.A. and McGINNIS, L. (1977). Some factors influencing the effects of temporary mother–infant separation — some experiments with rhesus monkeys. *Psycholog. Med.* **7**, 197-212.
HINDE, R.A. and SIMPSON, M.J.A. (1975). "Qualities of Mother–Infant Relationships in Monkeys", Ciba Foundation Symposium No. 33. Elsevier, Amsterdam.
HINDE, R.A. and WHITE, L. (1974). The dynamics of a relationship — rhesus monkey ventro-ventral contact. *J. Comp. Psychol.* **86**, 8-23.
HOBART, C.W. (1979). 'Changes in courtship and cohabitation in Canada, 1968-1977'. *In* "Love and Attraction (Eds M. Cook and G. Wilson), Pergamon, Oxford.
HOEHN, E. and SEIDEL, G. (1976, 4. Aufl.). "Das Soziogramm. Die Erfassung von Gruppenstrukturen", Hogrefe, Gottingen.
HOFFMAN, L.R. and MAIER, N.R.F. (1966). An experimental re-examination of the similarity-attraction hypothesis. *J. Personality Soc. Psychol.* **3**, 145-152.
HOFFMAN, M. (1968). "The Gay World: Male Homosexuality and the Social Creation of Evil", Bantam Books, New York.
HOFFMAN, M.L. (1970). Moral development. *In* "Carmichael's Manual of Child Psychology", Vol. 2 (Ed. P.H. Mussen), Wiley, New York.
HOGAN, R. and MANKIN, D. (1970). Determinants of interpersonal attraction: a clarification. *Psycholog. Reports* **26**, 235-238.
HOMANS, G.C. (1951). "The Human Group", Routledge and Kegan Paul, London.
HOMANS, G.C. (1961). "Social Behaviour: Its Elementary Forms", Routledge and Kegan Paul, London.
HONIGMAN, J.J. (1968). Perspectives on the atomistic-type society: Interpersonal relations in atomistic communities. *Human Organization,* **27**, 220-229.
HORNSTEIN, H. (1976). "Cruelty and Kindness: A New Look at Aggression and Altruism", Prentice Hall, Englewood Cliffs, NJ.
HUANG, L.J. (1977). Some patterns of non-exclusive sexual relationships among unmarried cohabiting couples. *Int. J. Sociol. Family* **6**,
HUBERT, L. and SCHULTZ, J. (1976). Quadratic assignment as a general data analysis strategy. *Br. J. Mathematical Statistical Psychol.* **29**, 190-241.
HUMPHREY, N.K. (1976). The social function of intellect. *In* "Growing Points in Ethology", ((Eds) P.P.G. Bateson and R.A. Hinde), Cambridge University Press, Cambridge.
HUNT, M. (1974). "Sexual Behavior in the 1970s", Dell, New York.
HURLBURT, R.T. (1979). Random sampling of cognitions and behaviour. *J. Res. Personality* **13**, 103-111.

HUSTON, T.L. (1974). A perspective on interpersonal attraction. *In* "Foundations of Interpersonal Attraction", (Ed. T.L. Huston), Academic Press, New York and London.

HUSTON, T.L. and LEVINGER, G. (1978). Interpersonal attraction and relationships. *In* Rosenzweig, M.R. & Porter, L.W. (eds.). *Annual Review of Psychology,* **29,** 115-156. Annual Reviews Inc.: Palo Alto, California.

HUYCK, M.H. (1977). Sex and the other woman. *In* "Looking Ahead", (Eds L. Troll, J. Israel and K. Israel), Prentice-Hall, Englewood Cliffs, NJ.

JOHNSON, C.L. (1977). Interdependence, reciprocity and indebtedness: an analysis of Japanese American kinship relations. *J. Marriage Family* **39,** 351-363.

JOHNSON, M.P. (1968). Courtship and commitment: a study of cohabitation on a university campus. Unpublished master's thesis, University of Iowa.

JOHNSON, M.P. (1973). Commitment: a conceptual structure and empirical application *Sociolog. Q.* **4,** 359-406.

JONES, E.E. and NISBETT, R.E. (1971). "The Actor and the Observer: Divergent Perceptions of the Causes of Behaviour", General Learning Press, Morristown, New Jersey.

JONES, R.W. and BATES, J.E. (1978). Satisfaction in male homosexual couples. *J. Homosexuality* **3,** 217-224.

JONES, S.C. (1973). The psychology of interpersonal attraction. *In* "Social Psychology: Classic and Contemporary Integrations", (Ed. C. Nemeth), Rand McNally, Chicago.

JOURARD, S.M. (1964). "The Transparent Self", Van Nostrand, Princeton, NJ.

JOURARD, S.M. (1971). "Self-disclosure", Wiley, New York.

JURICH, A.P. and JURICH, J.A. (1974). The effect of cognitive moral development upon the selection of premarital sexual standards. *J. Marriage Family* **36,** 736-741.

KANDEL, D.B. (1978). Similarity in real-life adolescent friendship pairs. *J. Personality Soc. Psychol.* **36,** 306-312.

KEAOUGH, D. (1975). Without knotting the tie. "The Arizona Republic", (July 27), 8-15.

KEIFFER, C. (1977). New depths in intimacy. *In* "Marriage and Alternatives: Exploring Intimate Relationships", (Eds R.W. Libby and R.N. Whitehurst), Scott, Foresman, Glenview, Ill.

KEISER, G.J. and ALTMAN, I. (1976). Relationships of non-verbal behaviour to the social penetration process. *Human Commun. Res.* **2,** 147-161.

KELLEY, H.H. (1971). "Attribution in Social Interaction", General Learning Press, Morristown, NJ.

KELLEY, H.H. (1977). An application of attribution theory to research methodology for close relationships. *In* "Close Relationships: Perspectives on the Meaning of Intimacy", (Eds G. Levinger and H.L. Raush), University of Massachusetts Press, Amherst, MA.

KELLEY, H.H. (1979). "Personal Relationships", Erlbaum, Hillsdale, NJ.

KELLEY, H.H. and THIBAUT, J.W. (1978). "Interpersonal Relations", Wiley, New York.

KELLY, G.A. (1955). "The Psychology of Personal Constructs", Norton.

KELLY, G.A. (1970). A brief introduction to personal construct theory. *In* "Perspectives in Personal Construct Theory", (Ed. D. Bannister), Academic Press, London and New York.

KELVIN, R.P. (1970). "The Bases of Social Behaviour", Holt, Rinehardt and Winston , London.

KELVIN, R.P. (1977). Predictability, power and vulnerability in interpersonal attraction. *In* "Theory and Practice in Interpersonal Attraction", (Ed. S.W. Duck), Academic Press, London and New York.

KENNY, D.A. (1975). Cross-lagged panel correlation: a test for spuriousness. *Psycholog. Bull.* **82**, 887-903.

KERCKHOFF, A.C. (1974). The social context of interpersonal attraction. *In* "Foundations of Interpersonal Attraction", (Ed. T.L. Huston), Academic Press, New York and London.

KHARTCHEV, A.G. (1964). "Marriage and the Family in the USSR", (Russian text).

KIEFER, T.M. (1968). Institutionalized friendship and warfare among the Tausug of Jolo. *Ethnology* **7**, 225-243.

KIMMEL, D.C. (1978). Adult development and aging: A gay perspective. *J. Soc. Issues* **34**, 113-130.

KING, M.D. (1975). "Cohabitation Handbook: Living Together and the Law", Ten Speed Press, Berkeley, CA.

KINSEY, A., POMEROY, W.B. and MARTIN, C. (1948). "Sexual Behavior in the Human Male", W.B. Saunders, Philadelphia.

KINSEY, A.C., POMEROY, W.B., MARTIN, C.E. and GEBHARD, P.H. (1953). "Sexual Behavior in the Human Female", Pocket Books, New York.

KIRKENDALL, L.A. (1961). "Premarital Intercourse and Sexual Relationships", Julian Press, New York.

KIRKENDALL, L.A. and LIBBY, R.W. (1966). Interpersonal relationships — Crux of the sexual renaissance. *J. Soc. Issues* **22**, 45-59.

KLEINKE, C.L., MEEKER, F.B. and FONG, C.L. (1974). Effects of gaze, touch and use of name on evaluation of engaged couples. *J. Res. Personality* **7**, 368-373.

KLING, J.W. and RIGGS, L.A. (Eds), (1971). *Exp. Psychol.* Holt, Rinehardt and Winston, New York.

KOMAROVSKY, M. (1946). Cultural contradictions and sex roles. *Am. J. Sociol.* **52**, 186-8.

KOMAROVSKY, M. (1971). "The Unemployed Man and his Family" Octagon Books, New York.

KOMAROVSKY, M. (1973). Cultural contradictions and sex roles: the masculine case. *Am. J. Sociol.* **78**, 813-884.

KON, I.S. (1974). The concept of friendship in ancient Greece. *Ancient History Herald* **3**.

KON, I.S. (1977). The place of history in the social sciences, *Philosophy and methodology of history.*

KRUEGER, H.-P. (1973). Masse Erlebte Interaktionshäufigkeit als soziometrische Mape (Tabellenteil). Dissertation, University of Erlangen-Nürnberg.

LA GAIPA, J.J. (1977a). "Interpersonal attraction and social exchange". *In* "Theory and Practice in Interpersonal Attraction", (Ed. S.W. Duck), Academic Press, London and New York.

LA GAIPA, J.J. (1977b). Testing a multidimensional approach to friendship. *In* "Theory and Practice in Interpersonal Attraction", (Ed. S.W. Duck), Academic Press, London and New York.

LA GAIPA, J.J. (1979). A developmental study of the meaning of friendship in adolescence. *J. Adolescence* **2**, 201-213.

LAING, R.D. (1962). "The Self and Others", Quadrangle Press, Chicago.

LAING, R.D. (1969). "The Divided Self", Pantheon Books, New York.

LASCH, C. (1977). "Haven in a Heartless World: The Family Besieged", Basic Books, New York.

LAUMAN, E. (1966). The relative associational contiguity of occupations in urban settings. *Am. Sociol. Rev.* **31**, 169-178.

LAUTENSCHLAGER, S.Y. (1972). A descriptive study of consensual union among college students. Unpublished master's thesis, California State University at Northbridge.

LENNARD, H.L. and BERNSTEIN, A. (1969). "Patterns in Human Interaction", Jossey-Bass, San Francisco.

LEONTIEV, A.I. (1977). "Activity, Consciousness and Personality", (Russian text).

LERNER, M. (1974). "Social psychology of justice and interpersonal attraction." *In* "Foundations of Interpersonal Attraction", (Ed. T.L. Huston), Academic Press, New York and London.

LERNER, M.J., MILLER, D.T. and HOLMES, J.G. (1976). Deserving and the emergence of forms of justice. *In* "Advances in Experimental Social Psychology", Vol. 9 (Eds L. Berkowitz and E. Walster) 133-162. Academic Press, New York and London.

LERNER, R.M. and SPANIER, G.B. (1980). The Child in the family. *In* "Developmental Psychology", (Eds E.B. Kipp and J. Krabow), Addison-Wesley, Reading, MA.

LEVINGER, G. (1966). Sources of marital dissatisfaction among applicants for divorce. *Am. J. Orthopsychiatr.* **36**, 803-807.

LEVINGER, G. (1972). Little sand box and big quarry: comment on Byrne's paradigmatic spade for research in interpersonal attraction. *Representative Res. Soc. Psycho.* **3**, 3-19.

LEVINGER, G. (1977a). Re-viewing the close relationship. *In* "Close Relationships", (Eds G. Levinger and H.L. Raush), University of Massachusetts Press, Amherst. MA.

LEVINGER, G. (1977b). The Embrace of Lives: changing and unchanging. *In* "Close Relationships", (Eds G. Levinger and H.L. Rausch), University of Massachusetts Press, Amherst , MA.

LEVINGER, G. (1979). A social exchange view of the dissolution of pair relationships. *In* "Social Exchange in Developing Relationship", (Eds R.L, Burgess and T.L, Huston), Academic Press, New York and London.

LEVINGER, G. and BREEDLOVE, J. (1966). Interpersonal attraction and agreement: a study of marriage partners. *J. Personality Soc. Psychol.* **3**, 367-372.

LEVINGER, G. and SNOEK, J.D. (1972). "Attraction in Relationship: A New Look at Interpersonal Attraction", General Learning Press, Morristown, New Jersey.

LEWIS, R.A. (1973). A longitudinal test of a developmental framework for premarital dyadic formation. *J. Marriage Family* **35**, 16-25.

LEWIS, R.A. and GUITTAR, E.C. (1974). Self concepts among some unmarried cohabitants. Paper presented at the Annual Meeting of the National Council on Family Relations, St. Louis, Missouri, 1974.

LEWIS, R.A., SPANIER, G.B., STORM ATKINSON, V.L. and LEHECKA, C.F. (1977). Commitment in married and unmarried cohabitation. *Sociolog. Focus* **10**, 367-374.

LIBBY, R.W. (1977). Creative singlehood as a sexual lifestyle: beyond marriage as a rite of passage. *In* "Marriage and Alternatives: Exploring Intimate Relationships", (Eds R.W. Libby and R.N. Whitehurst), Scott, Foresman, Glenview, Ill.

LINTON, R. (1936). "The Study of Man: An Introduction". Appleton-Century-Crofts: New York.

LIPETZ, M.E., COHEN, I.H., DWORIN, J. & ROGERS, L.S. (1970). Need complementarity, marital stability and marital satisfaction. In "Personality and Social Behaviour", (Eds K.J. Gergen and D. Marlowe), Addison-Wesley, Reading, Massachusetts.

LITWICK, E. and SZELENYI, I. (1969). Primary group structures and their functions: kin, neighbors, and friends. Am. Sociolog. Rev. 34, 465-481.

LOCKE, H.J. (1951). "Predicting Adjustment in Marriage: A Comparison of a Divorce and a Happily Married Group", Henry Holt, New York.

LOPATA, H.Z. (1975). Couple-companionate relationships in marriage and widowhood. In "Old Family/New Family", (Ed. N. Glazer-Malbin), Van Nostrand, London.

LORR, M. and McNAIR, D.M. (1963). An interpersonal behaviour circle. J. Abnormal Soc. Psychol. 67, 68-75.

LOTT, A.J. and LOTT, B.E. (1972). The power of liking: consequences of interpersonal attitudes derived from a liberalised new secondary reinforcement. Adv. Exp. Soc. Psychol. 6, 109-148.

LOTT, A.J., LOTT, B.E., REED, T. and CROW, T. (1970). Personality trait descriptions of differentially liked persons. J. Personality Soc. Psychol. 16, 284-290.

LOTT, A.J., LOTT, B.E. and WALSH, M.L. (1970). Learning of paired associates relevant to differentially liked persons. J. Personality Soc. Psychol. 16, 274-283.

LUCE, R.D. and PERRY, A.D. (1949). A method of matrix analysis of group structure. Psychometrika 14, 95-116.

LURIA, A.R. (1974). "On the Historical Development of Cognitive Processes", (Russian text).

LYNESS, J.F., LIPETZ, M.E. and DAVIS, K.E. (1972). Living together: an alternative to marriage. J. Marriage Family 34, 305-311.

MACCOBY, E. and JACKLIN, C. (1974). "The Psychology of Sex Differences", Stanford Press, Stanford, CA.

MACDONALD, A.P. and GAMES, R.G. (1974). Some characteristics of those who hold positive and negative attitudes toward homosexuals. J. Homosexuality 1, 9-27.

MACKLIN, E.D. (1972). Heterosexual cohabitation among unmarried college students. The Family Coordinator 21, 463-472.

MACKLIN, E.D. (1974). Students who live together: Trial marriage or going very steady? Psychology Today (November), 53-59.

MACKLIN, E.D. (1976). Unmarried heterosexual cohabitation on the university campus. In "The Social Psychology of Sex", (Ed. J.P. Wiseman), Harper and Row, New York.

MACKLIN, E.D. (1978a). Review of research on non-marital cohabitation in the United States. In "Exploring Intimate Life-styles", (Ed. B.I. Murstein), Springer, New York.

MACKLIN, E.D. (1978b). Non-marital heterosexual cohabitation. Marriage Family Rev. 1, 2-12.

MAKEPEACE, J.M. (1975). The birth control revolution: consequences for college student lifestyles. Unpublished doctoral dissertation, Washington State University.

MANGHAM, I.L. (1978). "Interactions and interventions in organizations", Wiley, Chichester, UK.

MANGHAM, I.L. (1979). "The politics of organizational change", Associated Business Press, London.

MANGHAM, I.L. (1980). Notes towards a theory of organizational change. University of Bath, Bath.

MANN, P.A. (1971). Effects of anxiety and defensive style on some aspects of friendship. *J. Personality Soc. Psychol.* **18**, 55-61.

MARCIANO, T.D. (1975). Qualitative studies on women with advanced degrees: Older women and their younger lovers; and postmarital living patterns among women with advanced degrees. Paper presented at the International Workshop on Changing Sex Roles in Family and Society, Dubrovnik, Yugoslavia, 1975.

MARKOWSKI, E.M., CROAKE, J.W. and KELLER, J.F. (1978). Sexual history and present behavior of cohabiting and married couples. *J. Sex Res.* **14**, 27-39.

MARLOWE, D. and GERGEN, K.J. (1969). Personality and social interaction. In "The Handbook of Social Psychology", (2nd edn), Vol. 3. (Eds G. Lindzey and E. Aronson), Addison-Wesley, Reading, Massachusetts.

MARWELL, G. and HAGE, J. (1969). Personality and social interaction. In "Handbook of Social Psychology", Vol. 3. (Eds G. Lindzey and E. Aronson), Vol. 3. Addison-Wesley, Reading, Mass.

MASTERS, W.H. and JOHNSON, V.E. (1966). "Human Sexual Response", Little, Brown, Boston.

MASTERS, W.H. and JOHNSON, V.E. (1976). "The Pleasure Bond", Bantam Books, New York.

MAYER, T.F. (1975). "Mathematical models of group structure", Bobbs-Merrill, Indianapolis.

McCALL, G.J. (1970). The social organization of relationships. In "Social Relationships", (Eds G.J. McCall, M. McCall, N.K. Denzin, G.D. Suttles and S.B. Kurth), Aldine, Chicago.

McCARTHY, B. (1978). Interpersonal behaviour of successful and unsuccessful acquainters. Paper delivered at the Annual Conference of the British Psychological Society, Social Psychology Section, Cardiff, September, 1978.

McCARTHY, B. and DUCK, S.W. (1976). Friendship duration and responses to attitudinal agreement-disagreement. *Br. J. Soc. Clin. Psychol.* **15**, 377-386.

McCARTHY, B. and DUCK, S.W. (1979a). When "I disagree" means "I will like you longer": attributions of causality in acquaintance. In "Love and Attraction", (Eds M. Cook and G. Wilson), Pergamon, Oxford.

McCARTHY, B. and DUCK, S.W. (1979b). Studying friendship: experimental and role playing techniques in testing hypotheses about acquaintance. *Br. J. Soc. Clin. Psychol.* **18**, 299-307.

McCAULEY, B. (1975). Sex roles in alternative lifestyles: Egalitarian attitudes in cohabiting relationships. Paper presented at the International Workshop on Changing Sex Roles in Family and Society, Dubrovnik, Yugoslavia, 1975.

McCAULEY, B. (1977). Self-esteem in the cohabiting relationship. Unpublished master's thesis, University of Delaware.

McCORD, W., McCORD, J. and HOWARD, A. (1961). Familial correlates of aggression in nondelinquent male children. *J. Abnormal Soc. Psychol.* **62**, 79-93.

McGUIRE, W.J. (1973). The yin and yang of progress in social psychology. *J. Personality Soc. Psychol.* **26**, 446-456.

McMURTRY, J. (1977). Monogamy: a critique. *In* "Marriage and Alternatives: Exploring Intimate Relationships" (Eds R.W. Libby and R.N. Whitehurst), Scott, Foresman, Glenview, Ill.

MEAD, G.H. (1934). "Mind, Self and Society", University of Chicago Press, Chicago.

MEHRABIAN, A. and KSIONZKY, S. (1974). "A Theory of Affiliation", Lexington Books, Lexington, Massachusetts.

MELLY, G. (1977). "Rum, Bum and Concertina", Weidenfeld and Nicholson, London.

MELVILLE, K. (1977). "Marriage and Family Today", Random House, New York.

MIKULA, G. and STROEBE, W. (Eds), (1977). "Freundschaft und Ehe", Huber, Bern.

MILARDO, R.M. and MURSTEIN, B.I. (1979). The implications of exchange orientation for the dyadic functioning of heterosexual cohabitors. *In* "Love and Attraction", (Eds M. Cook and G. Wilson), Pergamon, Oxford.

MILLER, A.G. (1972). Role-playing: an alternative to deception? A review of the evidence. *Am. Psychol.* **27**, 623-636.

MILLER, H.L. and RIVENBARK, W.H. (1970). Sexual differences in physical attractiveness as a determinant of heterosexual liking. *Psycholog. Reports* **27**, 701-702.

MISCHEL, W. (1968). "Personality and Assessment", Wiley, New York.

MISCHEL, W. (1973). Toward a cognitive social learning reconceptualization of personality. *Psycholog. Rev.* **80**, 252-283.

MITCHELL, H.E., BULLARD, J.W. and MUDD, E.H. (1962). Areas of marital conflict in successfully and unsuccessfully functioning families. *J. Health Human Behavior* **3**, 88-93.

MIXON, D. (1974). If you won't deceive, what can you do? *In* "Reconstructing Social Psychology", (Ed. N. Armistead), Penguin, Harmondsworth, Middlesex.

MONTGOMERY, J.P. (1972). Toward an understanding of cohabition. Unpublished doctoral dissertation, University of Massachusettes.

MONTGOMERYM, J.P. (1973). Commitment and cohabitation cohesion. Unpublished manuscript, University of Edmonton.

MORTON, T.L. (1978). Intimacy and reciprocity of exchange: a comparision of spouses and strangers. *J. Personality Soc. Psychol.* **36**, 72-81.

MURSTEIN, B.I. (1970). Stimulus-value-role: A theory of marital choice. *J. Marriage Family* **32**, 465-481.

MURSTEIN, B.I. (1971). A theory of marital choice and its applicability to marriage adjustment and friendship. *In* "Theories of Attraction and Love", (Ed. B.I. Murstein), Springer, New York.

MURSTEIN, B.I. (1972). Person perception and courtship progress among premarital couples. *J. Marriage Family* **34**, 621-626.

MURSTEIN, B.I. (1973). Perceived congruence among premarital couples as a function of neuroticism. *J. Abnormal Psychol.* **82**, 22-26.

MURSTEIN, B.I. (1974). "Love, Sex and Marriage through the Ages" Springer, New York.

MURSTEIN, B.I. (1976). A note on a common error in attraction and marriage research. *J. Marriage Family* **38**, 451-452.

MURSTEIN, B.I. (1977). The Stimulus-Value-Role (SVR) Theory of dyadic relationships. *In* "Theory and Practice in Interpersonal Attraction", (Ed. S.W. Duck), Academic Press, London and New York.

MURSTEIN, B.I. and CHRISTY, P. (1976). Physical attractiveness and marriage adjustment in middle-aged couples. *J. Personality Soc. Psychol.* **34**, 537-542.

MUSSEN, P. (1962). Long-term consequences of masculinity of interests in adolescence. *J. Consulting Psychol.* **26**, 435-444.

NAHEMOW, L. and LAWTON, M.P. (1975). Similarity and propinquity in friendship formation. *J. Personality Soc. Psychol.* **32**, 205-213.

NAVRAN, I. (1967). Communication and adjustment in marriage. *Family Process* **6**, 173-184.

NEALE, J.M. and LIEBERT, R.M. (1973). "Science and Behaviour: An Introduction to the Methods of Research", Prentice Hall, Englewood Cliffs, New Jersey.

NEWCOMB, M.D. and BENTLER, P.M. (1980a). Cohabitation before marriage: A comparison of couples who did and did not cohabit before marrying. *Alternative Lifestyles* **3**, 65-85.

NEWCOMB, M.D. and BENTLER, P.M. (1980b). Assessment of personality and demographic aspects of cohabitation and marital success. *J. Personality Assessment* **44**, in press.

NEWCOMB, P.R. (1979). Cohabitation in America: An assessment of consequences. *J. Marriage Family* **4**, 597-603.

NEWCOMB, T.M. (1952). "Social Psychology", Tavistock, London.

NEWCOMB, T.M. (1956). The prediction of interpersonal attraction. *Am. Psychol.* **11**, 575-586.

NEWCOMB; T.M. (1961). "The Acquaintance Process", Holt, Rinehardt and Winston, New York.

NEWCOMB, T.M. (1971). Dyadic balance as a source of clues about interpersonal attraction. *In* "Theories of Attraction and Love", (Ed. B.I. Murstein), Springer, New York.

NEWCOMB, T.M. (1978). The acquaintance process: looking mainly backward. *J. Personality Soc. Psychol.* **36**, 1075-1083.

NEWMAN, G. and NICHOLS, C.R. (1960). Sexual activities and attitudes in older persons. *J. Am. Med. Assn* **173**, 33-35.

NISBETT, R.E. and WILSON, T. De C. (1977). Telling more than we can know: verbal reports on mental processes. *Psycholog. Rev.* **84**, 231-259.

OGBURN, W.F. and NIMKOFF, M.F. (1955). "Technology and the Changing Family", Houghton-Mifflin, Boston.

OLDAY, D.E. (1977). Some consequences for heterosexual cohabitation for marriage. Unpublished doctoral dissertation, Washington State University.

OLSON, D.H. (1977). Insiders' and outsiders' views of relationships: research studies *In* "Close Relationships", (Eds G. Levinger and H.L. Raush), University of Massachusetts Press, Amherst, MA.

OVERTON, W.F. (1975). General systems, structure and development. *In* "Structure and Transformation", (Eds K.F. Riegel and G.C. Rosenwald), Wiley, New York.

PAINE, R. (1969). In search of friendship: an exploratory analysis in "middle-class' culture. *Man* **4**, 505-524.

PALMER, M. (1974). Marriage and the formerly fat: the effect weight loss has on your life together. *Weight Watchers* **7**, 23-50.

PANYARD, C. (1973). Self-discovery between friends. *J. Counselling Psychol.* **20**, 66-68.

PARKIN, D. (1978). "The Cultural Definition of Political Response", Academic Press, London and New York.

PATTERSON, G.R. (1976). The aggressive child: victim and architect of a coercive system. *In* "Behaviour Modification and Families, I. Theory and Research", (Eds L. Mash and L. Hamerlynck), Bruner/Mazell, New York.

PATTERSON, G.R. (1977). A three-stage functional analysis for children's coercive behaviors: a tactic for developing a performance theory. *In* "New Developments in Behavioral Research: Theory, Methods and Applications, In honor of Sidney W. Bijou", (Eds D. Baer, B.C. Etzel and J.J. LeBlanc), Lawrence Erlbaum, Hillsdale, New Jersy.

PATTERSON, G.R. (1979). "A performance theory for coercive family interaction". *In* "Social interaction: Methods, Analysis and Evaluation", (Ed. R. Cairns), Lawrence Erlbaum, Hillsdale, New Jersey.

PATTERSON, G.R. and REID, J.B. (1970). Reciprocity and coercion: two facets of social systems. *In* "The Experimental Analysis of Social Behavior", (Eds C. Neuringer and J. Michael), Appleton-Century-Crofts, New York.

PEARSON, G. (1974). Prisons of love: the reification of the family in family therapy. *In* "Reconstructing Social Psychology", (Ed. N. Armistead), Penguin, Harmondsworth, Middlesex.

PEAY, E.R. (1975). Nonmetric grouping: clusters and cliques. *Psychometrika* **40**, 297-313.

PEPLAU, L.A. (1976). Impact of fear of success and sex-role attitudes on women's competitive achievement. *J. Personality Soc. Psychol.* **34**, 561-568.

PEPLAU, L.A., COCHRAN, S., ROOK, K. and PADESKY, C. (1978). Loving women: attachment and autonomy in lesbian relationships. *J. Soc. Issues* **34**, 7-27.

PEPLAU, D.A., RUBIN, Z. and HILL, C.T. (1977). Sexual intimacy in dating couples. *J. Soc. Issues* **33**, 86-109.

PETERMAN, D.J. (1975). Does living together before marriage make for a better marriage? *Med. Aspects Human Sexuality* **9**, 39-41.

PETERMAN, D.J., RIDLEY, C.A. and ANDERSON, S.M. (1974). A comparison of cohabiting and non-cohabiting college students. J. Marriage Family, **36**, 344-354.

PETROVSKY, A.V. (1973). Constructing a Socio-psychological concept of group activity. *Questions of Psychology* (Russian Journal).

PFEIFFER, E. (1974). "Successful Aging", Duke University Center for the Study of Aging and Human Development, Durham, NC.

PFEIFFER, E., VERWOERDT, A. and DAVIS, G.C. (1972). Sexual behavior in middle life. *Am. J. Psychiatr.* **128**, 10.

PINEO, P.C. (1961). Disenchantment in the later years of marriage. *Marriage Family Living* **23**, 3-11.

PRESTON, S.H. and McDONALD, J. (1979). The incidence of divorce within cohorts of American marriages contracted since the civil war. *Demography* **16**, 1-25.

PRICE, R.A. and VANDENBERG, S.G. (1979). Matching for physical attractiveness in married couples. *Personality Soc. Psychol. Bull.* **5**, 398-400.

QUICK, E. and JACOB, T. (1973). Marital disturbance in relation to role theory and relationship theory. *J. Abnormal Psychol.* **82**, 309-316.

RADCLIFFE-BROWNE, A.R. (1962). "African Systems of Kinship and Marriage", Oxford University Press, London.

RAINWATER, L. (1964). Some aspects of lower class sexual behavior. *J. Soc. Issues* **22**, 96-108.

RANDS, M. and LEVINGER, G. (1979). Implicit theories of relationship: an intergenerational study. *J. Personality Soc. Psychol.* **37**, 645-661.

234   REFERENCES

RAPPOPORT, R. and RAPPOPORT, R. (1971). "Dual-career Families", Penguin, Baltimore.
RAUSH, H.L. (1977). Orientations to the close relationship. In "Close Relationships", (Eds G. Levinger and H.L. Raush), University of Massachusetts Press, Amherst, MA.
RAUSH, H.L., BARRY, W.A., HERTEL, R.K. and SWAIN, M.A. (1974). "Communication, Conflict and Marriage", Jossey-Bass, San Francisco.
REGAN, D.T. (1978). Attributional aspects of interpersonal attraction. In "New Directions in Attribution Research", Vol. 2. (Eds J.H. Harvey, W.J. Ickes and R.F. Kidd), Lawrence Erlbaum, Hillsdale, New Jersey.
REGAN, D.T., STRAUS, E. and FAZIO, R. (1974). Liking and the attribution process. J. Exp. Soc. Psychol. 10, 385-397.
REID, J.B. and TAPLIN, P. (1978). A social interactional approach to the treatment of abusive families. J. Pediatr. Psychol. (   ).
RICHEY, M.H., RICHEY, H.W. and THIEMAN, G. (1972). Negative salience in impression of character: effects of new information on established relationships. Psychonomic Sci. 28, 65-67.
RIDLEY, C.A., PETERMAN, D.J. and AVERY, A.W. (1978). Cohabitation: Does it make for a better marriage? "The Family Coordinator", (April), 129-137.
RIEGEL, K.F. (1976). The dialectics of human development. Am. Psychol. 31, 689-700.
RISKIN, J. and FAUNCE, E.E. (1970). Family interaction scales, III. Discussion of methodology and substantive findings. Arch. Gen. Psychiatr. 22, 527-537.
ROBERTSON, T.W. (1956). Caste. In "Victorian Melodramas", (Ed. G. Rowell), Oxford University Press, London.
ROBSON, K.S. and MOSS, H.A. (1970). Patterns and determinants of maternal attachment. J. Pediatr. 77. 976-985.
RODIN, M.J. (1978). Liking and disliking: sketch of an alternative view. Personality Soc. Psychol. Bull. 4, 473-478.
ROELOFS, H.M. (1967). "The Language of Modern Politics", Dorsey Press, Homewood, Illinois.
ROSENBLATT, P. (1974). Cross-cultural perspective on attraction. In "Foundations of Interpersonal Attraction", (Ed. T.L. Huston), Academic Press, London and New York.
ROSKAM, E.E. (1977). Fitting ordinal relational data to an hypothesized structure. In "Geometric Representations of Relational Data", (Ed. J.C. Lingoes), 511-527. Mathesis Press, Ann Arbor, Michigan.
ROY, D. (1955). "Making-out": A workers' counter-system of control of work situation and relationships. Am. J. Sociol. 60, 255-66.
ROY, R. and ROY, D. (1977). Is monogamy outdated? In "Marriage and Alternatives: Exploring Intimate Relationships", (Eds R.W. Libby and R.N. Whitehurst), Scott, Foresman, Glenview, Ill.
RUBIN, I. (1965). "Sexual Life After Sixty", Basic Books, New York.
RUBIN, Z. (1970). Measurement of romantic love. J. Personality Soc. Psychol. 16, 265-273.
RUBIN, Z. (1974). From Liking to Loving: Patterns of Attraction in Dating Relationships. In "Foundations of Interpersonal Attraction", (Eds T.L. Huston), Academic Press, New York and London.
RUBIN, Z. (1975). Disclosing oneself to a stranger: reciprocity and its limits. J. Exp. Soc. Psychol. 11, 233-260.

RUBIN, Z. and SHENKER, S. (1978). Friendship, proximity and self disclosure. *J. Personality* **46**, 1-22.

RUSSO, N.F. (1975). Eye-contact, interpersonal distance and the equilibrium theory. *J. Personality Soc. Psychol.* **31**, 497-502.

RUTTER, M. and BROWN, G.W. (1966). The reliability and validity of measures of family life and relationships in families containing a psychiatric patient. *Soc. Psychiatr.* **1**, 38-53.

RUTTER, D.R. and STEPHENSON, G.M. (1979). The functions of looking: effects of friendship on gaze. *Br. J. Soc. Clin. Psychol.* **18**, 203-205.

RYDER, R.G. (1968). Husband–wife dyads versus married strangers. *Family Process* **7**, 238-283.

SAFILIOS-ROTHSCHILD, C. (1970). The study of family power structure. *J. Marriage Family* **32**, 539.

SAFILIOS-ROTHSCHILD, C. (1976). A macro- and micro-examination of family power and love: an exchange model. *J. Marriage Family* **37**, 355-362.

SAGER, C. (1976). Sex as a reflection of the total relationship. *J. Sex Marital Ther.* **2**, 3-5.

SAGHIR, M. and ROBINS, E. (1973). "Male and Female Homosexuality", Williams and Wilkins, Baltimore.

SAMPSON, E.E. (1978). Scientific paradigms and social values. Wanted: a scientific revolution. *J. Personality Soc. Psychol.* **36**, 1332-1343.

SANDER, L.W. (1977). The regulation of exchange in the infant–caretaker system and some aspects of the context-content relationship. *In* "Interaction, Conversation and the Development of Language", (Eds M. Lewis and L.A. Rosenblum). Wiley, New York.

SANTROCK, J.W. (1975). Father absence, perceived maternal behavior, and moral development in boys. *Child Dev.* **46**, 753-757.

SCANZONI, J. (1972). "Sexual Bargaining", Prentice-Hall, Englewood Cliffs, NJ.

SCHACHTER, S. and SINGER, J. (1962). Cognitive, social and physiological determinants of emotional states. *Psycholog. Rev.* **69**, 379-399.

SCHRANK, R. (1978). "Ten Thousand Working Days", MIT Press, Cambridge, MA.

SCHUTZ, W.C. (1960). "FIRO: A Three-dimensional Theory of Interpersonal Behavior", Holt, Rinehardt and Winston, New York.

SCHWARTZ, T. (1977). Living together. *Newsweek* (August 1), 46-50.

SEARS, R.R. (1970). Relation of early socialization experience to self-concepts and gender-role in middle childhood. *Child Dev.* **41**, 267-290.

SEGAL, M.W. (1974). Alphabet and attraction: an unobtrusive measure of the effect of propinquity in a field setting. *J. Personality Soc. Psychol.* **30**, 654-657.

SEGREST, S.A. (1975). Comparison of the role expectations of married and cohabiting students. Unpublished master's thesis, University of Kentucky.

SEIDEN, A.M. and BART, P.B. (1975). Woman to woman: Is sisterhood powerful? *In* "Old Family/New Family", (Ed. Glazer-Malbin), Van Nostrand, London.

SEYFRIED, B.A. (1977).Complementarity in interpersonal attraction. *In* "Theory and Practice in Interpersonal Attraction", (Ed. S.W. Duck), Academic Press, London and New York.

SHOPE, D.F. (1975). "Interpersonal Sexuality", W.B. Saunders, Philadelphia.

SIGALL, H. and ARONSON, E. (1967). Opinion change and the gain–loss model of interpersonal attraction. *J. Exp. Soc. Psychol.* **3**, 178-188.

SIMONOV, P.V. (1971). *A theory of information and the psychophysiology of emotions.* (Russian text).
SIMPSON, M.J.A.S. and HOWE, S. (in press). Interpretation of individual differences in 8 week old rhesus monkey babies. *Behaviour.*
SINDBERG, R.M., ROBERTS, A.F. and McCLAIN, D. (1972). Mate selection factors in computer matched marriages. *J. Marriage Family* **34**, 611-614.
SKOLNICK, A. and SKOLNICK, J. (1974). "Intimacy, Family and Society", Little, Brown, Boston.
SLATER, P.E. (1968). "Some social consequences of temporary systems". *In* "The Temporary Society", (Eds W.G. Bennis and P.E. Slater), Harper and Row, New York.
SMITH, M.B. (1978). Perspectives on selfhood. *Am. Psychologist* **33**, 1053-1063.
SMITH, R.E. and CAMPBELL, A.L. (1973). Social anxiety and strain toward symmetry in dyadic attraction. *J. Personality Soc. Psychol.* **28**, 101-107.
SOEN, D. (1975). Primary relations in poor urban neighborhoods and development towns in Israel. *Jewish Social Studies* **37**, 333-343.
SONNESCHEIN, D. (1968). The ethnography of male homosexual relationships. *J. Sex Res.* **4**, 103-120.
SPANIER, G.B. (1979). The measurement of marital quality. *J. Sex Marital Ther.* **5**, 288-300.
SPANIER, G.B. and GLICK, P.C. (1980). Marital instability in the United States: some correlates and recent changes. Unpublished manuscript.
SPANIER, G.B., LEWIS, R.A. and COLE, C.L. (1975). Marital adjustment over the family life cycle: The issue of curvilinearity. *J. Marriage Family* May, 263-275.
SPREY, J. (1969). On the institutionalization of sexuality. *J. Marriage Family* **31**, 432-440.
STAFFORD, R., BACKMAN, E. and diBONA, P. (1977). The division of labor among cohabiting and married couples. *J. Marriage Family* **39**, 43-57.
STARK, R. and McEVOY J. III., (1970). Middle-class violence. *Psychol. Today* **4**, 52-65.
STAUB, E. (1974). Helping a distressed person: social personality and stimulus determinants. *Adv. Exp. Psychol.* **7**, 293-341.
STERN, D. (1977). "The First Relationship: Infant and Mother", Fontana/Open Books, London.
STEWART, A.J. and RUBIN, Z. (1976). The power motive in the dating couple. *J. Personality Soc. Psychol.* **34**, 305-309.
STRAUSS, A. (1977). *In* "Decisions, Organizations and Society", (Eds Castles *et al.*) Penguin, Harmondsworth, Middx.
STROEBE, W. (1977). Self esteem and interpersonal attraction. *In* "Theory and Practice in Interpersonal Attraction", (Ed. S.W. Duck), Academic Press, London and New York.
STRUHSAKER, T.T. (1965). Behavior of the vervet monkey *(Cercopithecus aethiops).* Ph.D. dissertation, University of California, Berkeley.
SUBBOTSKY, E.V. (1972). The formation of elements of altruistic behaviour among school-children. *Moscow State University Herald* (Russian Journal).
SULLIVAN, H.S. (1953). "Conceptions of Modern Psychiatry", Norton, New York.
TAJFEL, H. (1978). "Differentiation between Social Groups". Academic Press, London and New York.
TAYLOR, D.A. (1968). The development of interpersonal relationships: social penetration processes. *J. Soc. Psychol.* **75**, 79-90.

TAYLOR, F.W. (1911). "The Principles of Scientific Management", Harper Brothers, New York.

TEEVAN, J.J. (1972). Reference groups and premarital sexual behaviour. *J. Marriage Family* **34**, 283-291.

TERDHAL, L., JACKSON, R. and GERNER, A. (1976). "Mother-child interactions: A comparison between normal and developmentally delayed groups." *In* "Behaviour Modification and Families, I. Theory and Research", (Eds L. Mash, L. Hamerlynck and L. Handy), Bruner/Mazell, New York.

TERMAN, L.M., BUTTENWEISER, P., FERGUSON, L.W., JOHNSON, W.B. and WILSON, D.P. (1938). "Psychological Factors in Marital Happiness", McGraw-Hill, New York.

TERMAN, L.M. and WALLIN, P. (1949). The validity of marriage prediction and marital adjustment tests. *Am. Sociolog. Rev.* **14**, 497-504.

THARP, R.G. (1963). Psychological patterning in marriage. *Psycholog. Bull.* **60**, 97-117.

THIBAUT, J.W. and KELLEY, H.H. (1959). "The Social Psychology of Groups", Wiley, New York.

THORNGATE, W. (1976). Possible limits on a science of man. *In* "Social Psychology in Transition", (Eds L. Strickland, F. Aboud and K.J. Gergen), Plenum Press, New York.

TOLSDORF, C.C (1976). Social networks, support and coping: an exploratory study. *Family Process* **15**, 407-417.

TOMAN, W. (1971). The duplication theorem of social relationships as tested in the general population. *Psycholog. Rev.* **78**, 380-390.

TONNIES, F. (1957). "Community and Society (Gemeinschaft and Gesellschaft)", Translated by Loomis, C.P., Michigan State University Press, East Lansing, Michigan.

TRAUPMANN, J. (1979). Equity and intimacy in the lives of older women. Paper presented at the symposium on The Social Relationships of Older Women: Facts and Myths. Gerontological Society Meetings, Washington, D.C.

TRAUPMANN, J. (1978). Equity in intimate relations: an interview study of marriage. Unpublished Ph.D. dissertation, University of Wisconsin-Madison.

TRAUPMAN, J. and HATFIELD, E. (in press) The importance of "fairness" for the marital satisfaction of older women. *Res. Aging*.

TRAUPMANN, J., HATFIELD, E. and WEXLER, P. Equity and Sexual Satisfaction in Dating Couples. (in prep).

TRIPP, C.A. (1975). "The Homosexual Matrix", McGraw-Hill, New York.

TROST, J. (1978). Attitudes toward and occurrence of cohabitation without marriage. *J. Marriage Family* **40**, 393-400.

UDRY, J.R. (1974). "The Social Context of Marriage", Lippincott, Philadephia.

UTNE, M.K. (1978). Equity in intimate relations: a test of the theory in marital interaction. Unpublished Ph.D. dissertation, University of Wisconsin-Madison.

VALINS, S. (1966). Cognitive effects of false heart-beat feedback. *J. Personality Soc. Psychol.* **4**, 400-408.

VAN DEUSEN, E.L. (1974). "Contract Cohabitation: an Alternative to Marriage", Grove Press, New York.

VEISMAN, R.S. (1977). The connection between interpersonal relations and group efficiency. *Questions of Psychology*, (Russian Journal).

VERBRUGGE, L.M. (1979). Multiplexity in adult friendships. *Social Forces* **57**, 1286-1309.

WAGNER, R.V. (1975). Complementary needs, role expectations, interpersonal attraction, and the stability of working relationships. *J. Personality Soc. Psychol.* **32**, 116-124.

WALKER, H.M. and BUCKLEY, N.K. (1973). Teacher attention to appropriate and inappropriate classroom behaviour: an individual case study. *Exceptional Children* **5**, 5-11.

WALSTER, E.H. (1971). Passionate love. *In* "Theories of Attraction and Love", (Ed. B.I. Murstein), Springer, New York.

WALSTER, E. and WALSTER, G.W. (1978). "A New Look at Love", Addison-Wesley: Reading, Massachusetts.

WALSTER, E., WALSTER, G.W. and BERSCHEID, E. (1978a). "Equity Theory and Research", Allyn and Bacon, Boston.

WALSTER, E., WALSTER, G.W. and TRAUPMANN, J. (1978b). Equity and pre-marital sex. *J. Personality Soc. Psychol.* **37**, 82-92.

WARREN, C.A.B. (1977). Fieldwork in the gay world: Issues in phenomenological research. *J. Soc. Issues* **33**, 93-107.

WATERHOUSE, M.J. and WATERHOUSE, H.B. (1976). The development of social organization in rhesus monkeys (*Macaca mulatta*) — an example of bimodal attention structure. *In* "The Social Structure of Attention", (Eds M.R.A. Chance and R.R. Larsen), Wiley, Chichester, Sussex. 83-104.

WATZLAWICK, P., BEAVIN, J.H. and JACKSON, D.D. (1967). "Pragmatics of Human Communication", Norton, New York.

WEED, J.A. (1980). National estimates of marriage dissolution and survivorship. Unpublished manuscript, US Department of Health, Education and Welfare.

WEGNER, D.M. and VALLACHER, R.R. (1977). "Implicit Psychology: An Introduction to Social Cognition", Oxford University Press, New York.

WEICK, K. (1969). "The Social Psychology of Organizing", Prentice-Hall, Englewood Cliffs, New Jersey.

WEINBERG, M.S. and WILLIAMS, C.J. (1974). "Male Homosexuals: Their Problems and Adaptations", Oxford University Press, New York.

WEISS, L. and LOWENTHAL, M.F. (1975). Life-course perspectives on friendship. *In* "Four Stages of Life", (Eds M.F. Lowenthal, M. Thurnher and D. Chiriboga), Jossey-Bass, San Francisco.

WEISS, R.L., HOPS, H. and PATTERSON, G.A. (1973). A framework for conceptualizing marital conflict: a technology for altering it, some data for evaluating it. *In* Behavior Change: the Fourth Banff Conference on Behavior Modification, (Eds L.A. Hammerlynck, I.C. Handy and E.J. Mask), Research Press, Champaign, Michigan.

WEISS, R.S. (1974). The provisions of social relationships. *In* "Doing Unto Others". (Ed. Z. Rubin), Prentice-hall, Englewood Cliffs, NJ.

WEISS, R.S. (1975). "Marital Separation", Basic Books, New York.

WESTIN, A. (1967). "Privacy and Freedom", Atheneum, New York.

WHITEHURST, R.N. (1974). Sex role equality and changing meanings in cohabitation. Paper presented at the Annual Meeting of the North Central Sociological Association, Windsor, Canada, 1974.

WHITEHURST, R.N. (1977). The monogamous ideal and sexual realities. *In* "Marriage and Alternatives: Exploring Intimate Relationships", (Eds R.W. Libby and R.N. Whitehurst), Scott, Foresman, Glenview, Ill.

WIGGINS, J.S. (1979). Dynamic theories of social relationships and resulting research strategies. *In* "Social Exchange in Developing Relationships", (Eds R.L. Burgess and T.L. Huston), Academic Press, New York and London.

WILLCOX, W.F. (1891). The divorce problem. "Columbia University Studies in History, Economics, and Public Law", Vol. 1, No. 1.

WILLIS, R.H. and WILLIS, Y.A. (1970). Role playing versus deception: an experimental comparison. *J. Personality Soc. Psychol.* **16**, 472-477.

WILLS, T.A., WEISS, R.L. and PATTERSON, G.R. (1974). A behavioral analysis of the determinants of marital satisfaction. *J. Consulting Clin. Psychol.* **42**, 802-811.

WILSON, E.O. (1975). "Sociobiology: The New Synthesis", Harvard University Press, Cambridge, MA.

WINCH, R.F. (1958). "Mate-selection: A Study of Complementary Needs", Harper and Row, New York.

WISH, M., DEUTSCH, M. and KAPLAN, S.J. (1976). Perceived dimensions of interpersonal relations. *J. Personality Soc. Psychol.* **33**, 409-420.

WON-DOORNINK, M.J. (1979). On getting to know you: the association between the stage of a relationship and reciprocity of self disclosure. *J. Exp. Soc. Psychol.* **15**, 229-241.

WOZNIAK, R. (1975). Dialecticism and structuralism. *In* "Structure and Transformation", (Eds K.F. Riegel and G.C. Rosenwald), Wiley, New York.

WRIGHT, P.H. (1968). Need similarity, need complementarity, and the place of personality in interpersonal attraction. *J. Exp. Res. Personality* **3**, 126-135.

WRIGHT, P.H. (1969). A model and a technique for studies of friendship. *J. Exp. Soc. Psychol.* **5**, 295-309.

WRIGHT, P.H. and CRAWFORD, A.C. (1971). Agreement and friendship: a close look and some second thoughts. *Representative Res. Soc. Psychol.* **2**, 52-69.

WUERSIG, B. (1979). Dolphins. *Sci. Am.* **240**, 108-119.

YLLO, K.A. (1978). Nonmarital cohabitation beyond the college campus. *Alternative Lifestyles* **1:1**, 37-54.

YOUNG, M. and WILLMOT, P. (1957). "Family and Kinship in East London", Routledge and Kegan Paul, London.

ZARETSKY, E. (1973). "Capitalism, the Family, and Personal Life", Harper Colophon Books, New York.

ZIEGLER, R. (1972). "Theorie und Modell", Oldenbourg, München.

ZIMBARDO, P.G., HANEY, C., BANKS, W.C. and JAFFE, D. (1973). The mind is a formidable jailor: a Pirandellian prison. *The New York Times Magazine,* 18 April, Section 6, 38-60.

Author Index

A

Abbott, S. 111, *215*
Adelson, L. 79, 80, *221*
Ainsworth, M.D. 191, *217*
Ajzen, I. 6, 12, *215*
Albert, S. 36, *215*
Alexander, J.F. 192, *215*
Allan, G. 84, *215*
Allison, D. 29, *221*
Allport, F.H. 198, *215*
Altman, I. 13, 38, 42, 113, *215, 226*
Anderson, N.H. 34, *215*
Andreyeva, G.M. 61, *215*
Arafat, I. 142, *215*
Araji, S.K. 21, 22, *215*
Argyle, M. 9, *215*
Armistead, N. 27, 28, *215*
Aronson, E. 11, 38, 49, *215, 236*
Askham, J. 81, *216*
Austin, J.L. 9, *216*
Austin, W.G. 171, 172, *216*

B

Babchuk, N. 73, 83, 84, 85, *216*
Back, K.W. 35, *216*
Backman, C.W. 19, 49, *216*

Bailey, F.G. 212, *216*
Bailey, R.C. 32, *216*
Banfield, E.C. 74, *216*
Bannister, D. 13, *222*
Barnhart, J. 193, *216*
Bart, P.B. 83, 84, *235*
Bartram, M. 100, *216*
Bates, J.E. 112, *226*
Bateson, G. 10, 19, *216*
Baumrind, D. 191, *216*
Becker, W.C. 7, *216*
Befu, H. 80, *216*
Bell, A.P. 112, *216*
Bell, R.Q. 4, *216*
Bell, R.R. 173, *217*
Bell, S.W. 191, *217*
Bem, D. 140, *217*
Bem, S. 140, *217*
Bennis, W.G. 77, *217*
Bentler, P.M. 29, 32, 34, 131, 133, 135,
    138, 140, 141, 142, 143, 144, 145,
    146, 147, 148, 149, 151, 156, 179,
    217, 232
Berger, M.E. 132, 145, *217*
Berger, P. 79, 81, *217*
Bernard, J. 41, 185, 186, *217*
Berne, E. 173, *217*
Bernstein, A. 73, *228*
Berscheid, E. 24, 26, 31, 59, 177, *217*

Subject Index